C0-CEP-937

Professional Learning for

SCHOOL

LEADERS

Topics In Professional Learning Series

NATIONAL STAFF DEVELOPMENT COUNCIL

National Staff Development Council
504 South Locust Street
Oxford, OH 45056
513-523-6029
800-727-7288
Fax: 513-523-0638
E-mail: NSDCoffice@nsdc.org
www.nsdc.org

Professional Learning for School LEADERS
Editor: Valerie von Frank
Designer: Stacey D. Sanders

© National Staff Development Council, 2008.
All rights reserved.

Reproduction in whole or part without written permission is prohibited. Unless indicated otherwise, buyers of this book have permission to make up to 30 copies of up to 10 articles in this collection if they are to be used for instructional purposes as long as this book and NSDC are properly cited.

Requests for permission to reprint or copy any part of this book should be faxed to the NSDC business office at 513-523-0638 on organization letterhead. No e-mail requests will be accepted. All requests must specify the number of copies that will be made and how the material will be used. Please allow two weeks for a response.

Printed in the United States of America
Item #B395

ISBN: 978-0-9800393-5-1

TABLE OF CONTENTS

Contact information for authors printed with the original articles has been updated for this book in the Appendix.

Introduction

How much does leadership matter? Anyone who doubts the importance of a school leader need only look at a review of studies examining the effect of leadership on student achievement, done by McREL researchers J. Timothy Waters, Robert Marzano, and Brian McNulty (*Educational Leadership,* April 2004). They conclude that quality leadership contributes to raising student achievement by as much as 10 percentile points compared with schools with similar student and teacher populations.

Yet we sometimes think we don't know how to develop, or even describe, leaders. In conversations during the editing of this book, one person told me leadership isn't really describable, but "You know it when you see it." Another defined a leader as someone who "really takes charge to get things done."

Leadership, as the articles in this collection demonstrate, *can* be described. Leaders act in specific ways to achieve goals. Their actions are guided by clarity of thought and purpose, and thus they are able to create a culture and learning environment within schools that benefits both teachers and students. Leaders set the destination, and then they allow others to collectively map the best route.

Clarity of purpose and respect for teachers' professionalism are themes that run through interview after interview of principals of turnaround schools in the last several years of *The Learning Principal.* The articles in this collection show that we have been able to describe effective leadership — and how to create effective leaders — for some time.

This is the picture of sound leadership: school leaders engage in deep thought and reflection to distill what they value into a succinct vision, what Noel Tichy terms "Teachable Points of View" in the article, "Explain, inspire, lead" in Section III. Leadership requires that leaders be crystal clear about their values and purposes, speak powerfully and compellingly about those values and purposes, and persist in the face of resistance.

Dennis Sparks, NSDC's emeritus executive director, has often highlighed Visa founder Dee Hock's advice on leadership: "Have a simple, clear purpose which gives rise to complex, intelligent behavior, rather than complex rules and regulations that give rise to simplistic thinking and stupid behavior."

Joe Medina, principal of Torch Middle School in City of Industry, Calif., who was featured in the May 2008 issue of *The Learning Principal,* said much the same: "There was a time I thought a principal had to be a person with some God-like qualities. The closer I got to the position, the more it dawned on me that it wasn't the complexity of the solution that marked a good leader. It was the simplicity. A good solution had to be simple enough for everyone to understand. Now I don't shy away from simplicity, but embrace it."

Leaders, according to Sparks, promote deep change by encouraging educators to take time to reflect — to recognize the leverage points, the final 2% of action that coalesces the other 98% of our efforts.

"The final 2% is that cluster of experiences that literally change the brains of teachers and administrators," Sparks wrote in *On Common Ground* (Solution Tree, 2005, p. 159). "Educators have these experiences when they read, write, observe, use various thinking strategies, listen, speak, and practice new behaviors in ways that deepen understanding, affect beliefs, produce new habits of mind and behavior, and are combined in ways that alter practice. Such professional learning produces complex, intelligent behavior in all teachers and leaders and continuously enhances their professional judgment."

The articles in this book were selected to foster the kind of professional learning Sparks describes as the final 2%. Section I introduces the role of the principal as school leader. Articles in Section II provide greater depth. Section III includes articles that suggest school leaders create a vision, change culture, and create a learning environment. Other articles and pieces within the section are meant as tools to be used to discuss existing and ideal practices for school leaders. Section IV has numerous examples of how systems have been put in place to support principals in learning leadership skills. Section V lists additional resources for those who want to explore the topic more beyond the pages of this book.

Change is difficult. When leaders and those who coordinate leadership development programs make time to further their learning and to reflect on the effects of leadership in schools, they can foster the kind of collaboration, professionalism, and experimentation among leaders needed to accomplish NSDC's purpose: Every educator engages in effective professional learning every day so every student achieves.

— *Valerie von Frank*

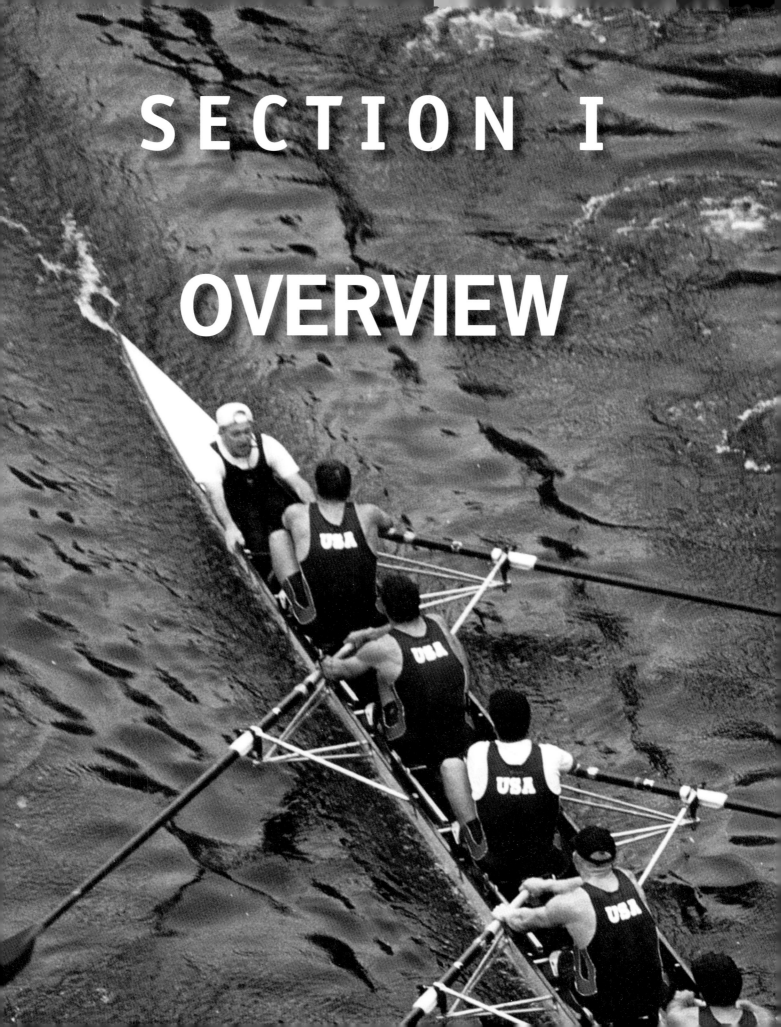

SECTION I

OVERVIEW

Teaching your principal
Top tips for the professional development of the school's chief

By Kent Peterson and Shelby Cosner

"The best staff development is in the workplace, not in a workshop."
— DuFour, 2004, p. 63

School success is influenced by many people. School principals remain one of the most important factors in this success. The research on effective schools, school restructuring, and instructional leadership point to the impact of principal leadership on student learning and improvement (Hallinger & Heck, 1996). But professional development for principals is often neither extensive nor job-embedded.

Learning the work of any occupation is difficult and time-consuming. Whether one is a surgeon, a teacher, or a school principal, acquiring the skills and knowledge to successfully accomplish daily tasks requires a variety of learning opportunities, from internships and professional development to on-the-job experience. While the more formal means of learning a set of tasks are centrally important, a large proportion of any occupational learning occurs on the job. Research suggests that on-the-job experience is a school leader's chief source of learning (Hamilton, Ross, Steinbach, & Leithwood, 1996).

While many staff developers have designed quality programs for school leaders, including walk-throughs and using data for decision making and planning, less attention has been directed at helping principals learn important problem-solving skills from the context of their daily work — the minute-by-minute skills principals need to survive and thrive in the stream of daily tasks they face. Given that much of principals' work involves problem solving within the school context (Coffin & Leithwood, 2000), principals must learn how to execute a daily list of complex, varied, and demanding work tasks. The daily realities make intuitive learning difficult and challenging. Professional development can enhance school leaders' ability to learn from experience.

DAILY REALITIES OF PRINCIPALS' WORK

Principals' daily work is characterized by brevity, variety, fragmentation, complexity, ambiguity, and uncertainty (Mintzberg, 1973; Peterson, 1982). The nature of their work may impede learning from experience:

JSD, Spring 2005 (Vol. 26, No. 2) © Kent D. Peterson. All rights reserved. Reprinted with permission.

- Principals' daily work comprises an enormous number of brief tasks. They engage in more than 2,000 separate interactions a day and the first and last hours of their days may include more than 50 to 60 separate interactions with multiple stakeholders needing answers to questions, problems solved, and concerns addressed (Peterson, 1982).

- Principals face a variety of problem arenas (instructional, political, psychosocial) and a mosaic of constituents (parents, teachers, students, community members). Task variety is a key variable.

- Their work is fraught with interruption, undermining their ability to accomplish tasks. They often begin one task (such as writing a teacher evaluation or planning next year's budget) only to be interrupted by pressing demands, problems, or emergencies.

- Their interactions often involve a range of cognitive complexity (simple memory vs. in-depth problem analysis) and require affective intensity (coping with conflict, interpersonal disagreements, emotional outbursts).

- Like doctors, psychologists, and teachers, principals face daily tasks that are incredibly complex with multiple, interlocking social, managerial, and cognitive features. From diagnosing and addressing faculty conflict or social anxiety to a literacy problem, their work involves intricate analysis.

- Many tasks and actions also are marked by ambiguity. The core problem is not immediately clear. For example, is a parent's lack of involvement in school due to poor relations with schools in the past, a lack of cultural competence and understanding, or simply the need for transportation?

- Principals face a high level of uncertainty each workday. Many report developing elaborate to-do lists only to be confronted with problems, issues, and immediate concerns that move such lists to the background.

While the worst challenges brought on by brevity, variety, fragmentation, and so forth can be improved, they do not go away. Even the most seasoned and effective principals face these work realities; it is the nature of the role.

Task brevity increases the number of problems principals encounter and shortens the time they have to analyze the situation and formulate a response. The brevity of tasks increases the difficulty of remembering, sorting, categorizing, and analyzing individual activities and sets of tasks.

Task variety increases the range of tasks principals encounter and impacts the repetition of such tasks within the overall scope of principals' work (Peterson, 1985).

Specifically, principals' work, like the work of other leaders, is comprised of a mix of "short wavelength" and "long wavelength" tasks (Sayles, 1979). Short wavelength tasks occur often (staff need additional funds; parents want to change their child's teacher) and can be quite routine. In contrast, long wavelength tasks occur only every several years, or once or twice in one's career (the death of a student or a major curriculum redesign).

Principals, like other managers, can learn short wavelength tasks more easily because they occur frequently enough for leaders to identify patterns, develop a common approach, and experiment with different actions. However, some of the most intense and difficult aspects of principals' work are long wavelength tasks. Those nonroutine tasks are difficult to analyze and learn. Professional development can help leaders learn both routine and nonroutine tasks.

Finally, task fragmentation segments task performance over multiple incidents that may span hours, weeks, or months. Task fragmentation can interfere with both the

JSD, Spring 2005 (Vol. 26, No. 2) © Kent D. Peterson. All rights reserved. Reprinted with permission.

analysis and the synthesis of multiple facets of a problem. But even coping with constant interruptions can be effectively addressed through learning and practice.

Collectively, brevity, variety, and fragmentation can substantially interfere with a principal's ability to reflect, making experiential learning difficult and undermining the leader's ability to develop problem-solving skills. Given the importance of experiential learning, what factors can help principals overcome obstacles to experiential learning, to learning on the job?

SUPPORTING PRINCIPALS' LEARNING
Collaborative learning

While many features of principals' work inhibit learning from experience, Coffin and Leithwood (2000, p. 21) suggest that "participating with others in authentic, nonroutine activities" fosters learning in work contexts. They suggest that professional development can be effective when it is collaborative, uses actual (i.e. authentic) problems and issues, and provides opportunities for principals to reflect on "nonroutine problems, those that occur irregularly, but can derail a school."

Staff developers and consultants can help design structured collaborative learning experiences embedded within the work context. These can provide critical opportunities for principals to draw on their past experiences as they consider current problems. Collaborative interactions around real problems and tasks also allow principals to be exposed to a broader, and perhaps richer, palette of ideas and approaches.

The role of school districts and outside organizations

School districts are in a unique position to support principals' experiential learning. School districts and their leaders can use the following four approaches to enhance school principals' opportunities to learn from experience.

1. **Structured interactions with superintendents.**

Coffin and Leithwood (2000) found that principals perceived interactions with their superintendents as supporting learning when the relationship between the superintendent and principal was strong and when the superintendent was viewed as in touch with the principal's school context. While principals from another study expressed similar opinions (Cosner, 2003), they also pointed to missed opportunities for job-embedded learning between superintendents and principals. Some principals described superintendents who seldom visited the schools to learn about the context of their organizations and who met with principals infrequently throughout the year, losing opportunities to provide guidance and support. Several principals interviewed in this study illustrate the point:

"There could be a great opportunity for learning with my superintendent, but that just hasn't happened. There aren't structured meetings during the year for us to meet. ... He and other members of the district leadership team know very little about my school. On a scale of one to 10, I would say that they are a two to three. They don't have a clue," one said.

Another said, "I think my superintendent is very good at a number of things. Instructional leadership isn't one of those things. I only have meetings with him a few times a year, but I need more than that. He needs to be much more involved in my school and more engaged with me."

In contrast, leadership development in another district centered around scheduled monthly meetings between the superintendent and either the elementary or secondary principals. The school leaders set the agendas for these meetings and designed the meetings to target and discuss in depth problems of practice.

Structured interactions between superintendents and principals can support principals' experiential learning

JSD, Spring 2005 (Vol. 26, No. 2) © Kent D. Peterson. All rights reserved. Reprinted with permission.

because they are in close proximity to school leaders' immediate context. Superintendents who recognize this opportunity and act in supportive ways can shape powerful on-the-job learning experiences for school principals. Superintendents can:

- Hold individual meetings monthly with principals or quarterly with veteran principals where agendas are jointly developed from current, immediate daily problems. Discuss and analyze these issues using a problem-based learning approach.

- Plan joint school tours with the superintendent and principal, followed by analysis of the interactions, interruptions, and issues that arise. Examine the particular school context and its impact on the daily realities of work.

2. Structured interactions with experienced administrators.

Interactions with other experienced administrators also can support learning from one's experiences. Using regularly scheduled administrative team meetings — when they are designed to address principals' context-specific learning needs — can be particularly helpful to enhancing job-embedded learning experiences. In many districts, focusing on principals' needs requires shifting the focus of an existing administrative team meeting from operational communication to reflective discussions on daily routines, unexpected problems, and exceptional interactions. These discussions should focus on long wavelength, unexpected events that senior administrators describe, or conversations may delve into the ways experienced principals cope with the daily press of activity.

Summer retreats also can provide a longer timeframe to discuss complex problems of daily practice and collaboratively reflect on the challenges of being a principal. Summer retreats, scheduled over multiple days, provide extended time for collaborative learning when principals are less likely to be pulled away for emergency situations in their schools. Given the extended time available, administrators, veteran principals, or outside leadership consultants can engage in deeper analyses of complex issues, personal reflection on the impact of daily pressures on stress, or ways to lessen interruptions.

District leaders also must consider the extent to which their administrative teams demonstrate deeper collegial skills and norms that result in concrete feedback. Ball and Cohen (1999) suggest that substantive collegial learning will require educators to "unlearn the politeness norms that dominate most ... discourse" (p. 27). Outside consultants or internal staff developers often are needed to help colleagues learn how to be "critical friends" in their discussions.

Whether through regular administrative meetings or retreats, professional development should legitimize the nature of the work while at the same time fostering deeper analysis, reflection, and interpersonal sharing about the principalship. While one's colleagues are frequently the best source of ideas, outside consultants can sometimes provide validation and multidistrict expertise that can boost learning.

3. Mentors and coaches.

A broad body of research calls for formal mentoring and coaching for school leaders (Coffin & Leithwood, 2000; NSDC, 2000; Tucker & Codding, 2002). Job-embedded mentoring and coaching can provide critical support to principals, particularly as they grapple with complex problem solving. Mentors and coaches who shadow principals and observe classrooms and school events gain important insights into principals' school contexts and are in good positions to support school leaders learning on the job.

JSD, Spring 2005 (Vol. 26, No. 2) © Kent D. Peterson. All rights reserved. Reprinted with permission.

While many school districts are introducing mentoring programs for beginning school leaders, few consider mentoring or coaching opportunities for all principals. In one Wisconsin system, district leaders used a massive redesign in the central office to initiate a coaching program for all school leaders, hiring several successful former school principals as coaches for all principals. The coaches meet regularly with individual principals and, importantly, have no evaluation responsibilities. Their role is to directly support principal learning at all stages of the individual's career.

4. Customized collaborative ventures.

Drawing from executive education approaches, school districts' collaborations with local universities or other professional development organizations can produce powerful learning opportunities for school leaders grounded in their current projects and problems (Tucker & Codding, 2002). The district/university partners often design professional development experiences customized to local contexts using case-based and problem-based learning. Analyzing learning cases, role-play, simulation, and structured discussion protocols developed and facilitated by an external consultant can help principals be more effective in their daily work.

School districts, consultants, and staff development professionals must work together to improve principals' opportunities for experiential, embedded, on-the-job learning. While instructional leadership skills should be a strong focus of professional development, it is also important to help principals learn how to deal effectively with the brevity, variety, and fragmentation of their daily work. Expanding both internal and external opportunities for learning will benefit school leaders, who help create more effective schools in which student learning is optimized.

REFERENCES

Ball, D. & Cohen, D. (1999). Developing practice, developing practitioners: Toward a practice-based theory of professional development. In L. Darling-Hammond & G. Sykes (Eds.), *Teaching as the learning profession: Handbook of policy and practice* (pp. 3-32). San Francisco: Jossey-Bass.

Coffin, G. & Leithwood, K. (2000). District contributions to principals' situated learning. In K. Leithwood (Ed.), *Advances in research and theories of school management and educational policy* (Vol. 4, pp. 19-38). Stamford, CT: JAI Press.

Cosner, S. (2003, November). *The district context for the professional development of high school principals.* A paper presented at the annual meeting of the University Council for Educational Administration, Portland, OR.

DuFour, R. (2004, Spring). The best staff development is in the workplace, not in a workshop. *JSD, 25*(2), 63-64.

Hallinger, P. & Heck, R. (1996). Reassessing the principal's role in school effectiveness: A review of empirical research. *Educational Administration Quarterly, 32*(1), 5-44.

Hamilton, D., Ross, P., Steinbach R., & Leithwood, K. (1996). Differences in the socialization experiences of promoted and aspiring school administrators. *Journal of School Leadership, 6*(4), 346-367.

Mintzberg, H. (1973). *The nature of managerial work.* New York: Harper and Row.

National Staff Development Council. (2000). *Learning to lead, leading to learn: Improving school quality through principal professional development.* Available at: www.nsdc.org/library/leaders/leader_report.cfm

Peterson, K. (1982). Making sense of principals' work. *The Australian Administrator, 2*, 1-4.

JSD, Spring 2005 (Vol. 26, No. 2) © Kent D. Peterson. All rights reserved. Reprinted with permission.

Peterson, K. (1985). Obstacles to learning from experience and principal training. *The Urban Review, 17*(3), 189-200.

Sayles, L. (1979). *Leadership: What effective managers really do . . . and how they do it.* New York: McGraw-Hill.

Tucker, M. & Codding, M. (2002). Preparing principals in the age of accountability. In M. Tucker & J. Codding (Eds.), *The principal challenge: Leading and managing schools in an era of accountability.* San Francisco: Jossey-Bass.

ABOUT THE AUTHORS

Kent Peterson is a professor in the Department of Educational Leadership and Policy Analysis at the University of Wisconsin-Madison.

Shelby Cosner is a doctoral candidate and senior teaching assistant in the Department of Educational Leadership and Policy Analysis at the University of Wisconsin-Madison.

JSD, Spring 2005 (Vol. 26, No. 2) © Kent D. Peterson. All rights reserved. Reprinted with permission.

High standards for principals bolster school performance

By Dennis Sparks

One of the most useful and cost-effective strategies for raising student learning is engaging principals in sustained standards-based professional study. Improvements in principals' performance are multiplied many times over through their affect on school culture, structure, and instructional programs. Designed properly to encourage principals to gain experience as instructional leaders and reflect on what they learn, these efforts to bolster principals' knowledge and skills can be the fulcrum for school improvement efforts.

A recent federal report underscores the fact that good schools require strong and stable leadership around achievement issues and that good principals are made, not born. The report, *Effective Leaders for Today's Schools: Synthesis of a Policy Forum on Educational Leadership*, concludes that principals have an "enormous influence over the environment in the school building, where the most meaningful actions take place." The real issue, the report says, "is how to structure leadership jobs and prepare people for them so that people who are proficient and committed, but not necessarily extraordinary, can succeed."

How should these proficient and committed but not necessarily extraordinary people be helped to do their important work? A critical starting point is adopting high standards for principals' performance. The Interstate School Leaders Licensure Consortium (under the aegis of the Council of Chief State School Officers) already has developed such model standards. These standards say principals:

- Must articulate and provide stewardship for a vision of learning shared by the school community;
- Must nurture and sustain a school culture and instructional program conducive to student learning and staff professional growth;
- Must manage the organization to promote an effective learning environment;
- Should know how to collaborate with families and community members to mobilize community resources; and

Results, December/January 1999

- Should act with integrity and fairness to influence each schools larger political, social, and cultural context.

In some states, prospective principals must successfully complete performance-based assessment processes developed by the Educational Testing Service.

New forms of professional development are required to help principals acquire new skills and grow intellectually so they can meet these standards. This professional development should be based on a few core standards for what leaders should know and be able to do, take place in participants' own school or context, and put participants to work solving real problems, says the Effective Leaders report. It should use a network of peers, be controlled by participants, and provide research findings about good teaching and productive schools.

The report cites several examples of such professional development including New York City District 2's principals' support groups which address a single topic for a year, such as evaluating student work. The report

also recognizes principals' networks in Boston in which participants collaborate in an important area, such as improving literacy in every school in the district. The report concludes that such professional development programs help "people learn leadership by actually leading ó and by having simultaneous opportunities to reflect on what they are doing, and to talk about the process with others."

School systems owe it to their communities to make certain that all principals meet high standards of performance and that they are engaged in sustained, serious study of the most effective ways to improve student learning. Standards for principal performance exist, and leading-edge professional development models for principals are available for adoption or adaptation. Now all that is required is the will to implement them.

ABOUT THE AUTHOR

Dennis Sparks is executive director of the National Staff Development Council.

Significant change begins with leaders

By Dennis Sparks

Leaders matter. Reform that produces quality teaching in all classrooms requires skillful leadership at the system and school levels. Such leadership is distributed in a broad and meaningful way to teachers and others in the school community. Because leaders are critical in transforming schools, it is important that school systems develop the habits of mind and practice essential in such transformation.

The habits that produce significant change in teaching and learning begin with significant change in what leaders think, say, and do. The implications of this are profound. It means, for instance, that leaders begin reform efforts by changing themselves before considering how others must change. It means that leaders carefully examine how their own assumptions, their own understanding of significant issues, and their own behaviors may be preserving current practices. It also means that leaders take on the intentional and disciplined process of changing professional habits that may be both ineffectual and deeply ingrained. In addition, it requires exposure and risk because new learning will often be public in nature and, like all learning of consequence, may sometimes lead to failure.

Professional development for school leaders, therefore, means something different than "parade of speakers" institutes or "sit and get" meetings during which leaders whose minds are rendered relatively inert receive "expertise" from others. Instead, professional development of a very different type will lead to deep understanding of important issues and practices, transformational learning at the level of beliefs and assumptions, and unrelenting action to apply this knowledge.

Leadership development that produces deep understanding is designed so administrators and teacher leaders explore subjects relevant to their day-to-day work — for instance, the nature of learning in the various subject areas and the methods of instruction that produce such learning — and elaborate on them in various ways. That means leaders will spend most of their time reading, writing, and considering ways to apply their professional learning. Leaders will also engage in simulations and real-life problem solving that will provide fresh perspectives on the issues at hand and not just formulaic answers.

Results, October 2003

Transformational learning may occur through dialogue as leaders explain their assumptions and consider the perspectives of others. Transformational learning may also occur when leaders experience strong emotions or cognitive dissonance as they make site visits to successful schools, interview students, or are confronted by disaggregated data that break through walls of denial.

Of course, deep understanding and transformational learning will mean little if they don't produce a continuous stream of powerful goal-focused actions. Consequently, workshops, meetings, and other such events will end with clear commitments to action and to mutually-held expectations that those actions will be carried out.

Because leaders matter and because as Gandhi put it, "We must become the change we seek in the world," the most powerful forms of leadership development will produce leaders who possess deep understanding, act from a core of clearly expressed and enabling beliefs and assumptions, and align their daily actions with those understandings. That is the type of leadership that creates high-performing cultures and outstanding teaching in all classrooms.

ABOUT THE AUTHOR

Dennis Sparks is executive director of the National Staff Development Council.

Expect the impossible

By Dennis Sparks

University of Kentucky Professor Tom Guskey tells this instructive story about his mentor, Benjamin Bloom. In 1981, Guskey left his position at the University of Kentucky to become director of research at the Center for Research on Teaching and Learning in Chicago. "One of my first tasks as director was to appoint a board of advisors and, naturally, I called upon my former doctoral advisor and dissertation committee chair, Prof. Benjamin Bloom.

"Together, we outlined an extremely ambitious research agenda for the Center. Our plan was to conduct an extensive series of small-scale, pilot studies testing the viability of various ways to improve student learning, especially at the post-secondary level. While the work was grueling, long hours and dedicated effort paid off, and we organized a conference in Chicago to discuss the research.

A STUNNING REVELATION

"On the morning the conference was to begin, Mr. Bloom met me at the Center and we walked together to the hotel where the conference was being held. On the way, our conversation reflected the excitement that both of us felt about what had been accomplished. At one point, however, he turned to me and said, 'You know, Tom, I never thought this would be possible.'

"His comment stunned me and I stopped mid-stride. 'What do you mean, you never thought this would be possible?' I asked him. 'You told me from the start that this is what you expected. I worked myself to a frazzle and now you tell me you never thought it would be possible!' Mr. Bloom sensed my anger but only smiled. 'Tom,' he said, 'I've never let my expectations be limited by what I thought was possible. You need to do the same.'

"As we walked on, I realized that in that simple, eloquent statement, he revealed to me the premise that guided his life's work. Our vision of what we can and should expect need not be narrowed to what we believe to be possible. Rather, it is by expecting the impossible that we attain our greatest achievements."

Results, February 2001

SELF-LIMITING BELIEFS

Guskey's story illustrates a powerful but little understood concept: that our mental constraints regarding what is possible are at least as significant in restraining our improvement efforts on behalf of all students as are the more obvious barriers of inadequate time, money, and research. Virtually all of us hold self-limiting beliefs that confine our ambitions and squander the potential we possess for making larger contributions to the world. And when school leaders hold those beliefs they can also limit the performance of teachers and students.

The most potent of those mental constraints — which are often invisible to those who hold them and can only be inferred from their actions — are those that claim that only some students can achieve at high levels and that teaching is a natural talent that cannot be improved through study and practice.

STAFF DEVELOPMENT AT ITS BEST

"It is no failure to fall short of realizing all that we might dream. The failure is to fall short of dreaming all that we might realize," VISA founder Dee Hock asserts. The consequences of that failure are nowhere more tragic than when school leaders fall short of dreaming all that teachers and students can realize together.

Benjamin Bloom reminds us of the link between expectations and achievement and of the human capacity to accomplish things that were once considered impossible. A wonderful thing about our beliefs, though, is that they can be changed in the blink of an eye, and that once altered, everything that flows from them changes forever. That's staff development at its very best!

ABOUT THE AUTHOR

Dennis Sparks is executive director of the National Staff Development Council.

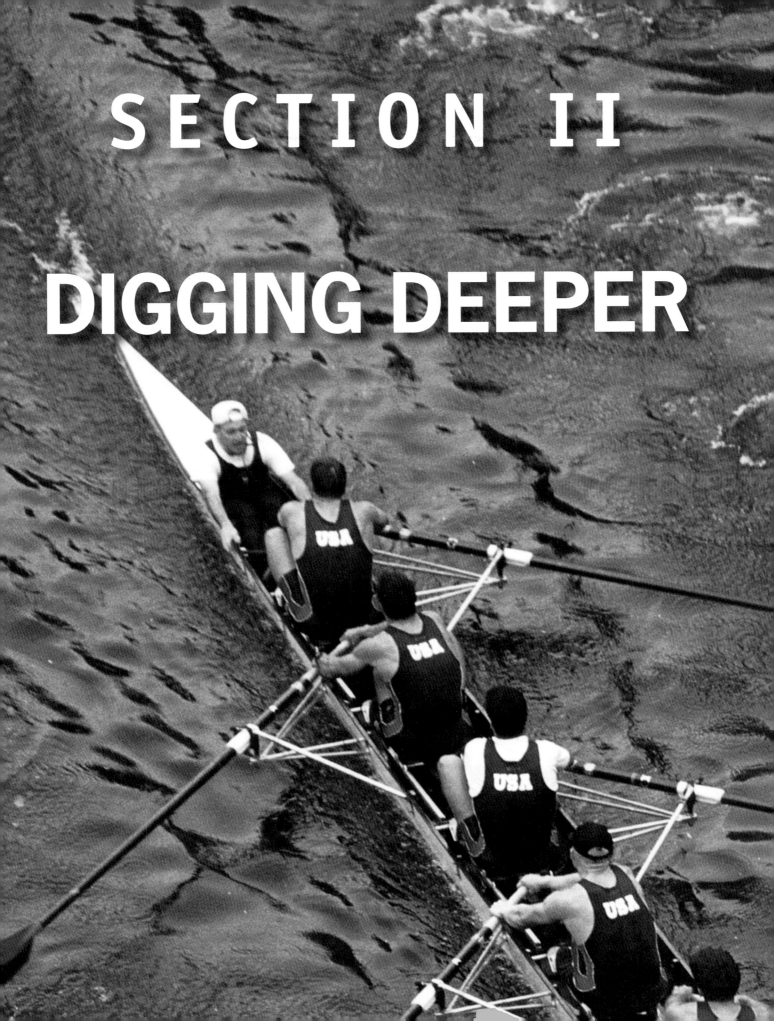

SECTION II

DIGGING DEEPER

The professional development of principals
A conversation with Roland S. Barth

By Dennis Sparks

SD: For many years, you have worked as either a principal or as director of the Principals' Center at Harvard. You've been in a unique position to trace the recent history of the evolution of the role of the principal as learner.

Barth: I've seen some important and heartening changes. Looking back over the years, we've had to remove several impediments that have interfered with principals becoming serious learners. One certainly was the view that it is immoral to take money out of the mouths of babes by using precious school resources for the principals' own personal and professional development. Another has been the admission that the principal who doesn't know how to do something, who is learning, is thereby flawed. Principals are hired because they are thought to know what to do and how to do it. In these days when respect for leadership is so fragile, who can stand up and announce that he or she does not know how to do something?

A third impediment to principals' learning has been their past experience. Staff development activities designed for principals have generally been so dreadful that few wanted more. Another barrier has been the realization that when a principal goes off and learns something — a new form of teacher supervision, perhaps — he or she has to *do* something with what has been learned. Thus, learning creates new work. Principals feel they already have too much. Why would they want more?

A decade ago, principals were seen as the learn*ed,* and others with whom they worked, namely students and teachers, were the learn*ers.* Principals were forbidden not to know. Indeed, many were trapped into playing the role that they knew everything from math and social studies to art and music.

I think some extraordinary things have happened in the last few years to change all of that. The work of Ron Edmonds and Larry Lezotte in the effective schools movement helped reassert the importance of the school principal. Qualities like strong leadership, continuous monitoring of performance, and providing a safe and orderly environment really constitute the job description of the school principal. Additionally, observations from the business world about the value of leadership at the local site have underscored the principal's central role.

Most observers of schools recognize that principals have a large influence on climate and morale. Too often,

Journal of Staff Development, Winter 1993 (Vol. 14, No. 1)

this influence has not been used, and sometimes it has been abused. It seems to me that the desirable way for principals to use their influence is to unlock the potential, energy, idealism, and learning of each member of the school community.

JSD: How do principals unlock that potential and energy?

Barth: First, they need to model important behaviors. For instance, to unlock energy and inventiveness, people have to take risks. I find teachers, students, and parents far more likely to risk when principals frequently and visibly take risks themselves.

Energy can also be unlocked through learning. Again, principals release this energy by becoming sustained, visible learners themselves. One definition of an "at-risk" student is "any student who leaves school before or after graduation with little possibility of continuing learning." Similarly, there is a phenomenon that might be called an "at-risk teacher," or an "at-risk principal" — any *educator* who leaves school at the end of the day with little possibility of continuing learning about the work they do. What's exciting for me to observe these days is that there are fewer and fewer school people who might be called "at risk" by this definition.

Energy and idealism are also unlocked when principals collaborate. Many wonderful ideas come forth when two or three people brainstorm and bounce thoughts of one another. The group will usually generate richer and more unusual ideas than will any of its members. Rather than going it alone or delegating, a principal can work with teachers, other principals, and parents.

JSD: What type of conditions have to exist for principals if they are to admit their vulnerability and take risks? I am thinking in particular about the conditions provided for principals by central office.

Barth: The most important job description for a superintendent, I believe, is that of head learner in the school system. This person must not only create conditions that promote the learning of adults and young people, but also nurture his or her own learning, as well. If the superintendent models risk-taking, collaborative work, and learning, then principals are more likely to do the same. I think principals will risk and learn when the environment within the school and within the district makes it not only permissible but essential to do so.

JSD: In your writing, you stress that schools ought to be communities of leaders and learners, but we know that relationships among adults in schools are often individualistic and sometimes adversarial. How do we get from where we are to the kind of school communities you advocate?

Barth: That's an important question. If nothing else comes from the work of W. Edwards Deming, it is that working alone is neither good for the quality of the product nor for the quality of life of those who produce the product. Working together, we can continually improve what we set out to do and at the same time get a great kick out of doing it. Ultimately, most of us find satisfaction in being a member of a successful team, not in being a solitary successful individual.

Unfortunately, school practitioners too often find themselves as competitors for increasingly scarce recognition and resources. Teachers and principals alike tend to hoard insights and good ideas the way they do magic markers. If they share them, someone else may do better and get more rewards and recognition. It's a cruel environment in which many school people work. To ask them to freely share their rich craft knowledge is really asking them to give away their slight advantage in gaining the recognition and resources they so desperately need.

We have to modify the reward system so that groups as well as individuals gain recognition and resources. When rewards are switched from the individual to the group, behavior becomes much more interdependent and cooperative.

JSD: You've written that the school ought to have a moral purpose. What do you mean by that?

Barth: Many critics of public schools point out that private schools have a moral purpose which is very clear and continually articulated, and that's why those schools are so good. Well, I am not so sure that all private schools are so good, nor do I know why they're good, but I would accept that there is a greater sense of direction and common overall purpose in many independent schools than in public schools. It's very difficult to come to a single moral purpose, one set of core values. Many schools and school systems are working hard to develop an institutional vision and are making a lot of headway. Educators are usually pleasantly surprised to learn how many values they hold in common and the subsequent effect a rich set of common values has upon the school culture.

JSD: What's the principal's role in identifying those core values?

Barth: Schools report several ways they come to a set of common values. Sometimes schools that are adrift with little sense of purpose mount a search for a new principal. Each candidate is asked to explain his or her vision. The system then hires the vision and the principal with the assumption that by next June, the school will reflect that vision. In this process, the principal projects — or inflicts — his or her vision onto the school community.

Another variation is that the principal is the facilitator, drawing from different constituencies the most firmly held pieces of their individual visions. Through some sort of alchemy, the principal weaves these threads together into a tapestry of principles. The job is basically one of mediating these different purposes, synthesizing them, and then putting them out to the school community.

A third way involves principals empowering teachers, parents, and children, and joining with them to grow a new vision for the school. In the former instance, the principal is the neutral facilitator whose vision is not expressed, while in the latter, the principal is an equal contributor to the process.

JSD: Do you have a preference among these processes?

Barth: My thinking has changed over the years. Early on, like many beginning principals, I had a messianic fervor and knew what was best for the unwashed. That approach was soon "staff developed" out of me by the school community! My preference now is toward the principal empowering others while remaining a first-class citizen — a player in this community of vision makers.

JSD: It sounds as if you are describing a consensus-building process in which the principal is part of the consensus. Sometimes principal have taken participatory management to mean that they should facilitate the decisions of others, but not be part of that consensus themselves. They abdicate their leadership responsibility to others.

Barth: Right. There's a tendency to say, "All right, you demand to have some say around here; why don't you go and do it?" Let someone else of the responsibility, the accountability, and the hassles. I find a certain anger here which really says, "You no longer want me to do it all. That's fine. You do it for yourselves then." It is far more powerful to join with others to do what needs to be done.

JSD: You wrote in *Improving Schools from Within* that "The moment of greatest learning is when we find ourselves responsible for a problem we care desperately to resolve. Then we seek assistance, we are ready to learn."

Barth: I believe the schoolhouse itself is the most powerful context for the continuing education of educators. You don't need to take a university course or go off to a workshop at the central office on Thursday afternoon. Schools are full of thoughtful people who are wrestling with significant problems, such as finding alternatives to ability grouping or how to move toward achieving racial integration as well as desegregation. Rather than facing our problems alone in what one teacher called "our separate caves," we can turn these problems into opportunities for sharing craft knowledge and for invention.

My experience working in schools as a teacher and as a principal is that schools provide a never-ending parade of issues and tough problems that can become growth-producing opportunities. You don't have to look hard for those moments of opportunity. For instance, a fire in the home kills two of the children in your school. All of a sudden, you are faced with an issue — and a moment of great learning opportunity. How a school responds and what learning the staff can bring to themselves and to others can be profound. Rather than avoiding discussion of death or having it become a depleting experience for the school, I have seen schools use this kind of common, tragic event to build communities and to reflect on how they might improve themselves.

JSD: You used the word "reflection" a moment ago. I assume that it's what separates the powerful learning experiences you describe from the many events that occur each day that seemingly have little effect on us. How do principals help themselves and the faculty become more reflective?

Barth: I've likened the life of a principal or a teacher in a school to that of a tennis shoe in a laundry dryer. It's hot, congested, turbulent, dark, and bumpy. How are we to slow the laundry dryer down and extract ourselves from it so that we can make some sense of the experience and improve subsequent experiences?

We must find imaginative ways of separating adults from youngsters at times during the school day for conversation, brainstorming, reflection, and replenishment. There are ways. Groups of students can be combined and student teachers, parents, or students themselves can provide leadership so that teachers may emerge from the laundry dryer and reflect on their actions.

JSD: You are an advocate of writing as a reflective process.

Barth: As a teacher and principal, I found writing to be the most powerful way for me to slow down the laundry dryer. It's a way of distancing yourself from the turbulence, even while in the midst of it. We adults need to engage in writing during the school day in ways that are visible to youngsters. We don't need to separate from students in order to have reflective time. Recent studies document just how little writing most youngsters do in the course of a school week. We can encourage students to write by doing more writing ourselves. I am familiar with schools where everyone from teacher to custodian to parent volunteers will read for one hour. I also know a few where everyone writes. It's a win-win situation.

JSD: You've said elsewhere that the most important and lasting changes come from within schools. There are people, however, who believe that forces external to the school — such as legislative or district mandates — can sometimes unfreeze the way things are traditionally done so that people will start looking at things in a new way. How does this view mesh with your belief that schools can find their own best solutions?

Barth: I have observed — both as an insider and an outsider — numerous attempts to change schools from the outside. It may have been new legislation, a program from a local university, or something initiated by the school board. These are attempts by outsiders to influence the insiders. We all know that school people are gifted at resisting these attempts, even the well intentioned ones, to be helpful to them.

I think we need to have more conversations between the residents of the schoolhouse — the teachers, students, parents, and principals — and some of these change agents from the outside about what needs to be improved and how best to go about it. Those inside the school and those outside should collaborate in the change process.

Many outside change attempts these days are far more thoughtful and involve more insiders. Ted Sizer's Coalition of Essential Schools is an example of an outside change agent that takes teachers and principals seriously right from the start. Outsiders can also provide a resource center — a group of responsive, caring adults — where help is available to those inside the school in their efforts to move toward a common purpose. What's outdated, of course, is the prescriptive, remote, authoritarian approach that says, "Here's what we want you do to and this is how we're going to evaluate you." Outdated, but not uncommon.

JSD: You believe that we need more inventive models and approaches to principal development. What are some examples of that?

Barth: There are many ways to promote leadership development in schools. Yet we seem to rely on the same tired method one staff developer called "sit 'n' get." Peer visits between principals is one way to promote leadership — you visit my building for a day and I'll visit yours for a day. I'll then reflect back to you and your faculty what I see going on and some questions I have. You do the same for my building. There's a lot of risk and time involved, but I've seen these visits have enormous effect.

Another option I'm familiar with is the work of principals' centers. We've found that when groups of principals gather together to take responsibility for promoting their own development, inventive ideas and exciting forms of staff development emerge. Because principals design the programs, it is uncommon to have a long parade of visiting speakers. Many centers begin

that way, but after awhile, the participants begin to recognize that thoughtful, honest conversations with one another about generic issues are more engaging and sustaining than listening to someone else talk. From these conversations frequently emerges the establishment of new relationships among principals.

When principals are responsible for their own learning, they design things they really enjoy, things that offer a new angle, and often things that are risky. I was once a part of a group that put together a team-building experience on board an 88-foot sailing vessel. Teams of teachers, principals, and superintendents came on board for a day. The crew demonstrated how to get the sails and anchors up and down, and then sailed the vessel out into Boston Harbor, whereupon they dropped both sails and anchor. We were told they wanted the schooner back at Charlestown Naval Yard by 4 p.m. Then the crew went below. Well, talk about team building! How does a group of people who don't know one another get an 88-foot sailing schooner back to the dock? Who does what? Meanwhile, tugboats blasted, destroyers came by, small recreational vehicles buzzed around us. A period of chaos gave way to some heady collaboration, after which we did get the boat back in by 4 p.m. We then spent the next five hours reflecting on that experience and what it said about team building. We talked about whether it was someone with rank, like a superintendent, who knew more about navigation, or someone with experience, or someone who might have been listening during the instructions. That's an example of a waterfront seldom sailed in staff development!

JSD: You've been involved with the Principals' Center at Harvard for over 10 years. What's the most important change you've seen in principal development over time?

Barth: Nowadays, principals are expected and challenged to be learners, to provide leadership *through* their own learning. In a brief decade, it has become legitimate,

Journal of Staff Development, Winter 1993 (Vol. 14, No. 1)

respectable, and essential for school and system leaders to invest time and attention to their own development in the belief that not only they, but the students and teachers within their schools will be the better for it. I think this trend will continue, and the ripple effects upon teachers and students will become more and more pronounced.

Not long ago, a principal told me, "Since I joined the Principals' Center, I've noticed that teachers in the building are taking their own professional development far more seriously." It's also clear that when youngsters see learning as something that their important role models do, they will also take learning far more seriously. Schools ought to be about finding the conditions under which learning curves go off the chart — *everyone's* learning curve. To me, that's the most important form

of "restructuring" a school can undergo. I'm confident that the next few years will contain even more reflection, inquiry, invention, and reform as schools blossom into communities of learners.

ABOUT THE AUTHOR

Dennis Sparks is executive director of the National Staff Development Council.

Roland S. Barth is the founding director of the Principals' Center and a senior lecturer in education at the Harvard Graduate School of Education.

What does leadership capacity really mean?

By Linda Lambert

Throughout this hemisphere, conferences, seminars, and academies are hosting events on leadership capacity. The Internet lists dozens of online courses about leadership capacity. Google reports more than 3 million hits under the title "leadership capacity."

What is really meant by leadership capacity? The term has been around for some time. What is my leadership capacity? What is the leadership capacity of individual teachers, our principal, our political figures? This personal usage, while central to school improvement, does not offer a framework or schema to sustain school improvement. Since the publication of *Building Leadership Capacity in Schools* (ASCD, 1998), educators use the term "leadership capacity" as an organizational concept meaning broad-based, skillful participation in the work of leadership that leads to lasting school improvement.

First, let's look closely at these terms.

- **Leadership** — and therefore the work of leadership as used within the definition of leadership capacity — means reciprocal, purposeful learning together in community. Reciprocity is essential to solving problems and working collaboratively. Purpose suggests values, focus, and momentum. Learning is mutually creating meaning and knowledge. Community is the essential environment for experiencing reciprocal, purposeful learning. These four ideas frame a definition of leadership in which all can see themselves reflected. It is the mirroring pool of a professional culture.

- **Broad-based participation** refers to who is at the table, whose voices are heard, and what patterns of participation exist. These patterns form the structure through which the work of the school or organization is done. Also, it is within these patterns of participation (teams, cadres, learning communities, study groups) that individuals develop lasting and

JSD, Spring 2005 (Vol. 26, No. 2)

Professional Learning for School LEADERS ■

respectful relationships. To be effective, participation requires skillfulness.

- **Skillful participation** is the understanding, knowledge, and skills that participants either develop or bring to their engagement in purposeful learning. The work of leadership involves developing skills in dialogue, inquiry, reflection, collaboration, facilitation, and conflict resolution. Leadership skills for adult learning parallel good teaching: A good leader is a good teacher who uses her knowledge and skills with colleagues.

By defining these terms and how they interact, we are able to understand schools' differing levels of ability to sustain improvement. Schools at varying stages of developing leadership capacity may be described as follows:

- Low leadership capacity schools tend to be principal-dependent, lack a professional culture and are significantly unsuccessful with children. Only the principal, serving as a top-down manager, is referred to as the "leader" in the school. Teacher leadership is not a topic of conversation, let alone interest. Educators in such cultures deflect responsibility while preferring blame; they avoid focusing on teaching and learning while holding fast to archaic practices. While professional relationships may be congenial, they lack the challenge of collegiality. Tests and test scores may be considered the only valid measures of student success, and promising products and performances revealed by student work are neglected. Absent an internal accountability system, these schools are subject to the whims, demands, and pressures of parents, districts, and states.

- Moderate leadership capacity schools lack a compelling purpose and focus, are governed by norms of individualism, hold few conversations among members of the whole community, and suffer from fragmentation and polarization. Concerns regarding teachers who will "not buy in" may arise when a small group of more skilled educators form an isolated inner core of decision makers. Either scenario — dispersed and individual action or corralled and exclusive action by a few — will leave the school without a focused, professional culture. The first scenario calls for a concerted effort to create a shared sense of purpose. The second scenario requires using broad-based, inclusive strategies (e.g. norms, collaborative action research, dialogue, inquiry) to involve everyone in the work of leading the school. In a school with moderate leadership capacity, disaggregating student scores inevitably reveals a lack of success for its more vulnerable or challenged students.

- High leadership capacity schools are learning communities that amplify leadership for all, learning for all, success for all. These schools have developed a fabric of structures (e.g. teams, communities, study groups) and processes (reflection, inquiry, dialogue) that form a more lasting and buoyant web of interrelated actions. The principal is only one of the leaders in the school community and models collaboration, listening, and engagement. Each participant shares the vision, understands how the school is moving toward the vision, and understands how he or she contributes to that journey. The quality of the school is a function of the quality of the conversations within the school. Student success is revealed by multiple measures of contribution, products, and performances, including the vivid presence of student voice. High leadership capacity schools hold great promise, but no guarantees, of sustainability.

In other words, schools that include everyone within collaborative patterns of participation are able to develop greater levels of leadership skillfulness. This achievement can move a school closer to lasting school improvement than would otherwise be possible.

SIX CRITICAL FACTORS

If high leadership capacity schools are good, why are they not always able to sustain improvement? That question usually leads to issues of values, authority, dependence, and identity within schools and districts. A study of high leadership capacity schools (Lambert, 2004) found several critical factors must be addressed to fully realize leadership capacity's promise:

1. **The school community's core values must focus its priorities.**

   Democratization and equity must be foremost among these values and are interdependent. Democratization is the means through which staff experience and honor equity. Members of high leadership capacity schools accept responsibility for all students' learning and include all voices.

2. **As teacher leadership grows, principals must let go of some authority and responsibility.**

   When principals lead for sustainability, teachers and principals become more alike than different. They share similar concerns, blend roles, and ask tough questions. They find leadership and credibility within each other through frequent conversations, shared goals, and, ultimately, collective responsibility.

3. **Educators must define themselves as learners, teachers, and leaders.**

   How we define leadership determines who will participate. This broad perspective encompasses sharing and distributing leadership. Leadership becomes a form of learning — reciprocal, purposeful learning in community. To learn is to be able to lead. Like children, all adults can learn, all adults can lead.

4. **We must invest in each other's learning to create reciprocity.**

   When principals engage teachers in problem solving rather than render them helpless through directives and granting or withholding permission, natural capacities for reciprocity come to life. Dependencies cause us to ask permission, to abdicate responsibilities, and to blame. Learning communities require reciprocity.

5. **The first tenet of leadership capacity is "broad-based participation."**

   Schools must create the structures through which participation occurs. Structures for broad-based participation include teams, study groups, vertical communities, and action research teams. These are the settings in which people deepen relationships, alter their beliefs, and become more skillful in the work of leadership. Without these structures, reculturing is unlikely.

6. **Districts must negotiate the political landscape to provide professional time and development, a conceptual framework for improvement, and tailored succession practices (fitting the principal to the school).**

This work requires engaging the board and the community in conversations that build an understanding of lasting school improvement. Without this groundwork, schools continually fight the same battles for time, for professional development, and for selecting principals who can take a school from where it is to where it ought to be without losing momentum or denying the worthy experiences of teacher leaders.

These factors are particularly challenging because they challenge our beliefs and traditional conceptions of leadership, how we relate to each other and ourselves and how we distribute power and authority. We consistently have called on ordinary people to do extraordinary work, and many times we succeed. We can succeed more often if we understand and implement the tenets of leadership capacity for lasting school improvement. The notion of "lasting" or sustainable improvement may well represent today's major learning edge.

REFERENCES

Lambert, L. (2004). *Lasting leadership: A study of high leadership capacity schools.* Oakland, CA: Lambert Leadership Development.

Lambert, L. (1998). *Building leadership capacity in schools.* Alexandria, VA: ASCD.

ABOUT THE AUTHOR

Linda Lambert is professor emeritus at California State University, Hayward.

A new view of leadership
Model focuses on educational and moral aspects of schooling

By Joseph Murphy

For most of the 20th century, we tended to think about school leadership in well-defined ways. We highlighted leaders' roles: the assistant principal, the associate superintendent. We featured academic and student-based domains of responsibility: department chair of mathematics, assistant superintendent for special education. We also defined leadership in terms of functions, such as personnel and guidance. And across all of these categories, the spotlight was directed to administrative tasks such as supervising teachers or communicating with parents. Over the last few decades, as our knowledge of leadership in general and our understanding of school administration in particular have deepened, we have learned that it is more helpful to scaffold school administration on broader concepts of leadership.

While tasks, roles, responsibilities, and functions continue to help us paint the landscape of school leadership, they become secondary to broad orientations or perspectives that significantly reset the work of the women and men in various school administration positions. In our broader understanding of leadership for the 21st century, it makes more sense to talk about providing others with a seat at the power table than to talk about school public relations. In a similar vein, it makes more sense to home in on learning-focused leadership than it does to talk about supervising and evaluating teachers. Equally important, we find that these core broad orientations (see diagram above) or perspectives wrap around, stretch across, or define all administrative positions.

Over the last 15 years, my colleagues and I have worked to forge a framework that features these more fundamental and more essential orientations. The ideas of leadership focused on empowerment, entrepreneurship, environmental sensitivity, and educational and ethical grounding have not always been central in school improvement efforts, just as teacher leadership has not been at the forefront of the larger issue of professionalization.

Over time, colleagues from all domains of the school administration family have turned their lenses on one or more of these orientations. Meanwhile, more comprehensive foundational views of school leadership that provide alternative ways of thinking about who we are and the work we undertake remain rare in our profession.

One foundational view of school leadership is what we refer to as the 5E model of leadership. At the heart of

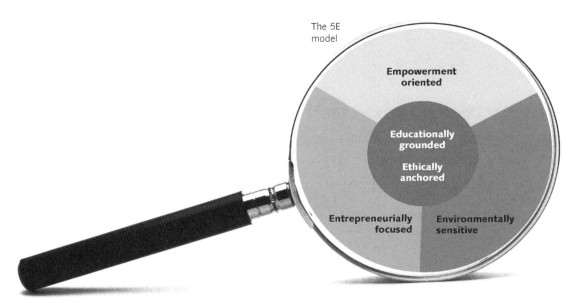

The 5E model

Empowerment oriented

Educationally grounded

Ethically anchored

Entrepreneurially focused

Environmentally sensitive

the model are five orientations that define work across tasks, functions, and roles — orientations that potentially give meaning to and bring coherence to the complex and multifaceted nature of school administration. The model, we believe, helps recenter the work of those who lead our schools.

The model defines leadership in terms of five core orientations, perspectives that an abundance of recent evidence helps us understand are at the center of effective management and high-performing organizations. At the heart of the framework are two key pillars that provide the central support structure of school leadership in a post-industrial world, and in the process give meaning to the other three orientations.

To switch metaphors, the 5E model tells us that school leaders need glasses with orientations (not tasks), and that the lenses in these spectacles should direct attention to the educational and moral aspects of schooling. Using the educational lens, the model tells us that the basis for administration must be learning, teaching, and school improvement (education) — not organization, or politics, or administration, or governance. These latter issues are important, often critically so, but only to strengthen the

educational program at the school or district, not as center stage players in the educational drama.

The framework tells us that a key to great leadership is the ability to focus on the hundreds of decisions school leaders make every day using the educational lens, not to allow decisions to be made primarily on organizational, financial, and political grounds.

The center of the model also shows us that effective leadership grows from an ethical core, the ethics of care and justice in particular. While the demands for scientifically based evidence are important, school leaders, the model tells us, also must build their leadership on a robust platform of values. While no scientific evidence tells us that we must focus on children from poor communities if we are to enhance student performance, a moral and ethical obligation would lead us to do so. We have had scientific evidence for decades about how to close achievement gaps and keep students from low-income families in school. The problem was less that we didn't know how to close the gap than it was a lack of willingness to challenge the moral bankruptcy of organizational routines (e.g. the ways students were grouped for instruction, the guidance that low-income families received, the methods used to assign teachers to students, and so forth). Thus the model tells us that one lens of leaders' spectacles must direct attention to the moral implications of the routine decisions, practices, behaviors, structures, and policies that engage school leaders — regardless of their roles, tasks, or areas of responsibility.

The other three E's in the model also help to reforge the meaning of school leadership. Schools in this country were built from raw material that came out of organizational and institutional ideas about schooling. School administration literature throughout the 20th century is full of discussions of hierarchical and bureaucratic pillars of management — authority, control, impersonality, division of labor. Contrary to what is increasingly portrayed in the literature (see Murphy, 1992, for a review), hierarchy and bureaucracy are not evil twins. In many fundamental ways, they provide the structure and the glue to hold schools and school systems together. It is when they occupy center stage rather than a supporting role that there is a problem.

The 5E model helps us see that these basics — hierarchy and bureaucracy of schooling — must be yoked to larger purposes and goals. We can no longer allow them to distort education for youngsters. The model tells us that a primary focus on hierarchy and administrative control will fail schools much more frequently than it helps them. It tells us that leadership, whether by an assistant principal or a director of assessment, is about empowering others — providing direction, building capacity, removing barriers — to carry the school to more productive places.

The fourth E in the model informs us that effective school leadership must be entrepreneurial, if not by preference, then through serious training. The entire foundation of schooling in the U.S. is being fundamentally and structurally reshaped to governance influenced less by government agents than by market forces, ideas not even in existence 15 years ago. The public monopoly

dominated by education service providers (i.e. us) has given way and is being replaced by systems more responsive to customers and clients. As we continue to find this very DNA of school governance changing, it is imperative, the model asserts, that administrators learn and practice the art of entrepreneurship — risk taking, innovativeness, and proactiveness, elements that have rarely defined a field dominated by concern for roles, responsibilities, and tasks.

Finally, the 5E model of leadership tells us that school leadership needs to be rooted as much in understanding the education environment as in internal school operations. The current era of accountability, marketization, and community-driven reform has made it even more critical that leaders are environmentally sensitive. An environmental orientation is now more important than many of the ways of thinking about leadership that dominated the practice and academic domains of school administration for most of the 20th century.

Leaders today, regardless of role or function or task, need broader and more powerful ways to think about who they are and what they do. Older ways of conceptualizing leadership and describing their efforts will not disappear. But, we believe, they must occupy less of the stage in the school leadership play. More importantly, they will continue to be of use only when they are informed by more powerful leadership orientations. One such set of orientations can be found in the 5E model of leadership.

REFERENCE

Murphy, J. (1992). *The landscape of leadership preparation: Reframing the education of school leaders.* Newbury Park, CA: Corwin Press.

ABOUT THE AUTHOR

Joseph Murphy is associate dean and professor of education in the Peabody College of Vanderbilt University.

Challenging role
Playing the part of principal stretches one's talent

By Rick DuFour

What is the role of the school principal in a professional learning community? Principals have been called upon to:

- Celebrate the success of their schools and to perpetuate discontent with the status quo;

- Convey urgency regarding the need for school improvement and to demonstrate the patience that sustains improvement efforts over the long haul;

- Encourage individual autonomy and to insist on adherence to the school's mission, vision, values, and goals;

- Build widespread support for change and to push forward with improvement despite resisters;

- Approach improvement incrementally and to promote the aggressive, comprehensive shakeup necessary to escape the bonds of traditional school cultures.

Principals have been portrayed as middle managers in the school district hierarchy and as leaders of their respective buildings. They have been lauded as the critical element in a school improvement initiative and criticized for making their schools overly dependent upon them.

Confronted with these conflicting messages, what is a principal to do?

The message to principals is particularly confusing is the area of leadership styles. On the one hand, the importance of the principal serving as a strong instructional leader has almost become a cliche. On the other hand, there are increasing calls for principals to delegate, collaborate, and empower others to make decisions (Lezotte, 1997; Lieberman, 1995). As one study concluded:

"Principals in schools with strong professional communities delegate authority, develop collaborative decision-making processes, and step back from being the central problem solver. Instead they turn to the professional

community for critical decisions." (Louis, Kruse, & Marks, 1996.)

Can a principal be a strong instructional leader and empower others to make important decisions?

NEED FOR STRONG PRINCIPALS

There is little question that the role of the principal has changed since the days when the effectiveness of the principal was based primarily on his or her ability to "run a tight ship." The National Association of Secondary School Principals acknowledged that the authoritarian leadership style that distinguished principals of the past is ineffective in an era of site-based decision making and shared responsibility (1996). But while the role of the principal has changed, the importance of the principalship has not. Schools need strong principals more than ever.

Principals can promote the shared decision-making and collaborative culture of a learning community and demonstrate strong instructional leadership if they attend to the following leadership responsibilities.

1. **Lead through shared vision and collective commitments rather than rules and authority.** A learning community, by definition, is a group of people working together toward a shared vision. Therefore, building a shared vision and a collective commitment to act in ways that advance that vision is one of the most important responsibilities of principals in learning communities. When teachers have reached consensus on the questions, "what do we want our school to become," and "what are we prepared to do to get it there," principals can exercise "loose-tight" leadership. They can be "loose" on the particular strategies teachers might use to advance the vision, but passionately "tight" on upholding the vision and demanding adherence to the collective

commitments. Rather than emphasizing rules or resorting to the authority of the position to control the work of teachers, they provide staff with a sense of direction by promoting and protecting shared vision and collective commitment.

2. **Create collaborative structures that focus on teaching and learning.** Principals must recognize two important facts: (1) A collaborative culture is essential to a learning community, and (2) inviting people to collaborate will not create such a culture. Principals must develop structures and strategies that systematically embed collaboration into the daily life of the school. They must:
Provide time for teachers to collaborate in teams during the school day and year;
• Help each team develop effective working relationships by facilitating the development of protocols for how members will operate with one another;
• Clarify the purpose of the collaboration and the products that should be generated as a result of teachers working together; and
• Insist that each team identify specific, measurable performance goals to create the results orientation essential to a learning community.

3. **Pose the questions that help the school focus on issues of teaching and learning.** In schools that have been most successful in creating a professional learning community, principals have focused on posing questions rather than dictating solutions (Louis, Kruse, & Raywid, 1996). The questions convey their priorities and point people in the right direction. When principals engage faculty in substantive dialogue on key questions such as those listed below, they develop the capacity of the staff to function as a learning community.

- Do we have a shared vision of the school we are trying to create?
- What commitments must each of us demonstrate for our vision to be realized?
- What goals should we establish this year to move closer to the school we desire?
- Are we clear on what students should know and be able to do as a result of each grade level, course, unit of instruction?
- What strategies are in place for responding to students who are having difficulty in achieving the intended learning?
- Have we clarified the criteria we will use in assessing student work?
- How will we know if we are becoming more effective as a school? What evidence is important to us?

4. **Provide staff with the training, information, and parameters they need to make good decisions.**

There is no reason to believe that simply involving teachers in decision making and providing high levels of teacher autonomy will improve a school. Uninformed people do not make good decisions. Principals must provide staff with relevant background information and research findings. They must ensure that teachers receive the training and support to master the skills that will make them more effective in achieving the school's goals. They must develop monitoring procedures that supply teacher teams with the data, information, and feedback that enable them to make necessary course corrections and improvements. In short, they must recognize that they must function as staff developers.

CONCLUSION

Principals must do more than encourage teacher autonomy and then hope for the best. Effective principals recognize that they do not empower others by disempowering themselves. Empowered teachers and strong principals are not mutually exclusive; the learning community must have both.

REFERENCES

Lezotte, L. (1997). *Learning for all.* Okemos, MI: Effective School Products.

Lieberman, A. (Ed.). (1995). *The work of restructuring schools.* New York: Teachers College Press.

Louis, K.S., Kruse, S., & Marks, H. (1996). Schoolwide professional community. In Fred Newmann and associates (Eds.), *Authentic achievement: Restructuring schools for intellectual quality.* San Francisco: Jossey-Bass.

Louis, K.S., Kruse, S., & Raywid, M.A. (1996). Putting teachers at the center of reform. *NASSP Bulletin, 80*(580), 9-21.

National Association of Secondary School Principals. (1996). *Breaking ranks: Changing an American institution.* Reston, VA: Author.

ABOUT THE AUTHOR

Rick DuFour is superintendent of Adlai Stevenson High School District 125.

Make principal development a priority

By Dennis Sparks

So much has been written in recent years about the importance of a competent, caring teacher in every classroom that we seem to have forgotten that this goal cannot be reached unless we have a skillful principal in every school. That challenge is particularly acute given the current difficulties many districts face in filling principal vacancies.

In this situation, the professional development of principals becomes particularly important. Unfortunately, principal development, which has traditionally been given an even lower priority by school systems than teacher development, too often turns participants into passive recipients of information rather than active participants in solving important educational problems.

These observations are prompted by a speech given by Anthony Alvarado in December at NSDC's 1999 Annual Conference. "The truth is that the preparation of supervisors makes the preparation of teachers look outstanding," Alvarado argued. "Principals and vice principals and superintendents rarely have good places to learn."

In his speech, Alvarado outlined the key elements of a well-designed principal development program. First, he urged conference participants to increase the budget for all professional development each year, citing New York City's Community School District 2's decade-long growth in this area from one tenth of a percent to nine percent. "We exponentially underestimate what people need to learn to do something different and better," he said.

The budget for principal development must provide funds for regular visits to other schools and for ongoing coaching, Alvarado argued. "One thing that we need is massive inter-visitation . . . to go places, to see practice that is actually the kind of practice that we want to implement."

Regarding coaching Alvarado said, "You cannot change behavior, change practice in organizations, without large-scale coaching by people who know the content, who know how to do it, and who know how to help people learn. At the heart of it is the simple notion that you need someone working with you to model, to give feedback, to assist in the actual trying of the new practice, to support in the ongoing habituation of new

Results, April 2000

practice. It is impossible to improve practice without access to high quality coaching."

A final important ingredient proposed by Alvarado is study groups in which principals consider problems, particularly those in the critical areas of reading and mathematics, and figure out what to do about them. "This sense of organizing ourselves through study groups, action research groups, or a wide variety of practitioner-related structures is essential to making progress in organizations," he said.

School systems that are serious about standards-based student learning and the quality of teaching will ensure that all principals:

- Join ongoing study groups that delve deeply into the most important instructional issues in their schools;
- Visit one another's schools to learn about outstanding practice, critique colleague's improvement efforts, and support one another in improving instruction; and
- Receive frequent in-school coaching on critical skill areas such as working with teachers to improve instruction, analyze data, and critique student work.

- Districts can be guided in these efforts by the Interstate School Leaders Licensure Consortium Standards for School Leaders. These six standards, which have been adopted or adapted by 30 states, have student learning at their core and describe the knowledge, dispositions, and performance expected of school leaders.

The development of principals cannot continue to be the neglected stepchild of state and district professional development efforts. It must be standards-focused, sustained, intellectually rigorous, and embedded in the principal's work day. Nothing less will lead to high levels of learning and performance for all students and teachers.

ABOUT THE AUTHOR

Dennis Sparks is executive director of the National Staff Development Council.

It's lonely at the top

By Pat Roy

We often ask whether colleges have done a sufficient job of preparing teachers for the classroom. A similar question needs to be asked of principals, namely, did your collegiate training prepare you to be an instructional leader? Based on the incredulous expressions and laughter that I hear whenever I pose that question, it seems that most certificate programs still focus primarily on the management tasks of the school leader rather than the critical leadership skills that make the principal essential to high levels of student learning. McREL has conducted a meta-analysis of 35 years of school leadership research and identified 21 leadership responsibilities as well as 66 leadership practices that have been shown to impact student learning (Marzano, Waters, & McNulty, 2005). We are clearer than ever about how the principal can improve student learning.

As a result, the principal needs to **participate in professional learning to become a more effective**

Leadership:
Staff development that improves the learning of all students requires skillful school and district leaders who guide continuous instructional improvement.

instructional leader (Roy & Hord, 2003, p. 67). But, this development work needs to be designed using job-embedded, collegial experiences similar to the learning that NSDC recommends for instructional staff. First, the principal would **participate in facilitated learning teams that problem solve and learn together.** Principals confide in me that their job is a lonely one. They have few colleagues available to them to talk with and fewer yet in whom they have established the trust necessary to reveal challenges and solve nagging problems. Participating in a facilitated learning team can build professional relationships while assisting principals to learn and apply new strategies while working with colleagues who understand their situations and circumstances.

The learning team should be designed so that principals **participate in extensive, ongoing learning activities that include hands-on, problem-based, and multiple practice opportunities.** One of the primary objectives of this development work is not merely to help principals learn about new strategies but also create opportunities for them to feel comfortable enough to **implement** new leadership practices during their workday. Using active, real-life, job-embedded strategies with principals will help accomplish that objective.

Finally, principals need to commit to **allocating time to explore and practice specific behaviors and strategies and receive feedback on the implementation of new skills.** One of the conclusions of the McREL meta-analysis is that principals do matter! This research means that there are leadership actions that shape and focus a school so that high levels of student learning result. In order to get those results, principals need to learn to use those essential skills. A leadership coach can provide constructive feedback on new behaviors. But once trust has been established among principals, they can be a powerful source of feedback to their colleagues

as well. The benefits of participating in collegial learning teams are enormous — improved student learning, increased job satisfaction, and stronger collegial relationships will result.

REFERENCES

Marzano, J., Waters, T., & McNulty, B. (2005). *School leadership that works: From research to results.* Alexandria, VA: ASCD & McREL.

Roy, P. & Hord, S. (2003). *Moving NSDC's staff development standards into practice: Innovation Configurations, Vol. 1.* Oxford, OH: NSDC & SEDL.

ABOUT THE AUTHOR

Pat Roy is co-author of **Moving NSDC's staff development standards into practice: Innovation configurations** *(NSDC, 2003).*

Leadership is intensely personal

By Dennis Sparks

Leadership development is an essential and often-neglected task in the process of creating schools in which all students and teachers learn and perform at high levels. It is important that principals, teacher leaders, and district administrators acquire the knowledge and skills to be instructional leaders and to create and sustain high-performance cultures in their organizations. And because instructional and cultural change is intensely interpersonal, it is also important that leaders develop the communication and problem-solving skills that promote positive, productive relationships and that school systems provide individualized support to guide leaders' efforts and to maintain their motivation over many years.

Because of NCLB and state and school system initiatives, leadership development efforts in the past few years have often focused on raising test scores by instituting strong literacy and mathematics programs and by assisting principals to improve teaching in those areas. While those activities are worthwhile, unless school systems simultaneously address the complex and emotionally-laden interpersonal demands of leadership, schools will be unable to sustain improvements in teaching and student achievement.

Many principals say that a great deal of their time and emotional resources these days are devoted to upset parents, disaffected staff members, and unrelenting pressures from outside the school. They also report few opportunities for sustained conversations about important issues. Teacher leaders who serve on school improvement teams or as school-based staff developers may face anxious and frustrated colleagues, experience internal doubts about their own capacity to effectively serve in new roles, and feel torn by conflicting expectations for their work held by teachers, principals, and district staff.

Some methods of personal interactions have proven more effective than others in addressing such issues. School leaders can develop clarity regarding their purposes and values, become more powerful speakers and writers, learn to listen deeply and with empathy to others in the spirit of dialogue (which is particularly challenging when they feel unfairly attacked), acquire the ability to stay focused on possibilities rather than falling prey to resignation and dependency, and develop the resourcefulness to generate multiple pathways to achieve goals. NSDC has conducted pilot programs that have demonstrated that these are teachable skills that

Results, December 2003/January 2004

can improve the results achieved by even experienced, sophisticated leaders.

Individualized support can take the form of mentoring for new leaders and of "executive coaching" for veteran administrators of the type that has become increasingly prevalent in businesses. Such support can provide leaders with the insights and wisdom of successful, experienced educators and offer opportunities for leaders to clarify their intentions, strengthen their planning and problem-solving capacities, develop stronger communication and interpersonal skills, and maintain energy and enthusiasm for their critically important work.

Such leadership development efforts will not only improve teaching and learning throughout the school, they will also serve as a valuable recruitment tool to attract the best candidates to difficult-to-fill positions. These efforts will also contribute to the long-term retention of leaders who feel that the challenges they face are understood by their employers, who believe that they are being adequately supported in meeting those challenges, and who perceive that their efforts are truly making a difference.

Instructional improvement and culture building are relationship intensive and emotionally demanding. Establishing productive, trusting relationships is a critically important aspect of the improvement journey for which school leaders are often ill-prepared and under supported. The ultimate success of school reform, I believe, will be determined to a large extent by our ability to support leaders in addressing these demanding interpersonal challenges.

ABOUT THE AUTHOR

Dennis Sparks is executive director of the National Staff Development Council.

Job-embedded, collaborative principal learning

By Pat Roy

Does it seem that there has been an explosion of leadership development programs in the past few years? Federal and state departments of education, universities, and regional assistance centers are paying attention to the principal's important role in improving student learning. The content for that development work is becoming clearer as a result of a meta-analysis of leadership research. McREL's meta-analysis covered 35 years of work on school leadership and identified 21 leadership responsibilities as well as 66 leadership practices that have been shown to impact student learning (Marzano, Waters, & McNulty, 2005).

Central office staff have a role in this work as well. Central office staff need to provide professional learning experiences to enable principals to function as instructional leaders (Roy & Hord, 2003, p. 118). But rather than arranging for an outside consultant to plow through research results that identify essential

Leadership:
Staff development that improves the learning of all students requires skillful school and district leaders who guide continuous instructional improvement.

practices, central office staff can use job-embedded, collaborative strategies to build principal skills and knowledge. Central office staff begin by creating facilitated learning teams for principals in which they problem solve and learn together. In order for principals to understand and value learning teams within their own schools, they need first-hand experience of working within a learning team. Providing a facilitator will be important to help principals work cooperatively with each other because many school leaders feel that they are in competition with each other for recognition, resources, and respect. This perception of competition makes cooperation difficult and the sharing of problems or challenges almost impossible.

Within the learning team, principals would be involved in extensive, ongoing learning activities that include hands-on, problem-based, and multiple practice experiences. In other words, principals need to learn about new strategies and then practice using those new strategies. This development work is best accomplished for principals — just as for teachers — when it is designed within the context of their daily work and based on real-life issues and challenges. Using a problem-based learning approach, for example, might mean presenting a case study of a typical challenge facing principals. The group recommends actions based on research and best practice — not merely past experience.

Given the identification of 66 specific leadership skills, principals will also need time to explore and practice those behaviors and strategies and receive feedback on the implementation of new skills. An implementation imperative is clear for this work. Principal cannot just "know" about these leadership skills; they also need support to help them begin to change their daily leadership practices. Many development programs include principal coaches who provide constructive feedback to school leaders as they reconceptualize and enact their roles.

It is clear that principals matter when they focus on and use the essential responsibilities and practices identified in the leadership research. Effective professional development should support principals as they learn these new skills.

REFERENCES

Marzano, J., Waters, T., & McMulty, B. (2005). *School leadership that works: From research to results.* Alexandria, VA: ASCD & McREL.

Roy, P. & Hord, S. (2003). *Moving NSDC's staff development standards into practice: Innovation Configurations, Vol.1.* Oxford, OH: NSDC & SEDL.

ABOUT THE AUTHOR

*Pat Roy is co-author of **Moving NSDC's staff development standards into practice: Innovation configurations** (NSDC, 2003).*

SCHOOL
LEADERSHIP

We want to enable people to lead change, but you can't lead change unless you've got a profound sense of appreciation and respect for learning. And you need to have something to aspire to that's bigger and more compelling than what you've got.

—Rayona Sharpnack (Dahle, 2000, p. 278)

"T"he principal is the key person in determining whether a school succeeds." "Good principals are focused on instruction and student learning." "It's harder and harder to find good principals to replace those who are retiring." "Our best teachers don't aspire to be principals. We think that's because the job is getting more difficult to do each year."

Comments such as these have filled educational publications for the past few years and can be overheard in the hallways wherever school leaders gather. At the same time, we hear: "The job of the principal is too big for one person. No one can be expected to do all those things." "Teachers have leadership talents we don't tap." "It's important to find ways that teachers' leadership abilities can be used without them leaving the classrooms to become administrators."

The "vision" described in Part I—high levels of learning for all students, all students with competent teachers, all teachers receiving the powerful new forms of professional development they require to be effective with an increasingly diverse student body—requires principals who are consensus builders, strong instructional leaders, and skillful in

Designing Powerful Professional Development for Teachers and Principals, by Dennis Sparks (NSDC, 2002)

Designing Powerful Professional Development For Teachers and Principals

chapter seven

forming and sustaining the professional learning communities as described in Part II. It also requires that principals distribute leadership among teachers who then perform key roles in the school improvement process.

This chapter explores new conceptualizations of the principal's role. It also considers the role of teacher leadership in creating high-performing schools. Chapter 8 will discuss the type of professional learning that is essential if principals are to fulfill their new responsibilities and if teachers are to play various critical leadership roles in their schools and in district offices.

NEW CONCEPTUALIZATIONS OF THE PRINCIPAL'S ROLE

While there seems to be universal agreement on the importance of the principal, school systems report that they are finding it difficult to attract qualified candidates to the vacancies created by retiring "boomer" administrators. And because few districts have "aspiring principal" programs to identify and begin developing prospective leaders, more and more districts find themselves between the proverbial rock and a hard place—while skillful principals are essential in the reform efforts they are harder than ever to come by.

Concurrently, as we will see below, expectations for principals continue to increase. Principals are expected today to create learning communities in their schools and to engage the broader school community in creating and achieving a compelling vision for its schools, which typically serve increasingly diverse student populations. They are asked to give up "command-and-control" views of leadership and to be instructional leaders steeped in curriculum, instruction, and assessment who can coach, teach, develop, and distribute leadership to those in their charge.

Roland Barth (2001) offers a simple definition of leadership: "Making happen what you believe in" (p. 446). But more complex conceptions of leadership are also taking hold. For instance, the Task Force on the Principalship of the School Leadership for the 21st Century Initiative (Institute for Educational Leadership, 2000) based its work on this premise: "[P]rincipals today also must serve as *leaders for student learning*. They must know academic content and pedagogical techniques. They must work with teachers to strengthen skills. They must collect, analyze, and use data in ways that fuel excellence" (p. 2).

Implementing such an ambitious set of tasks takes its toll on principals, however. "Creating a learning community requires planned pursuit, yet principals can be easily consumed by everyday 'urgent but unimportant' matters," Milli Pierce observes (2000).

Designing Powerful Professional Development for Teachers and Principals, by Dennis Sparks (NSDC, 2002)

Designing Powerful Professional Development For Teachers and Principals

"Their quandary is whether to learn to carve out time to supervise and coach teachers and work with them on professional development plans that support real school improvement, or to risk leading a disaffected, low-performing school community" (p. 1). In addition, principals' responsibility for improvement is typically not matched by authority in critical areas such as personnel and budgets (Johnston, 2000). As a result, principals experience intense job stress, excessive time requirements, difficulty in satisfying parents and community members, and social problems that make it difficult to focus on instructional leadership, *Leadership for Student Learning: Reinventing the Principalship* (IEL, 2000) reports.

As we saw in Part II, rising expectations for principals require that school systems modify their policies and practice to support principals as instructional leaders. Christopher Cross and Robert Rice (2000) concur. "Enabling principals to put instructional leadership first," they write, "requires a realignment in school districts of the practices, responsibilities, and duties assigned to principals, and will entail delegating many of the nonacademic tasks to assistant principals or other staff members" (p. 62). Indeed, some school systems are experimenting with dividing the duties of principals into two positions, one which addresses the instructional leadership of teachers while the other focuses on non-instructional tasks such as food services and building maintenance.

PRINCIPALS AS INSTRUCTIONAL LEADERS

The National Association for Elementary School Principals' (2001) report, *Leading Learning Communities: Standards for What Principals Should Know and Be Able to Do*, advocates that principals provide time for teacher reflection on their own practice; invest in teacher learning; connect professional development to school learning goals; provide opportunities for teachers to work, plan, and think together; and recognize the need to continually improve their own professional practice.

Richard Elmore (2000) offers a definition of school leadership comparable to Roland Barth's in its brevity: "Leadership is the guidance and direction of instructional improvement" (p. 13). One of the most important instructionally-focused areas for school leaders, according to Elmore (2000), is helping others acquire new values and behaviors. Sounding a bit like Linda Lambert in Chapter 8, Elmore writes: "People make these fundamental transitions, by having *many* opportunities to be exposed to the ideas, to argue them into their own normative belief systems, to practice the behaviors that go with these values, to

chapter seven

Designing Powerful Professional Development For Teachers and Principals

observe others practicing those behaviors, and, most importantly, to be successful at practicing in the presence of others ... " (p. 31).

Elmore (2000) emphasizes the importance of a coherent set of school goals "... that give direction and meaning to learning and collegiality" (p. 16) and notes that collegial interaction has little value "... except in a school where the principal and teachers explicitly created a normative environment around a specific approach to instruction" (p. 17).

According to Andreae Downs (2000), if all teachers are to perform at high levels, principals must serve teachers and students as instructional leaders who keep school activities focused on student learning and build learning communities among staff members (and sometimes parents and community members as well). Just as they believe in the capacity of all students to learn at high levels, so, too, do instructional leaders believe they can learn to be more effective. These principals regularly visit classrooms, meet with teachers in large and small groups to discuss teaching and learning, discuss student work with teachers, alter the daily schedule to provide time for teacher learning, and use faculty meetings for professional development. They also shape school norms to promote an ongoing discussion of teaching and learning and to encourage reflection in the use of new practices.

Phil Schlechty (2001) advises principals to see themselves as part of a district-level team as well as head of a school team. He also asks them to focus the school on creating quality work for students and to remove barriers that inhibit that focus. "You are as responsible for what teachers do in the classroom as are the teachers themselves," he reminds principals. "Good leaders do not exist outside the context of good followers, and good followers do not exist unless they have the potential to be good leaders. Developing that potential is what good leadership is all about" (p. 214).

In a study of elementary school leadership in Chicago, Penny Sebring and Anthony Bryk (2000) found three common elements among the principals of productive schools: leadership style, their strategies, and the issues on which they focus. Principals had a leadership style that was inclusive and facilitative, focused the institution on student learning, provided efficient management, and combined pressure with support. The strategies used by these principals included making "quick hits" (attacking a highly visible problem and solving it quickly); having a long-term focus on the instructional core; having a strategic orientation through a comprehensive, coherent plan for school development; and by attacking incoherence. Key issues addressed by these principals were the strengthening of parent/ community ties to the school, developing teachers' knowledge and skills, and promoting a

Designing Powerful Professional Development for Teachers and Principals, by Dennis Sparks (NSDC, 2002)

Designing Powerful Professional Development For Teachers and Principals

school-based professional community.

Lew Smith (2001) tells of a Fordham University study of schools that make significant improvements. The researchers noted that these schools had newly-assigned experienced principals who provided strong leadership that helped create internal dissonance combined with outside pressure. These leaders also initiated internal and external collaborative relationships, had a commitment to school-based professional development with a sharp focus on how well students were learning, and shifted from top-down management to teachers' making decisions about curriculum and teaching methods. Smith closes his essay with the question, "Can we muster the will to make change happen?" (p. 33), a subject I will address in Part V.

Tom Guskey (2000) argues that principals must help teachers make better use of assessment data, particularly that data that is produced in their own classrooms. He says that principals should emphasize the use of classroom assessments as learning tools that are part of the instructional process, regularly review classroom assessment results with teachers to identify potential instructional problems, and provide opportunities for teachers to plan collaboratively, examine their students' assessment results and work samples to identify areas of difficulty, and develop shared strategies for improvement.

Likewise, Richard Stiggins (2001) believes principals must cultivate "assessment literacy" within their schools by being assessment literate themselves and ensuring that classroom assessments serve instructional purposes. "Leadership is needed," he writes, "to create an instructional environment that expects and supports competence in assessment, as well as the effective application of that competence in the service of students' academic well being" (p. 25).

Principals also play an essential role in establishing a school culture that promotes quality teaching, according to Sandra Harris (2000). She found that teachers value empowering behaviors such as treating teachers professionally and involving teachers in decision making; supporting behaviors such as providing emotional and moral support and being visible during the school day; and communicating behaviors such as active listening, providing encouragement, and establishing clear expectations.

"The bottom line is that the leader is the primary culture carrier for the organization," Carol Schweitzer (2000) concludes. "If the leader's attitudes and behaviors do not match the culture that you are intending to build, it will not work. The leader and the culture must be in sync" (p. 35).

Designing Powerful Professional Development for Teachers and Principals, by Dennis Sparks (NSDC, 2002)

Dave Wheat, James Cramer, and Mary Kay Cramer (2000) offer yet another important task for principals: supporting teachers who are seeking National Board of Professional Teaching Standards certification. Principals can assist these teachers, the authors point out, by monitoring candidate's progress, celebrating the completion of small steps along the way, providing released time for candidates to prepare portfolios, and critiquing videotaped lessons.

TEACHER LEADERSHIP

A common view of leadership is that leaders are strong, often charismatic individuals. They alone persuade others through their forceful personalities or induce compliance through fear. They know what needs to be done and they transform their workplaces into high performance organizations by the force of their will. Peter Senge (1999) argues, however, that leadership for deep change requires replacing the myth of the "hero leader" with the concept of leadership communities. These communities, he believes, enable the building of leadership capacity throughout the organization so the organization can continually adapt and reinvent itself.

If schools are to be places in which students and educators are successful in their respective roles, teachers must be at the core of the leadership communities that Senge envisions. Teacher leadership can take many forms. It may include advocating the vision for staff development described in this book as part of collective bargaining, participating on school and district improvement teams to help determine goals and strategies, conducting classroom and schoolwide action research to determine if changes are improving the learning of all students, mentoring new teachers, serving on peer review panels to provide support and assistance to new and veteran teachers, and working on special assignment as coaches or instructional guides to provide ongoing professional learning for their peers.

Fullan (2001) explains the value of teacher leadership this way: "The teacher in a collaborative culture who contributes to the success of peers is a leader; the mentor, the grade-level coordinator, the department head, the local union representative are all leaders if they are working in a professional learning community" (p. 266).

Teacher leadership provides clear benefits to schools and to the individuals who assume those responsibilities. But significant barriers to the fulfillment of these roles exact an emotional and physical toll on teacher leaders. Many of these barriers can be traced to antiquated mental models—"deeply ingrained generalizations, and even images that influence how we understand the world and how we take action" (Senge, 1990, p. 8). For example, the common

Designing Powerful Professional Development for Teachers and Principals, by Dennis Sparks (NSDC, 2002)

Designing Powerful Professional Development For Teachers and Principals

and tacit view that teaching is semi-skilled labor with an emphasis on nurturing undermines both the need for intellectually rigorous staff development and the value of teacher leadership in the school improvement process. The assumptions that teachers' responsibilities should be limited to the classroom with students, that teachers should work alone, and that all teachers should be viewed as equal in their knowledge and skills are other significant barriers. More will be said about barriers to teacher leadership in Chapter 8.

DISTRIBUTING LEADERSHIP IN SCHOOLS

Mary Neuman and Warren Simmons (2000) observe that, "In the most effective schools that we have worked with, every member of the education community has the responsibility—and the authority—to take appropriate leadership roles. ... The definition of 'leader' has been broadened to encompass teachers, staff members, parents, and members of the entire education community" (pp. 9-10).

Elmore (2000) lists five principles of distributed leadership in schools: (1) the purpose of leadership is the improvement of instructional practice and performance, regardless of role, (2) instructional improvement requires continuous learning, (3) learning requires modeling, (4) the roles and activities of leadership flow from the expertise required for learning and improvement, not from the formal dictates of the institution, and (5) the exercise of authority requires reciprocity of accountability and capacity.

Jonathan Supovitz (2000) describes three specific forms of distributed leadership: the preparation of teacher specialists within schools who act as advocates for new forms of teaching and serve as coaches to their peers, the devolution of authority to teams of teachers who are responsible for making instructionally-related decisions and whose leaders serve on school councils, and the employment of full-time design coaches and literacy or math coordinators within comprehensive school reform designs.

Neuman and Simmons (2000) offer other ways in which teachers provide leadership within schools. "Other structures that enhance shared leadership and responsibility," they note, "include networks of teachers who gather regularly to share their own or their students' work, study groups that focus on learning about and understanding particular issues, action research that provides both continuous feedback to practitioners and summative data about performance, and 'critical friends' who can offer needed but often difficult observations on the work of a school" (p. 12).

Ann Lieberman (Sparks, 1999) points out that leadership roles enable teachers to move

Designing Powerful Professional Development for Teachers and Principals, by Dennis Sparks (NSDC, 2002)

chapter seven

Designing Powerful Professional Development For Teachers and Principals

out of the isolation even good teachers feel in their classrooms. "It's extremely liberating," she says, "for teacher leaders to go to places where people are talking about learning and the issues of the day" (p. 56). Roland Barth (2001) agrees: "These teachers win something important. They experience a reduction in isolation; the personal and professional satisfaction that comes from improving their schools; a sense of instrumentality, investment, and membership in the school community; and new learning about schools, about the process of change, and about themselves. And all of these positive experiences spill over into their classroom teaching. These teachers become owners and investors in the school, rather than mere tenants. They become professionals" (p. 449).

MY ASSUMPTIONS

■   Principals play an essential role in creating schools that promote quality teaching in all classrooms and high levels of student learning.

■   Effective schools distribute leadership responsibilities among many individuals.

■   Teacher leaders benefit as they serve the school, its faculty, and its students.

FOR DISCUSSION

Write your assumptions regarding the areas addressed by my assumptions. Be specific and succinct. Dialogue with your group regarding your assumptions, remembering that the intention of dialogue is the nonjudgmental surfacing of assumptions rather than critiquing or seeking to change the assumptions of others.

Discuss your views regarding Roland Barth's definition of leadership: "Making happen what you believe in."

Describe how your district supports or does not support principals as strong instructional leaders in their schools.

Designing Powerful Professional Development for Teachers and Principals, by Dennis Sparks (NSDC, 2002)

Designing Powerful Professional Development For Teachers and Principals

Discuss school or district policies and practices that enable teacher leadership in your district or school.

Specify what actions will be taken as a result of this discussion, who will take them, and by what date.

REFERENCES

Barth, R. (2001). *Learning by heart*. San Francisco: Jossey-Bass.

Cross, C. & Rice, R. (2000). The role of the principal as instructional leader in a standards-driven system. *NASSP Bulletin, 84*(620), 61-65.

Dahle, C. (2000). Natural leader. *Fast Company,* 41, 268.

Downs, A. (2000, March/April). Leadership for student achievement: Successful school reform efforts share common features. *Harvard Education Letter, 16*(2), 1-5.

Elmore, R. (2000). *Building a new structure for school leadership*. Washington, DC: Albert Shanker Institute.
www.shankerinstitute.org/education.html

Elmore, R. & Burney, D. (1999). Investing in teacher learning. In L. Darling-Hammond & G. Sykes (eds.), *Teaching as the learning profession*. San Francisco: Jossey-Bass.

Fullan, M. (2001). *The new meaning of educational change (3rd ed.)*. New York: Teachers College Press.

Guskey, T. (2000, Nov.). Twenty questions? Twenty tools for better teaching. *Principal Leadership: High School Edition, 1*(3), 5-7.

Designing Powerful Professional Development For Teachers and Principals

Harris, S.L. (2000, Nov.). Behave yourself. *Principal Leadership: High School Edition, 1*(3), 36-39.

Johnston, R. (2000, Sept. 20). British 'heads' reign with broad power. *Education Week, 20*(3), 1, 14, 16-17.
www.edweek.org/ew/ewstory.cfm?slug=03england.h20

Institute for Educational Leadership. (2000, Oct.) *Leadership for student learning: Reinventing the principalship*: A report of the task force on the principalship. Washington, DC: Author.

National Association for Elementary School Principals. (2001). *Leading learning communities: Standards for what principals should know and be able to do*. Alexandria, VA: Author.

Neuman, M. & Simmons, W. (2000, Sept.). Leadership for student learning. *Phi Delta Kappan, 82*(1), 9-12.

Pierce, M. (2000, Sept./Oct.). Portrait of a 'super principal.' *Harvard Education Letter, 16*(5), 1-5.

Schlechty, P. (2001). *Shaking up the schoolhouse*. San Francisco: Jossey-Bass.

Schweitzer, C. (2000, Dec.). Creating a dot-com compatible culture. *Association Management, 52*(13), 28-35.

Sebring, P.B. & Bryk, A.S. (2000, Feb.). School leadership and the bottom line in Chicago. *Phi Delta Kappan, 81*(6), 440-443.

Senge, P. (1999). *The dance of change: The challenges to sustaining momentum in learning organizations*. New York: Doubleday.

Designing Powerful Professional Development for Teachers and Principals, by Dennis Sparks (NSDC, 2002)

Designing Powerful Professional Development For Teachers and Principals

Senge, P. (1990). *The fifth discipline: The art and practice of the learning organization.* New York: Doubleday.

Smith, L. (2001, Feb. 7). Can schools really change? *Education Week, 20*(21), 30 & 32-33. *www.edweek.org/ew/ewstory.cfm?slug=21smith.h20*

Sparks, D. (1999, Winter). Real-life view: An interview with Ann Lieberman. *Journal of Staff Development, 20*(4), 53-57. *www.nsdc.org/library/jsd/lieberman204.html*

Stiggins, R. (2001). The principal's role in assessment. *NASSP Bulletin, 85*(621), 13-26.

Supovitz, J.A. (2000, Nov.). Manage less, lead more. *Principal Leadership: High School Edition, 1*(3), 14-19.

Wheat, D., Cramer, J., & Cramer, M.K. (2000, Nov.). A standard of support. *Principal Leadership: High School Edition, 1*(3), 33-35.

SECTION III

MAKING CHANGE, TAKING ACTION

The principal as instructional leader

CREATE A VISION

People developer
A new role for principals

By Joellen P. Killion, Judith P. Huddleston, and Margaret A. Claspell

P rincipals have emerged as a key link in the process of providing professional development for teachers (Brookover & Lezotte, 1979; Purkey & Smith, 1985). School effectiveness research (Edmonds, 1979; Purkey & Smith, 1985; Weber, 1971) confirms the importance of the principal as the school's instructional leader. Since the primary responsibility of principals is to help teachers teach effectively, their role in the continued renewal of teachers is paramount in school improvement efforts.

In this article, we identify the knowledge, skills, and beliefs that principals need to guide the professional development of their staff members. We also examine the incongruence between the role of the principal as a manager and the principal as a staff developer. Further, we suggest some strategies for helping principals to become principal-staff developers.

THE PRINCIPALSHIP: A LOOK BACK

Many principals who are currently in schools were hired because they were strong managers. Their expertise lies in directing people and resources, assessing the needs of their school, identifying the needs they wish addressed, and planning strategies to do so. They are organizers, delegators, monitors, and evaluators.

When the principal-as-instructional-leader movement emerged, principals who were managers often made only minor changes in their behavior. They continued to lead by controlling decisions about curriculum, instruction, and evaluation. They decided which new instructional programs to sanction and support, which teachers to reward with extra responsibilities and growth opportunities, and which staff development classes to allow in their building. On the other hand, principals who came to see themselves as instructional leaders developed the human potential of their staff members, acknowledged their own strengths and weaknesses, trusted rather than managed, sanctioned rather than controlled, and mentored rather than directed.

Today all these principals — no matter what their previous orientation — are expected to be people developers, a role that may require a new set of skills, knowledge, and beliefs.

QUALITIES OF PRINCIPAL-STAFF DEVELOPERS

To be effective in supporting and encouraging staff development, principals need certain qualities as well as

Journal of Staff Development, Winter 1989 (Vol. 10, No. 1)

appropriate knowledge, skills, and beliefs. Theses qualities can be cultivated in some individuals through training and practice. For others, however, they may not be easy to acquire because they are so basic to one's personality and value system that they may not be learnable. From our experiences, we have identified what we believe to be some of the essential qualities of principal-staff developers.

KNOWLEDGE

An important source of knowledge required of principal-staff developers is *self-awareness.* Principals who are successful staff developers are more likely to have an accurate perception of their personal and professional strengths and limitations. They know who they are, how they operate, and what they believe in. They know their leadership style and are able to adjust it to match the needs of their staff.

Principals also need to have a thorough knowledge of their staff members. They must strive to know the professional strengths and areas for growth of each staff member almost as well as they know their own. In essence, principal-staff developers are like omniscient narrators who know and understand the thoughts, behaviors, and interactions of each character. With this information, principals can tailor their interactions and provide personalized support to individuals rather than to the masses.

SKILLS

Principals need many skills to be successful as a staff developer in addition to traditional skills such as communication, goal setting, and conflict resolution.

Maintaining flexibility. The principal needs to have a full range of behaviors at his or her disposal. A principal needs to choose when to be a cheerleader, who encourages, motivates, and builds enthusiasm; a coach, who facilitates growth through questioning, advising, or suggesting; an expert, who directs and sets standards; or

a resource who provides access to information, people, budget, time, or space.

Modeling. To demonstrate their commitment to professional renewal, principals must demonstrate their belief in the value of continued growth (Little, 1982). These characteristics include a willingness to admit to weaknesses and failures, openness to suggestions for improvement, active participation in administrator development programs, eagerness to share what they have learned, and a celebration of successes with others. Another important modeling behavior for principals is attendance and active participation in the staff development programs in which their teachers participate. Principals complete all assignments and activities that others are expected to do.

Supporting. Principals who take their roles as staff developer seriously support their teachers and expect reciprocal support when they need it. They confront rather than avoid problems. They engage in problem solving by encouraging discussion about contributing factors and ways for dealing with these factors. Willing to admit that they may not have all the answers, principals work to help their teachers find appropriate resources and support.

Using resources creatively. Principal-staff developers view resources as possibilities rather than limitations. They do not allow the budget to block opportunities for enrichment, but rather work around it. They are eager to do their fair share in covering classes while teachers participate in inservice programs or observe colleagues. In addition, these principals say yes more often than they say no. The ask the right questions and assist teachers in analyzing the implications of their actions. Principal-staff developers encourage teachers to make their own decisions.

Reflecting and analyzing. Principals who succeed as staff developers help their staff members teach reflectively rather than reflexively. They help teachers see themselves as rational decision makers who can and do make a difference with students (Ashton, 1984). They

Journal of Staff Development, Winter 1989 (Vol. 10, No. 1)

use reflective questioning (Killion & Harrison, 1988) to model and guide teachers in analyzing their decisions and the actions that result from those decisions. When observing teachers and holding instructional conferences with them, these principals refrain from telling what they observed; instead they question teachers on their decisions (Garmston, 1988). Through modeling, these principals instill the skills and value of self-analysis and reflection so that teachers begin to engage in these activities independently for their own benefit.

Hero-making. According to Heider (1985), "A wise leader settles for good work and then lets others have the floor. The leader does not take all the credit for what happens and has no need for fame" (p. 17).

Principals who support their staff members in professional growth are hero-makers. They allow teachers to be experts. These principals encourage, support, and push teachers into the limelight and reward them for their efforts. For example, these principals encourage teachers to present school programs in workshops and at conferences. They share district political secrets that help teachers have access to the appropriate people and resources to achieve their goals. These principals also provide teachers with opportunities to become teachers of other teachers. They ask teachers to share their particular expertise with one another through both formal and informal staff development activities.

These principals also refrain from rescuing. If a teacher fails, the principal does not rush to rescue the teacher and remove the consequences. Instead, the principal will stand by the teachers as a supportive partner, helping the teacher solve the problem or rectify the situation. These principals know the value of learning from one's experiences. They recognize that giving teachers opportunities to make decisions in difficult situations is one way they can help the teacher become stronger.

Collaborating. If they believe in professional development, principals encourage collaboration among staff members. They prefer to influence through collegiality rather than to control through power. They build networks among other principals to extend the resources they are able to offer staff members. They share resources and engage teachers in discussions about their teaching practices.

These principals recognize the need to combat the negative influence of classroom isolation. They structure time at faculty meetings for teachers to talk about their teaching (Valencia & Killion, 1988). These principals also increase the number of occasions which require shared work (Purkey & Smith, 1985). Teachers are encouraged to learn from and with each other.

Sanctioning. Supportive principals give their staff permission to explore, take risks, and change. Principals make it clear that the status quo is unacceptable when they encourage teachers to try new strategies (Hord, Rutherford, Huling-Austin, & Hall, 1987); Valencia & Killion, 1988). They compliment and publicly acknowledge efforts of their teachers in professional development. They may make informal mention of these efforts to colleagues or make formal presentations about them.

Mentoring. Mentoring gives principals a special opportunity to demonstrate that they are the key staff developers in their schools. In this role, they consult with teachers, provide them comfort and care, coach them, and gently push them to explore new possibilities. Mentoring includes meeting with teachers to give them instructional feedback, personalizing assistance to teachers' specific needs, and doing joint problem-solving with them. Most importantly, these principals are accessible to teachers and are willing to give them their time. They recognize that the success of their teachers is the single most important way to improve the quality of education for students.

BELIEFS

While principals need knowledge and skills to be successful staff developers, they are also believers in the potential of students and their staff members. The principal-staff developer is a believer dedicated to quality education and committed to school improvement (Achilles, 1987, p. 20). Principals strive to craft a culture which reflects their belief in continuous professional development. They work to develop beliefs shared among all staff members (Deal & Kennedy, 1981). They confirm that continuous professional development is a natural part of working in their schools (Little, 1982). Some of the beliefs that principals hold regarding professional development are described below.

Openness and trust. Principal-staff developers believe in openness and trust. They strive to create a culture that promotes acceptance and validation of everyone. This caring sense of community (Cohen, 1983) permits people to share both success and failure without fear of reprisal. Principal-staff developers trust their staff members and the decisions they make. They maintain confidentiality and respect the dignity of each person. They recognize and value each individual as an important member of the school community.

Congruence. Principal-staff developers strive to ensure congruence between their actions and their beliefs. These leaders are reflective, giving careful consideration to how their actions will be read. They recognize that their actions symbolize the meaning of their beliefs. The principals' actions also serve as a model of the behaviors expected in the building.

Potential of people. Principal-staff developers believe everyone wants to grow and succeed, and they maintain an efficacy expectation, the conviction that one can succeed (Bandura, 1977). They promote change and recognize that satisfaction with the status quo blocks opportunities for growth (Valencia & Killion, 1988). Risk taking is encouraged and supported.

View of the principalship. Principals who support staff development minimize the managerial functions of their jobs and eagerly embrace the role of people

developer. They consider matters related to instruction and the classroom performance of teachers the major focus of their work activity (Manasee, 1985). These principals are goal-oriented, proactive, and create conditions for effective instruction (Blumberg & Greenfield, 1980; Edmonds, 1979).

THE PRINCIPALSHIP: A LOOK AT THE PRESENT

There is today a mismatch between principals' managerial skills and the necessary knowledge, skills, and beliefs of a principal-staff developer. Many principals who were hired for their managerial skills do not possess the knowledge, skills, and beliefs to become school-based staff developers. They do not believe that the empowerment of teachers or the relinquishment of control is in the best interest of students. As a result, they consciously or unconsciously block improvement. Since a large number of these principals currently serve in our schools, what can be done to address this problem?

There are two possible approaches. First, school districts can assist these administrators in acquiring the appropriate knowledge, skills, and beliefs. Another approach is to help principals identify other individuals in their buildings who have the knowledge, skills, and beliefs to carry out the staff development functions, and then to work with the principal to ensure the success of that designee.

PROGRAMS FOR ASSISTING PRINCIPALS IN BECOMING STAFF DEVELOPERS

To make the transition from principal-managers to principal-staff developers, principals first must recognize the need for change and the benefits that can be gained for themselves and their schools. They must then receive assistance and support as they change their behaviors and relationships with their staff. Principals need numerous opportunities to discuss the principal-staff developer philosophy and role and to compare it to their own beliefs and behavioral systems and to internalize it. They also need to understand the research and practices which support this approach.

Programs. Staff development processes for principals might include:

Administrator development academies. These academies provide workshops and classes based on the needs of the administrators. Topics might include participatory decision-making, instructional leadership, conflict resolution, peer coaching, clinical supervision, cooperative learning, and group facilitation.

Peer-assisted leadership. This cooperative leadership program is designed to help principals understand and analyze their leadership behaviors (Dwyer, 1984). It involves the use of shadowing and reflective interviewing for data collection that allows principals to view their behavior from another's perspective.

Collegial teams. These teams allow for the establishment of trust and openness among a small group of administrators. Meetings have no set agenda but allow for the examination of personal and professional issues and problems, and provide a forum for discussion and to receive honest, constructive feedback.

Cluster groups. These groups involve 10-12 principals in addressing school improvement issues and problems and reflecting upon their actions in relation to district expectations. The goal for cluster groups is to increase collegiality and collaboration among principals and throughout the district.

Principal-peer observation teams. These teams have less structure than the peer-assisted leadership process, but allow administrators to shadow each other, obtain feedback, and discuss professional goals and concerns in a collaborative manner.

Principals' centers. Centers provide another forum for principals to learn about and to discuss the role of the principal-staff developer. A center may be a regional or statewide alliance of administrators that provides participants with opportunities to examine educational research and practices and that encourages discussion and self-examination.

Benefits for principals. These programs have several advantages for principals. They:

- Establish a research base for principals' actions and provide the opportunity for participants to develop a sound rationale for decision making.
- Allow for the sharing of experiences and facilitate the transfer of theory to practice.
- Promote self-analysis and provide opportunities to get support and feedback from colleagues.
- Create a collaborative environment that reinforces the concept that everyone in the district is working through the change process together.
- Provide examples of what is occurring in other educational settings that might be adapted for local use.

DELEGATING THE STAFF DEVELOPMENT ROLE TO OTHERS

The previous programs are based upon the assumption that the knowledge, skills, and beliefs necessary for becoming a principal-staff developer can be cultivated. While many principals can acquire the necessary skills and knowledge, their beliefs may be immutable; therefore, they cannot make the transition from a manager to a staff developer. As a result, these administrators may need encouragement to allow others to assume staff development responsibilities.

Like their colleagues, these principals must be assisted to recognize the need for change and the benefits of this change to their schools and to themselves. Communication of district expectations and of things that are being done in other schools can help increase principals' awareness of the need for change. These principals should be paired with someone they trust and whom they acknowledge as expert in staff development.

Journal of Staff Development, Winter 1989 (Vol. 10, No. 1)

This person might be a supervisor, colleague, or a district staff developer. They should begin by discussing with their trusted colleagues the value of staff development for themselves and their staff members.

Further, principals need assistance in addressing the issues related to delegating the staff development function to others. These issues include:

Power and control. The relationship between the principal and the school's staff developer will need to be discussed. For example, how will the principal be involved in the staff development program? How much control will be exercised over the staff developer?

Communication. Reporting and information networks will need to be clarified. For example, how will the principal be included and kept informed?

Trust. Selection and/or placement of a staff developer must include consideration of the staff developer's skills, the principal's personality, and the school's needs. Several questions need to be addressed: How can trust be established in the school? What kind of an individual would work most effectively with this principal and this staff? Should the staff developer be a current staff member or someone from outside the building?

Identifying the staff developer is only the first step. After the staff developer begins to work in the school, principals need continued support, encouragement, and acknowledgment for their efforts. They need assistance in working through the problems which arise in their buildings. They need encouragement to discuss the program with their staffs on an ongoing basis. Both the principals and the staff developers should have opportunities to network with other buildings.

RECOMMENDATIONS

Successful staff developers, whether they be principals or others, have specific knowledge, skills, and beliefs. Since the role of a staff developer at the building level is critical for teachers' professional growth and renewal, we recommend the district establish formal staff development programs which provide for the acquisition of principal-staff developer skills.

These programs should incorporate an assessment component so that districts can determine where their administrators are in relationship to staff development skills. In addition, districts should design intervention programs for principals who are having difficulty making the transition from managers to staff developers. These programs should provide support, assistance, and recognition for changes which are made.

To make the transition from principal-managers to principal-staff developers, some principals will need opportunities to refine the skills that will make them effective in that effort. Other principals, however, will need encouragement in allowing others to assume the staff development role. A thoughtful district plan, with a variety of options, can provide the support necessary to principals to assume their responsibilities as people-developers.

REFERENCES

Achilles, C.M. (1987). A vision of better schools. In W.D. Greenfield (Ed.), *Instructional leadership: Concepts, issues, and controversies.* Boston, MA: Allyn & Bacon.

Ashton, P. (1984). Teacher efficacy: A motivational paradigm for effective teacher education. *Journal of Teacher Education, 35*(5), 28-32.

Bandura, A. (1977). Self efficacy: Toward a unifying theory of behavioral change. *Psychological Review, 84*(2), 191-215.

Blumberg, A.C. & Greenfield, W.D. (1980). *The effective principal.* Boston, MA: Allyn & Bacon.

Brookover, W.B. & Lezotte, L.W. (1979). *Changes in school characteristics coincident with student achievement.* East Lansing, MI: Michigan State University Institute of Research on Teaching. (ERIC Document Reproduction Service ED 181 005).

Cohen, M. (1983). Instructional, management, and social conditions in effective schools. In A.O. Webb &

L.D. Webb (Eds.), *School finance and social improvement: Linkages in the 1980s.* Cambridge, MA: Ballinger.

Deal, T.E. & Kennedy, A.A. (1981). *Corporate culture: The rites and rituals.* Reading, MA: Addison-Wesley.

Dwyer, D.C. (1984). The search for instructional leadership: Routines and subtleties in the principal's role. *Educational Leadership, 41*(5), 32-37.

Edmonds, R.R. (1979). Effective schools for the urban poor. *Educational Leadership, 37*(2), 15-27.

Garmston, R. (1988, August). A call for collegial coaching. *The Developer*, pp. 4-6.

Heider, J. (1985). *The tao of leadership: Lao Tzu's Tao Te Ching adapted for a new age.* Atlanta, GA: Humanics New Age.

Hord, S.M., Rutherford, W.L., Huling-Austin, L., & Hall, G.E. (1987). *Taking charge of change.* Alexandria, VA: Association for Supervision and Curriculum Development.

Killion, J.P. & Harrison, C.R. (1988). Evaluating training programs: Three critical elements for success. *Journal of Staff Development, 9*(1), 34-38.

Little, J.W. (1982). The effective principal. *American Education, 18*(7), 38-43.

Manasee, A.L. (1985). Improving conditions for principal effectiveness: Policy implications of research. Elementary School Journal, 85(3), 439-463.

Purkey, S.C. & Smith, M.S. (1985). School reform: the district policy, implications of the effective schools literature. *Elementary School Journal, 85*(3), 353-389.

Valencia, S.W. & Killion, J.P. (1988). Overcoming obstacles to teacher change: Direction from school-based efforts. *Journal of Staff Development, 9*(2), 2-8.

Weber, G. (1971). *Inner city children can be taught to read: Four successful schools.* Washington, DC: Council for Basic Education.

ABOUT THE AUTHORS

Joellen P. Killion is a staff developer and curriculum specialist at the Staff Development Training Center in Northglenn, Colo.

Judith P. Huddleston is director of curriculum for School District No. 12, Adams County, in Northglenn, Colo.

Margaret A. Claspell is principal of Eastlake Campus Alternative School, Eastlake, Colo.

New images of school leadership
Implications for professional development

By Ginny V. Lee

Those of us involved in the professional development of school administrators are witnessing significant changes in conceptions of school leadership. Top thinkers in school administration are moving away from the dominant paradigm of the past decade — the image of principal as instructional leader. In its place they are proposing an image that is more congruent with new visions of schools and classrooms, with new visions of schools and classrooms, an image in which the school is viewed as a learning community and the principal is regarded as the central person in the development of school culture. This shift toward a new image of school leadership — one that emphasizes collaboration and school culture — has significant implications for the professional development of school administrators.

The purpose of this article is to discuss promising professional development strategies which promote the development of leaders in this new image. (While other individuals in the school play important leadership roles, this article is limited to the formal site leader, the school principal.) The article begins with some recent shifts in conceptions of schools and implications of these shifts for school leadership in bringing such conceptions of schools to life. These leadership qualities are then connected to strategies for professional development. Principles of professional development are discussed in relation to their ability to develop the leadership qualities needed for schools to operate as learning communities. Finally, these principles are connected to recommendations for staff developers.

THE CHANGING VIEW OF SCHOOLS AND SCHOOL LEADERSHIP

The current thinking of experts in school administration has moved away from a concept of instructional leadership that is focused on hierarchy, supervision, and technical solutions to problems of instruction and management. In his most recent writings, Tom Sergiovanni (1992a, 1992b) proposes that the metaphor of "schools as communities" would better serve educators as the dominant conceptual frame for thinking about their work.

Sergiovanni's argument is echoed by Michael Fullan (1991, 1992), whose work on school change emphasizes the importance of collaborative cultures. Similarly, Kenneth Leithwood's (1992) most recent

Journal of Staff Development, Winter 1993 (Vol. 14, No. 1)

research of the school leader has focused on the concept of "transformational leadership," which emphasizes, among other tasks, the principal's role in developing a collaborative school culture.

NEW VISIONS OF LEADERSHIP

For schools to operate more as communities characterized by collaborative cultures, new visions of leadership are required. A prominent and overarching characteristic of such leadership, one that serves as a foundation for all others, is the notion of shared responsibility and power (Glickman, 1992; Leithwood, 1992; Sarason, 1990; Sergiovanni, 1992b). While descriptions of specifics vary concerning what shared responsibility and power might look like in a school, the changing conceptions of schools and leadership generally call for less hierarchical distance between the principal and staff.

Sharing responsibility and power supports the development of schools as learning communities in at least two ways. First, it contributes to the achievement of a common vision and shared goals by providing opportunities for the involvement and contributions of all staff members. This, in turn, helps develop a shared culture and a sense of cohesiveness among staff. Second, sharing responsibility and power supports the technical side of teaching and learning by making it possible to pool staff expertise for better outcomes. Everyone benefits when the combined expertise of the group addresses specific challenges and problems faced by the school as a whole and by individual teachers.

When responsibility and power are shared, leadership takes on a new meaning. The principal then becomes an "enabler of solutions" (Fullan, 1992), a facilitator and collaborator (Leithwood, 1992), and a "leader of leaders" (Brandt, 1992).

Leadership of schools that are communities (a) supports negotiation rather than confrontation, (b) aids in developing an environment for inquiry and open exploration of ideas, (c) helps build consensus when needed, and (d) leads to win-win solutions. In schools as communities, the administrator promotes collegial professional relationships, including peer support and assistance, in place of isolation or competition among teachers (Fullan, 1992; Sergiovanni, 1992b). These processes require different modes of communication between the administrator and staff, and they may require that the administrator assist in developing new communications and interaction modes among staff members (Lee, 1991a).

QUALITIES OF THE NEW LEADER

While it would be impossible to identify a single list of skills or attributes to describe this new leader, a number of qualities can be derived form the vision of schools and leadership that have been portrayed thus far. First, the knowledge and skills needed by "instructional leaders" would still be important (e.g., knowledge about teaching, learning, curriculum, and student assessment). However, the way in which the leader makes use of this knowledge would differ considerably in a school that operates as a learning community.

Direct supervision of instruction, for example, would be replaced by collaborative, collegial strategies to support improved teaching and learning (Glickman, 1992). Many decisions about school management, particularly those affecting teachers directly, would no longer be made by the leader alone (Sarason, 1990; Sergiovanni, 1992a, 1992b). Much of the leader's work would focus on creating and supporting new ways for the staff of the school to collaborate as a professional community (Fullan, 1992; Leithwood, 1992; Sergiovanni, 1992b).

From this perspective, a cluster of qualities can be identified that would be useful to administrators in creating professional communities within the schools. These qualities include but are not limited to:

- The ability to tolerate ambiguity and uncertainty. This includes the recognition of many possible ways to deal with an issue, with less emphasis on finding the single best way.

- A respect for, and valuing of, differences and diversity among individuals. Thus, colleagues are viewed as assets rather than deficits.

- Expertise in communication processes, particularly those that support inquiry, cooperation, the development of consensus, and the achievement of win-win solutions. Valued communication skills include open-ended questioning, listening, clarifying, and acknowledging others' ideas.

- A willingness to reflect on his or her own practices and beliefs and to recognize others as sources of learning.

IMPLICATIONS FOR PROFESSIONAL DEVELOPMENT

If staff developers acknowledge the need to support the growth of the qualities listed above, then professional development programs and activities for school leaders must shift to accommodate this goal. This shift needs to occur not only in program content (what is presented) but also in program delivery (the strategies and processes used to present ideas and engage the participants).

The type of leadership described above cannot be reduced to a set of technical skills; it involves dealing with the evolving and organic elements of school culture, including complex networks of interaction among members of a community. Solutions to practical application problems (e.g., how to accomplish this in a specific school) will vary with context, values, and preferences of those involved.

For these reasons, the content of professional development to support this type of leadership will not lend itself to a "training" or "direct instruction" model of delivery. Rather, staff developers will need to model and

illustrate the principles and processes outlined above when working with administrators. Thus, to support principals in providing this type of leadership in their schools, staff developers will need to provide the same type of leadership in their professional development programs.

MODELING OF NEW LEADERSHIP

Modeling is important for at least three reasons. First, professional development that emphasizes this new leadership represents a significant departure from existing models and concepts of leadership. Learning (or even thinking about) an alternative way of doing business can be uncomfortable for participants. One of the most powerful ways to demonstrate the appropriateness of this leadership approach is to engage participants in a firsthand experience of it and let them discover the benefits.

For example, a group of professional development participants who have a direct experience of working interdependently on a series of tasks can identify for themselves the value of being part of a community of learners and imagine how this concept would apply in their own setting. Any conclusions they reach will be more valid than if they were simply being told about the community of learners concept (e.g., in a direct instruction format).

A second, closely related reason for using delivery strategies that model the new leadership resides in the value of providing a direct demonstration for participants. While the demonstration strategy is generally useful in professional development, it is especially useful when addressing an unfamiliar and complex concept. By seeing new leadership principles and processes modeled throughout program delivery, participants have a much clearer and more specific idea of how these new ideas look in action. More importantly, when the demonstration is coupled with reflection and sharing about what they are witnessing and experiencing, participants achieve a deeper understanding of the power of the principles and processes.

Journal of Staff Development, Winter 1993 (Vol. 14, No. 1)

A third reason for modeling is the need for the staff developer to be perceived as credible and legitimate to the audience. One way of accomplishing this is by "walking the talk." If a staff developer claims to endorse these new leadership ideas (the talk), his or her demonstration of what that "talk" looks like demonstrates clearly and concretely that the person's work is based on deeply held knowledge, beliefs, and values, and that the work has integrity.

What do such professional development programs look like? How does a staff developer model collaboration and community for administrators? For the past nine years, the staff at the Far West Laboratory has worked with administrators and staff developers in the way described above (Lee, 1998, 1991b). Our experience includes delivery of the Peer-Assisted Leadership (PAL) Program for administrators, the PAL Instructor Preparation and Certification Program, and numerous workshops on administrator peer coaching, administrator mentoring, and similar topics.

From our experience in these activities, we have been able to identify principles and strategies that support the models of collaboration and community described here. The remainder of this article discusses two important principles which guide the programs and describes some of the strategies we use. These strategies focus on the processes of learning and of interaction, and can be employed by staff developers working in a variety of contexts with school administrators and other adult audiences.

Principle No. 1: Work for deep and authentic personal/professional engagement and ownership of the learning. For participants to be fully engaged with the substance of programs, they must use their professional development experiences as a means for greater clarity about their own knowledge, beliefs, and values. Because learning experiences must penetrate beyond a superficial encounter with new knowledge, individuals need opportunities to consider how new information makes sense for them, how it makes sense for others, and

how it can be incorporated into their own professional development (Lee, 1991a). There are a number of strategies that can produce this engagement.

Build from the experiences and skills of the group. Help participants identify what and how much they already know; demonstrate how "expert" knowledge and research are connected to their experiential, "common sense" knowledge; provide multiple small-group activities that allow individuals to learn from others in the group; and create tasks that require group interdependence and that draw upon multiple abilities (or "intelligences") of group members.

Put learning activities directly in the hands of participants. Minimize up-front explanations by the staff developer; have participants engage themselves directly with the skills or information being presented by allowing them to read source materials, practice new skills, learn by experimenting, and other hands-on types of learning; use open-ended, divergent tasks to maximize learning outcomes; and let participants teach each other and also teach you.

Push for the "so what?" Create opportunities for individuals and small groups to reflect on the process and content; encourage reflection not only about what was learned but how it was learned; focus discussion at regular intervals on how participants' experiences might have an impact on their work; encourage divergent thinking; and acknowledge multiple uses for the new information. Strategies such as these, when used consistently, increase the likelihood that participants will leave the session with significant learning. They demonstrate respect for diversity in the group and promote inquiry, cooperation, and self-reflection.

Principle No. 2: Create a climate that supports a sense of professional community among participants. The kind of engagement and ownership described above cannot occur without collaboration and professional dialogue among the participants, including the facilitator. To support such dialogue, the climate of any staff development program must support norms of professional interaction and positive regard. With groups of administrators who are accustomed to having to "look good" and/or to compete with other administrators, this may require a significant shift in the norms of the group. This type of shift can be encouraged with strategies that:

Encourage risk-taking. Establish and model clear norms of behavior (such as keeping comments nonjudgmental) that make the environment safe for everyone; acknowledge everyone's contribution and require participants do to the same by building on each other's input; assume everyone is doing the best he or she can; point out the strengths of individuals and of their contributions; provide opportunities for participants to discuss concerns; be willing to reveal your own limitations; and solicit feedback and show that you are willing to use it.

Avoid having the "right" answer. Acknowledge that there is no one best answer; accept a range of responses to any question; turn participant questions back to the individual and/or the group for an answer; and admit when you don't know.

Developing a sense of professional community goes beyond simple cordiality and small group discussion activities. It requires revealing who we are as professionals — what we know, what we believe, and what we value. It demands that we not only listen to each other, but that we *hear* what others are saying. The ideas clustered under this principle help create conditions that foster a sense of professional community. In carrying out these ideas, the staff developer is exhibiting many of the leader qualities described earlier: the need to tolerate ambiguity and uncertainty, the respect for others' points of view, regard for everyone as a contributor, and win-win communication strategies. Allowing participants to experience involvement in this type of learning climate is imperative for developing

their capacity to support professional community in their own schools.

RECOMMENDATIONS AND CONCLUSION

Putting these principles and strategies into action requires that staff developers relinquish their positions of absolute authority and their control of outcomes. This can be an unnerving experience, one that may at first feel risky. In addition, this approach may create discomfort among participants, especially those who want the presenter to "just tell us what to do."

Yet, the more staff developers are able to let go and to work with and through the group, the more effective they will be in empowering administrators to move away from the old leadership paradigm toward a model of collaboration and culture-building in action. For the staff developer, the two guidelines described below can support this kind of work.

Focus on service. The measure of a successful program for the development of new leaders should be how well it serves participants Sergiovanni (1992a) writes of "servant leadership," and the concept has relevance here. It means relinquishing self-interest and letting go of ego; it requires a vulnerability that does not always feel comfortable. But a service orientation is absolutely essential to the development of the climate in which administrators can move toward new ideals.

Demonstrate flexibility. Letting go of preconceived outcomes or of preconceived notions of how experiences will look and be processed by participants is central to achieving the kinds of authentic, personalized learning necessary for the new leadership. The staff developer engaged in the practices and processes identified above must be able to work with whatever the group presents. This requires continual reflection-in-action and a willingness to deviate from the lesson plan.

When professional developers bring into administrator professional development programs the kinds of

Journal of Staff Development, Winter 1993 (Vol. 14, No. 1)

experiences, processes, and interactions that characterize a community of learners, they are creating the best opportunities for today's leaders to become the kind of administrators who will help develop schools in new image.

REFERENCES

Brandt, R. (1992). On rethinking leadership: A conversation with Tom Sergiovanni. *Educational Leadership, 49*(5), 46-49.

Glickman, C.D. (1992). Introduction: Postmodernism and supervision. In C.D. Glickman (Ed.), *Supervision in Transition* (pp. 1-3). Alexandria, VA: Association for Supervision and Curriculum Development.

Fullan, M.G. (with Stiegelbauer, S.) (1991). *The new meaning of educational change* (2nd ed.) New York: Teachers College Press.

Fullan, M.G. (1992). Visions that blind. *Educational Leadership, 49*(5), 19-20.

Lee, G.V. (1998). Reaching broader audiences: Training trainers to deliver Peer-Assisted Leadership. Paper presented at the annual meeting of the American Educational Research Association. New Orleans, LA.

Lee, G.V. (1991a). Instructional leadership as collaborative sense-making. *Theory Into Practice, 30*(2), 83-90.

Lee, G.V. (1991b). Peer-assisted development of school leaders. *Journal of Staff Development, 12*(2), 14-18.

Leithwood, K.A. (1992). The move toward transformational leadership. *Educational Leadership, 49*(5), 8-12.

Sarason, S. (1990). *The predictable failure of educational reform.* San Francisco: Jossey-Bass.

Sergiovanni, T.J. (1992a). *Moral leadership: Getting to the heart of school improvement.* San Francisco: Jossey-Bass.

Sergiovanni, T.J. (1992b). Why we should seek substitutes for leadership. *Educational Leadership, 49*(5), 41-45.

ABOUT THE AUTHOR

Ginny V. Lee is director, Peer-Assisted Leadership Program, Far West Laboratory for Educational Research and Development, San Francisco, Calif.

Journal of Staff Development, Winter 1993 (Vol. 14, No. 1)

Measuring a leader
The standards provide a measure for making a difference

By Eddy J. Van Meter and Cynthia A. McMinn

Improving the quality of school leaders needs to start with leadership standards. The Interstate School Leaders Licensure Consortium (ISLLC) recognized that need nearly a decade ago.

In 1996, ISLLC adopted a set of standards to "help link leadership more forcefully to productive schools and enhanced educational outcomes." Since then, the group has out-lined a process to encourage school leaders to make those standards part of their individual professional development.

The standards are used throughout the United States. In the most recognized use, the standards have been used in assessment for licensing beginning principals (Latham & Pearlman, 1999). Kentucky and Mississippi have used the standards to help universities restructure school leader preparation programs. State professional associations, particularly in Illinois, have used them to design new professional development programs for practicing school leaders. And ISLLC is developing new ways to use the standards in principals' professional development, both for training and to enhance current skills.

FOCUS ON THE PRINCIPAL

Although the ISLLC standards apply to all school leadership positions, they target school principals and associate principals. The standards provide a "road map" for practicing principals, a blueprint for making a difference in fundamental areas such as fostering teacher professional growth, engaging sustained parental and community involvement, and accomplishing successful student learning.

The six ISLLC standards focus on (1) developing a vision of learning that is shared by all school stakeholders; (2) fostering a productive school culture and instructional program; (3) managing school in an efficient and effective manner; (4) enhancing collaboration with families and the community; (5) administering in a legal and ethical fashion; and (6) influencing the socioeconomic, legal, political, and cultural contexts of schooling through proactive leadership.

Under each standard, indicators define what the school leader should know, highlight education-related beliefs and values to which the individual should be committed, and point out what the individual should be able to do to perform the job.

In addition to providing a job performance assessment, the standards emphasize the principal's emerging role in serving the school community rather than attempting to direct and control the school community (Murphy & Shipman, 1999).

As with other sets of educational standards, ISLLC intended for its standards to be put into practice. To date,

Journal of Staff Development, Winter 2001 (Vol. 22, No. 1)

PROPOSITIONS FOR PRINCIPAL DEVELOPMENT

In 1998, the ISLLC consortium appointed a 15-member design team including practicing school leaders, professional association representatives, and university school leadership faculty to develop the ISLLC Collaborative Professional Development Process. This team worked throughout 1998 and the first half of 1999, using the following set of propositions to guide the design effort. The process should be:

- Linked to the ISLLC standards.
- Linked to the day-to-day work of the school leader.
- Based on an assumption that school leaders are competent and, as professionals, routinely and in numerous ways improve their knowledge, dispositions, and performance.
- Based on an assumption that the primary responsibility for professional growth ultimately rests with the school leader himself or herself.
- Based on an assumption that collaboration is required between a school leader and others in order to examine and reflect on leadership and to promote personal growth.

the standards have been used primarily in three ways: to prepare school leaders, to assess existing school leaders, and to guide school leaders' professional development.

PREPARING LEADERS

Preparing to become a successful school leader obviously begins well before one is appointed to the job and includes skills learned from childhood on through building experiences as a teacher.

However, formal university preparation is important, and the ISLLC addresses four areas in this preparation

1. **Selecting individuals for the preparation program.** The standards can help determine whether an applicant's beliefs are compatible with current school-based values, especially whether an aspiring school leader believes certain groups of children have the capacity to learn at relatively high levels, or whether the individual is committed to other important education values.

2. **Deciding appropriate curricula.** The ISLLC standards guide curricula that target student success, offer performance indicators essential to school leaders' success, and encourage aspiring school leaders to advocate for students and their families.

3. **Guiding instruction for prospective school leaders**. The standards encourage preparation programs that are anchored in practice, emphasize context when presenting information, and provide real-world examples.

4. **Evaluating the preparation program**. Preparation programs can be measured against the ISLLC standards.

LICENSURE ASSESSMENT

In addition to providing a framework for preparation programs, the standards guided the design of a licensing assessment (Reese & Tannenbaum, 1999).

The School Leaders Licensure Assessment (SLLA), a performance-based exam, is being used in Illinois, Kentucky, Missouri, Mississippi, North Carolina, and the District of Columbia. Other states also are considering adopting the exam.

The exam has four parts. The first is brief vignettes of situations a principal might encounter, and the examinee reacts to them. The second module consists of longer

Journal of Staff Development, Winter 2001 (Vol. 22, No. 1)

cases. The prospective principal reviews documents related to each case and identifies appropriate action. In the third portion, the individual analyzes school documents and answers questions about school improvement. Finally, the examinee answers focused questions about longer cases based on documents.

ISLLC STANDARDS

The ISLLC program set out to define and improve school leadership and raise school leaders' competence. In the beginning, the consortium focused on defining leadership standards and strengthening preparation and licensing of school administrators. In the late 1990s, with additional funding, the group began to emphasize the professional development of practicing school leaders through two initiatives.

The first initiative is the ISLLC Assessment Portfolio. Candidates for re-licensure develop and analyze data on their school, community, staff, and students and then offer ideas for making improvements at the school. The Educational Testing Service is field testing these modules in Mississippi, North Carolina, Indiana, Ohio, and Missouri.

The second initiative is the ISLLC Collaborative Professional Development Process for School Leaders. It is available from the Council of Chief State School Officers office in Washington, D.C.

In this process, the school leader takes a step-by-step series of actions. He or she:

- Establishes a preliminary plan of personal and professional development goals that emphasize teaching and learning consistent with school improvement plans, district goals, and the ISLLC standards.
- Identifies colleagues to serve as a professional development team. This team critiques the school leader's work toward accomplishing goals and helps identify resources and strategies to assist.

7 PRINCIPLES

Seven principles were used to guide the development of the ISLLC standards. Standards should:

- Reflect the centrality of student learning.
- Acknowledge the changing role of the school leader.
- Recognize the collaborative nature of school leadership.
- Be high, upgrading the quality of the profession.
- Inform performance-based systems of assessment and evaluation for school leaders.
- Be integrated and coherent.
- Be predicated on the concepts of access, opportunity, and empowerment for all members of the school community.

- Presents the professional development plan to the professional development team, receives feedback, and revises the plan before developing products for review.
- Prepares a professional development portfolio, comprising work products the school leader develops to address his/her personal and professional goals. Each goal relates to specific needs or important challenges facing the school or district. The school leader's written reflections on team meeting discussions also are part of the portfolio. This portfolio documents the leader's progress toward the personal and professional goals.
- Presents work products for review and discussion at regular meetings of the professional development team. At these meetings, team members provide feedback to help the school leader refine ideas, constructively review the portfolio work products,

review product and professional development goal alignment with the ISLLC standards, and monitor the principal's progress toward his or her personal growth and professional development goals.

• Prepares a self-evaluation, including a critique of that plan by the professional development team, and revises the plan to begin the process anew.

The professional development team provides the school leader with direct and personal assistance. The whole process is closely linked to school-based improvements, along with individual professional development. These characteristics make the ISLLC Collaborative Professional Development Process different from other professional growth approaches.

THE ISLLC PROCESS IN PRACTICE

As a design plan and also as a process, the ISLLC Collaborative Professional Development Process can be used in a variety of ways (Van Meter, Shipman & Murphy, unpublished manuscript). Districts might use it in a non-evaluative manner to promote administrators' personal and professional growth or as part of a formal performance appraisal program for district leaders. Education agencies and professional associations might use it within programs to promote school leadership development. And individual school leaders might find it helpful for managing their own professional growth.

CONCLUSION

The ISLLC Standards for School Leaders build on a concept of standards-based school leadership preparation and practice that has evolved over two decades and been fostered by individuals, organizations, and professional associations, including the American Association of School Administrators, the National Association of Secondary School Principals, and the National Association of Elementary School Principals (Hoyle, English & Steffy, 1998).

FOR MORE INFORMATION

The Council of Chief State School Officers is a nationwide, nonprofit organization composed of public officials who lead departments responsible for elementary and secondary education in the states, the U.S. extra-state jurisdictions, the District of Columbia and the Department of Defense education activity. In representing the chief education officers, CCSSO works on behalf of the state agencies that serve pre-K-12 students throughout the nation.

• The Council's offices are at One Massachusetts Ave., NW Suite 700, Washington, D.C. 20001-1431, (202) 408-5505, fax (202) 408-8072.

• The Council's web site is www.ccsso.org.

• To obtain the standards, contact the CCSSO, or see publications.ccsso.org/ccsso/publication_list.cfm

These standards differ from similar previous efforts because of their specific focus on high expectations of success anticipated for "all" students, their emphasis on teaching and learning as the primary grounding for school leadership, and because of the importance the standards place on beliefs and values in providing direction for school leaders.

REFERENCES

Hoyle, J.R., English, F.W., & Steffy, B.E. (1998). *Skills for successful 21st century school leaders: Standards for peak performers.* Arlington, VA: American Association of School Administrators.

Latham, A.S. & Pearlman, M.A. (1999). From standards to licensure: Developing an authentic

Journal of Staff Development, Winter 2001 (Vol. 22, No. 1)

assessment for school principals. *Journal of Personnel Evaluation in Education, 13*(3), 245-262.

Murphy, J. & Shipman, N. (1999). The Interstate School Leaders Licensure Consortium: A standards-based approach to strengthening educational leadership. *Journal of Personnel Evaluation in Education, 13*(3), 205-224.

Reese, C.M. & Tannenbaum, R.J. (1999). Gathering content-related validity evidence for the School Leaders Licensure Assessment. *Journal of Personnel Evaluation in Education, 13*(3), 263-282.

Van Meter, E., Shipman, N., & Murphy, J. (2000). The ISLLC collaborative professional development process for school leaders: A standards-based approach to support the professional growth of practicing school leaders. Manuscript submitted for publication.

ABOUT THE AUTHORS

Eddy J. Van Meter is a professor of educational leadership at the University of Kentucky.

Cynthia A. McMinn is director of leadership development and enhancement for the Mississippi Department of Education.

Principals first change themselves

By Dennis Sparks

"Others will choose to change more readily from the example set by our own transformation than by any demand we make of them."

— Peter Block

What principals think, say, and do profoundly affects the quality of teaching and learning in their schools, the satisfaction they and the teachers with whom they interact derive from their work, and their ability to remain deeply engaged over many years in the demanding tasks of continuous improvement. Therefore, principals who desire significant changes in teaching, learning, and relationships within their schools begin by making significant changes in what they think, say, and do. As Gandhi expressed it, "We must become the change we seek in the world."

Principals have the capacity to make a tremendous difference in their organizations through the values they embody, the beliefs they hold, the intentions they express, the depth of their understanding of critical issues, the clarity of their thought and speech, and the ways in which they interact with others. Such attributes can have a substantial affect — for good or for ill — on the moods and performance of countless individuals within the school community.

Some values, beliefs, intentions, understandings, and actions establish trust and respect, focus and energize staff members, tap and develop talents, and stimulate creativity. Others can have the opposite effect. This subject is addressed by Jim Loehr and Tony Schwarz in the *Power of Full Engagement* (Free Press, 2003). "Every one of our thoughts, emotions, and behaviors has an energy consequence, for better or for worse," they note. Jane Dutton adds another dimension in *Energize Your Workplace* (Jossey-Bass, 2003). "[L]eaders can make a profound difference in activating and renewing energy by building and sustaining high-quality connections ... ," she writes. "High-quality connections contribute substantially to individuals' well-being and work performance. They also contribute significantly to an

Results, October 2004

TOOL 3.1

organization's capacity for collaboration, coordination, learning, and adaptation, as well as its ability to keep people committed and loyal."

Energy is created and performance improved when principals think, speak, and act in ways that connect the school community to larger, compelling purposes and strengthen relationships among teachers and between teachers and students and the families of those students. Energy is dissipated when principals and teacher leaders hold beliefs and act in ways that express resignation ("There's nothing we can do" or "They won't let us") and dependency ("Tell us what to do"). Resignation and dependency undermine genuine collaboration, professional learning, and a school's ability to find innovative solutions to pressing problems.

I recommend that principals and teachers develop a detailed vision of the school which they wish to create that is consistent with their values and then adopt beliefs,

intentions, understandings, speech forms, and behaviors that are consistent with that result. In that way, the creation of schools with higher levels of purpose, energy, and performance begins with principals first changing themselves.

By beginning with the end in mind and first changing themselves, principals are far less likely to be interested in blaming or "fixing" others. Because they have experienced profound change themselves, they are far more likely to see possibility and opportunity in situations in which others may only see limitations. As they empower themselves, they empower everyone with whom they interact.

ABOUT THE AUTHOR

Dennis Sparks is executive director of the National Staff Development Council.

Results, October 2004

10 steps to success
Principals need to remember that instruction is the key purpose of the school

By Harold Brewer

Nothing fails like success. To become better leaders, we can't rely simply on what's been successful in the past. Applying past solutions to current problems leads to failure. Instead, we must open ourselves to the possibility that we may have to change based on new research, new knowledge, or a deeper understanding. We must question why we believe what we believe.

A successful principal is alert to current realities, getting the questions right, being open to solutions that match the circumstances, and involving as many stakeholders as is reasonable in the process of defining the appropriate solution.

Consider these suggestions on the pathway to success:

1. **Focus on instruction.** Management concerns and the logistics of budgets, schedules, meetings, extracurricular activities, and all the things that consist of "doing school" can be distracting. Unless a principal is careful, these things represent what he or she becomes as a principal. The principal may pass off to a talented assistant principal the essentials of the instructional process and tell that person to "keep me posted." In delegating this task, the principal has just handed over the key influence of the school to a subordinate and set upon a path that leads away from the school's true mission. A focus on instruction is a focus that puts children first. It is a focus on teaching and learning. It is a focus on climate and culture. Yes, the logistics of school are important, and the principal is evaluated on their effectiveness. The successful principal will have thought through those essentials and will delegate the logistics, wherever possible, to the assistant principal to focus on learners' needs. For the principal who does not have an assistant, maintain an instructional orientation. Anything less and the principal will be seen as a good manager, someone who tries hard but is not the real leader of the school. Have a say in what this school will become. Stay planted on instructional soil and grow from there. Anything less is not worthy of the principal's time.

2. **Build a community of learners.** Create a school climate focused on student success. Spend time

Journal of Staff Development, Winter 2001 (Vol. 22, No. 1)

and energy focusing on those things recognized as having value and which are most likely to create desired outcomes. We must help the community understand the roles and relationships between school and community, and the supports and collaboration necessary to bring children to school ready to learn.

3. **Share decision making.** Allow ideas to be expressed, opinions shared and reflected back to stakeholder groups, and brought back to the decision-making body before decisions are made. Involve stakeholders at all levels and guard against having decisions reported to the School Improvement Team as "the way it is going to be" and then passed through stakeholder representatives back to the departments as team decisions. This route clearly demonstrates the real power is not in the leadership team but in the principal. Such behavior alienates staff members and undermines the improvement process. When stakeholders own the process and are committed to a shared vision, the energy and initiative to be successful will be there. Take the time and do the hard work to develop opportunities for meaningful participation.

4. **Sustain the basics**. Management, budget, discipline, the logistics of schedules, personnel, time, and all the details inherent in these areas are key to the principal's success. Being able to "do school" and all of the things that implies cannot be overlooked. "Doing school" is paramount to being a good school. Yet within that issue is the question of how to sustain the initiative for change that is so necessary in our quest to be better, not just for some, but for all students.

5. **Leverage time.** Identify essential processes, align those processes, and integrate the language of change and improvement into the school's daily routines.

While everyone cries, "We don't have time," the successful principal determines how to make time, take time, and use time.

6. **Support necessary and ongoing professional development for all staff.** Targeted professional development is essential to generate the skills and awareness that will build conditions which support the school's and community's desired goals.

7. **Assess and redirect resources necessary to support a multifaceted school plan.** Don't try to do this alone. Great conversations can build around these issues. Share opportunity and responsibility.

8. **Be a person of integrity.** Stephen Covey identifies integrity as comprising character and competence. A principal is elevated to a position within the community that requires one to have a strong moral character and to be an example of community values. This is not an optional component of the job. Think and listen to see what this means in your community.

9. **Remain competent.** To become competent requires both a knowledge and mastery of essential skills. To remain competent requires wisdom based on continuous learning and experience. To sustain competence requires an unending commitment.

10. **Develop a climate of inquiry and continuous improvement.** The process of improvement in organizations is as much a function of knowing what questions to ask as it is getting the answer right. Don't just look for answers. Making the connections is the work of leadership.

ABOUT THE AUTHOR

Harold Brewer is superintendent of the Montgomery County (Md.) Schools.

Inside the journal of an administrator
Aspiring administrators learn to reflect

By Michelle Contich

Journaling is an integral part of staff development because it allows individuals to consider their own learning thoughtfully. Journaling helps participants analyze their own and other's thought processes and think about how one thinks and learns.

When Williamson County Schools in Franklin, Tenn., had several openings for principal positions in 2003, leaders found that the applicant pool barely produced the quality of administrators the district wanted. Leaders decided to create an academy to "grow" their own future administrators who would be equipped with the knowledge, skills, and beliefs to create a high-achieving learning environment.

The academy's two-year design mirrored the rigor of graduate work. Interstate School Leaders Licensure Consortium (ISLLC), International Society for Technology in Education (ISTE), National Educational Technology Standards (NETS), and National Staff Development Council (NSDC) standards served as the framework for the model. After a structured application and interview process, the district accepted 20 educators for the academy. Aspiring administrators met each month during the school year for two consecutive years to learn techniques they could use to develop as quality school administrators, including reflecting on practice, accessing and using research, identifying problems and appropriate solutions, and understanding operational leadership. Current administrators and government officials, including the director of schools, principals, central office staff, the county mayor, and county chief financial officer worked with participants to share perspectives from their roles and jobs. Embedded within the work was constant reflection through journaling.

Participants used journals to record essential information and reactions throughout the academy. Each was asked to date, title, and connect entries to real-life experiences and ongoing research. The entries also recorded action plans participants would implement in their schools, based on a topic/subject each chose aimed at increasing student achievement and professional learning in their respective schools. The journal entries recorded aspirants' new learning, understanding, and actions taken toward the project.

THE ACADEMY

Academy participants began by reading Michael Fullan's book *Leading in a Culture of Change* (Jossey-Bass,

TOOL 3.3

2001) to spark conversations. Their discussions centered on leading with a moral purpose, creating and sustaining a positive culture, creating and promoting a vision, making connections, understanding and fostering change, and becoming results-oriented and data-driven.

They then demonstrated leadership in their schools by developing and implementing the individual projects that addressed a particular area of concern: assessment; classroom instruction; classroom management; use of resources, including personnel and volunteers; integrating technology; the standards-based county curriculum; budget management; quality staff development connected to proven results; and communication.

Some of the topics the administrators chose included the impact of student goal setting on achievement, integrating technology to increase student performance, and effective mentoring of first- through third-year teachers.

Each selected a project that was job-embedded. The project had to include: identifying a problem and designing appropriate responses; identifying others to work toward common goals; assessing and using educational research; using baseline data to determine student cognitive and affective needs; identifying instructional strategies and materials aligned with identified student needs; frequent assessments of student progress that result in action based on identified needs; and a timeline for implementation and results.

The tool of reflective writing helped participants clarify their thoughts and solidify their learning. Journaling allowed them to analyze their personal strengths and areas they wanted to strengthen in relation to the concepts and skills they were learning.

Journaling improved participants' metacognitive skills as they analyzed their own and others' thought processes.

Essential questions used to structure the reflective writing were:

Williamson County Schools
Franklin, Tenn.

Number of schools: 20 elementary schools (K-5), 7 middle schools (6-8), 8 high schools (9-12), and 1 K-8 school
Grades: K-12
Enrollment: 23,616
Staff: 1,442
Racial/ethnic mix:

White:	90.3%
Black:	4.4%
Hispanic:	24%
Asian/Pacific Islander:	2.9%
Native American:	0.1%
Other:	0%

Limited English proficient: 1.7%
Languages spoken: 67 languages and dialects
Free/reduced lunch: 7.6%
Special education: 14.2%
Contact:
Michelle Contich
1320 W. Main St., Stuie 202
Franklin, TN 37064
Phone: (615) 472-4081
Fax: (615) 595-4898

- What did I already know?
- How did I know this?
- Did I conduct my own research?
- On what sources of information did I base my beliefs?
- What do I think about the ideas and information presented?
- How did I reach my interpretation?
- What new information would make me change my mind?
- How does understanding this concept help me do my job more effectively?
- What do I value and why?
- What other information do I need?

The academy participants then self-assessed their journals using a rubric (see box). Each was ultimately responsible for posing questions and seeking answers

JSD, Summer 2006 (Vol. 27, No. 3)

to those questions by conducting action research and holding themselves accountable for finding the answers.

Journal entry — Aug. 12, 2003

"Moral purpose must be accompanied by strategies that energize people to pursue a desired goal and vision. Leaders inspire people to make a commitment to the moral purpose of the organization."

— Charlotte Pitcher, assistant principal

Journal entry — May 13, 2005

"Mike Schmoker in The Results Fieldbook (ASCD, 2001) stresses the need for teachers meeting regularly and collectively to review data specific to their building.

"Schools should begin focusing their goals this way. Through common goals, a school can begin to concentrate its efforts on the needs of its specific population and affect change directly."

— Victoria Roark, teacher

USING TECHNOLOGY

Academy participants learned to create a digital portfolio to structure their reflection and track their work. The portfolio included work the aspiring administrators collected as part of their projects, such as photographs and videos of work and artifacts specifically produced for the portfolio to demonstrate evidence of their growth and development over time. Their journals were an essential piece of the electronic portfolio.

As Kay Burke (1997) said, "Without written commentaries, explanations, and reflections, the portfolio is no more than a notebook of artifacts or a scrapbook of teaching mementos." Participants had to link their plans for instructional improvement and evidence of how they implemented their plans to reflections on ISLLC standards and to their individual and school goals.

SELF-EVALUATE YOUR JOURNAL

Place a check mark next to the level that best describes the entry in your journal. Review the elements of higher-level writing and work to meet the standards in subsequent entries.

Level A _____

My journal exhibits a developing understanding of critical issues in leadership today. The writing documents a small to moderate amount of research and action. The writing demonstrates organization and analysis without in-depth synthesis or evaluation. The reflections do not have any or have limited supporting resources or visible action.

Level B _____

My journal contains writing that includes information, resources, strategies, events, viewpoints, and anecdotes. The content of the writing demonstrates that action was taken at the school level, reflected on, analyzed, and improved upon for future implementation. My journal details my plans for an organized, effective project that, after being successfully implemented, could be duplicated. It demonstrates knowledge, analysis, and synthesis of information.

Level C _____

My journal contains a broad spectrum of writing to include information, resources, strategies, events, viewpoints, and anecdotes. The content transfers concepts from multiple sources that are critically analyzed, synthesized, investigated, and acted upon. The critiquing of information is sophisticated and exhibits originality, leadership, vision, and concrete steps for action. A high level of expertise and understanding is evident. It details a project that has a positive impact on the school.

JSD, Summer 2006 (Vol. 27, No. 3)

Summaries of the six Interstate School Leaders Licensure Consortium (ISLLC) Standards:

Standard 1

A school administrator is an educational leader who promotes the success of all students by facilitating the development, articulation, implementation, and stewardship of a vision of learning that is shared and supported by the school community.

Standard 2

A school administrator is an educational leader who promotes the success of all students by advocating, nurturing, and sustaining a school culture and instructional program conducive to student learning and staff professional growth.

Standard 3

A school administrator is an educational leader who promotes the success of all students by ensuring management of the organization, operations, and resources for a safe, efficient, and effective learning environment.

Standard 4

A school administrator is an educational leader who promotes the success of all students by collaborating with families and community members, responding to diverse community interests and needs, and mobilizing community resources.

Standard 5

A school administrator is an educational leader who promotes the success of all students by acting with integrity, fairness, and in an ethical manner.

Standard 6

A school administrator is an educational leader who promotes the success of all students by understanding, responding to, and influencing the larger political, social, economic, legal, and cultural context.

Source: Interstate School Leaders Licensure Consortium Standards for School Leaders, by Council of Chief State School Officers. Washington, DC: Council of Chief State School Officers, 1996.

Journal entry — Oct. 22, 2004

"We devote much of our time to preparing students for high-stakes testing. Often students know and understand that these tests do not affect their grade in a class and therefore are not compelled to do their best work. I chose to focus on the writing assessment and am working with teachers to set writing goals with their students. Through this study, we should be able to determine if student goal setting has an effect on their academic growth in the area of writing over time."

— Julie Sparrow, assistant principal

At the end of the project, participants shared their electronic portfolios with each other and used an assessment protocol to debrief and receive feedback on ways to implement their projects and the ISLLC standards in the future.

RESULTS

The journey through the projects and their reflections on the effort helped enlighten these administrators as they learned together the importance of collegial conversations, data collection and analysis, research-based decision making, and journaling.

The job of principal is often lonely, isolated, and demanding. Although they were and are competing for the same jobs, the academy recruits developed close relationships.

Having a support structure for reflection and dialogue helped them form a genuine learning community that will continue to benefit them as they become leaders within the school district.

Another critical result of the academy was the impact these aspiring leaders had on student achievement. Each project produced authentic results for students and helped nurture leadership skills. Journal entries reflected some of the results the aspiring administrators achieved.

Journal entry — May 23, 2005

"The participants had a mean growth equivalency rate of 1.19. It is also worthy of note that none of the participants' classes averaged less than a year's worth of growth, while 60% of the nonparticipants' classes did show less than a year's worth of growth."

— Victoria Roark, teacher

The first 11 academy participants graduated in 2005 understanding how to begin school improvement planning by looking at data; how to develop teachers in areas where they need to grow in order to get student results; how to ensure that teachers implement strategies by providing incentives such as technical equipment and released time, and monitoring results; and how to measure the impact of the project. Additionally, they now know the importance of reflecting and how to create a tool that collects and shows their learning.

Journal entry — June 2, 2005

"As I reflect, I wholeheartedly believe that this project has been a worthwhile endeavor. The faculty is better equipped to meet the needs of the students we serve by providing them with more of the tools they need to thrive in a future competitive workplace. Furthermore, I am better prepared to meet the needs of my faculty by being involved in this project. This project has been a long eventful journey, and I strongly believe that positive change has taken place in our school. We have now established a baseline on which future professional development can be planned and implemented:"

— Bill Toungette, assistant principal

Journal entry — May 31, 2005

"This project is ongoing in that several components have been added. First, a web site through the WCS Intranet is being developed to meet the needs of mentor leaders. The web site will contain workshop PowerPoint presentations, links to current online research, and the monthly newsletter. It will also have a link to the WCS bulletin board for new teacher mentors. This web site is due to become available in fall 2005."

— Melonye Lowe, teacher

REFERENCE

Burke, K. (1997). *Designing professional portfolios for change.* Thousand Oaks, CA: Corwin Press.

ABOUT THE AUTHOR

Michelle Contich is professional development coordinator for the Williamson County Schools.

The principal sets the tone

CHANGING CULTURE

Explain, inspire, lead
An interview with Noel Tichy

By Dennis Sparks

JSD: *In The Cycle of Leadership: How Great Leaders Teach Their Companies to Win* (HarperBusiness, 2002), you write, "The essence of leading is not commanding, but teaching." You define a teaching organization as "one in which everyone is a teacher, everyone is a learner, and as a result, everyone gets smarter every day." In such organizations, "everyone in the organization is expected to be constantly in a teaching and learning mode. ... [T]rue learning takes place only when the leader/teacher invests the time and emotional energy to engage those around him or her in a dialogue that produces mutual understanding."

Tichy: People agree that great teachers don't stand at podiums with a megaphone yelling at students. Instead, they engage with students in ways in which both they and their students learn.

I work in health care settings, as well as in business and education. In a good residency program, attending doctors both teach and learn from the residents. But the minute doctors become administrators, they have a lobotomy, forget what worked with residents, and act as if command and control is the way to run a hospital.

The same thing is true with principals who may have been incredible teachers. As teachers, they created a culture in their classrooms in which everyone learned and everyone taught. Students who were better at something coached other students. When they become principals, all of a sudden they act as bureaucrats rather than as teachers who create a learning environment for other teachers.

STRETCH GOALS WITH MILESTONES

JSD: I'd like to talk for a moment about the value of ambitious goals. You argue for "goals that stretch people's abilities" and write, "Winning leaders set goals that people think are impossible to achieve, and then help them to achieve them." Some leaders would argue that that's a recipe for discouragement and failure rather than motivation.

Tichy: That's true if there aren't milestones along the way through which confidence can be built. Without actions and milestones to measure progress, stretch goals are a recipe for disaster. When we link stretch goals, actions, and milestones, we can tap incredible emotional energy. Martin Luther King's "I Have a Dream" speech is a perfect example of a stretch goal — people being judged by the content of their character, not the color of their

JSD, Spring 2005 (Vol. 26, No. 2)

skin — that has motivated individuals and groups over several decades.

GREAT PRINCIPALS

JSD: You've recently applied your ideas with educators at the New York City Principals' Academy.

Tichy: New York City principals can impact 90,000 teachers and 1.2 million kids. I am convinced that if you want to leverage improvement in a school system, the most critical role is the principal. When you have a great principal, you can affect the culture of the school and teaching. Our goal is to help principals clarify their Teachable Points of View and for them to create Virtuous Teaching Cycles with various stakeholder groups ranging from parents to the union to students and teachers.

TEACHABLE POINTS OF VIEW

JSD: You just used two terms — Virtuous Teaching Cycles and Teachable Points of View — that I'd like to discuss in more detail. About Virtuous Teaching Cycles you wrote, "a leader commits to teaching, creates the conditions for being taught him- or herself, and helps the students have the self-confidence to engage and teach as well." The starting point of these cycles is leaders developing a Teachable Point of View, or TPOV for short. A TPOV, you say, is "a cohesive set of ideas and concepts that a person is able to articulate clearly to others." It is critical, you believe, that leaders have a TPOV on an "urgent need that is clear and palpable to everyone in the organization," "a mission that is inspiring and clearly worth achieving." Teachable Points of View can undoubtedly serve other purposes as well.

Tichy: The key elements about which leaders create Teachable Points of View are ideas, values, ways to energize people, and making tough yes-no decisions, which I call edge. In a school, the ideas may relate to the curriculum or instruction. The Teachable Point of View is an intellectual framing of a leader's key ideas in important areas. Values describe how stakeholders are going to behave in support of those ideas. It's also critically important that principals have a Teachable Point of View regarding how they will motivate various stakeholders. Because money is in short supply in schools, motivation comes instead from engagement, encouragement, and cheerleading. School principals also have to apply edge around the behavior of individuals, saying what behavior will and won't be allowed and enforcing those decisions.

ACT AND REFLECT

JSD: In *The Cycle of Leadership*, you wrote, "The very act of creating a Teachable Point of View makes people better leaders. … [L]eaders come to understand their underlying assumptions about themselves, their organization, and business in general. When implicit knowledge becomes explicit, it can then be questioned, refined, and honed, which benefits both the leaders and the organizations."

Tichy: The great leaders I've observed have the ability to both act and reflect. If all they do is reflect, they suffer from analysis paralysis. If all they do is act, they are hip-shooters. I had the privilege of working for and then with Jack Welch, the former CEO of GE, who was a great leader-teacher. People saw the action side of him, but the side very few people saw was him closing the door in his office to reflect, write, and bounce his ideas off people. I saw the same with Roger Enrico at PepsiCo and Larry Bossidy at Honeywell. They have the ability to do the hard reflective work and to put it in writing.

CLARIFY THOUGHTS BY WRITING

JSD: You acknowledge in your book that creating a TPOV is not a simple or easy process, noting, "It requires first doing the intellectual work of figuring out what our point of view is, and then the creative work of putting it into a form that makes it accessible and interesting to others." You recommend that leaders write their Teachable Points of View and observe, "The process of articulating one's Teachable Point of View is not a one-time event. It is an ongoing, iterative, and interactive process."

Tichy: Far too few leaders write. Writing requires that we make a decision. Speaking our thoughts allows us to slip around quite a bit, which affects clarity and crispness. Poor leaders also have staff people do this work, and they react to it. That's very different than doing the first draft yourself. Welch never had a speechwriter. He prepared his own presentations and wrote his own annual report letters. That may not sound like much, but 90% of CEOs have someone else do it for them.

CREATE A VISION

JSD: As you well know, busy, action-oriented people often resist writing and the processes involved in refining it. I'm curious how you engage leaders in this difficult intellectual work.

Tichy: I'm on my 12th book, and I avoid writing as much as anyone. I'm supposed to be writing right now, which makes this interview a form of avoidance. So I know firsthand how painful writing can be.

When I take a group of senior leaders away for three days to work on their Teachable Points of View, I begin by asking each of them to write about the business ideas they believe are driving or will drive their organizations. After they write, we get their ideas out on flip charts. People cannot hide, and it gives the group something to talk about. We spend three or four hours on each of the elements of Teachable Points of View — ideas, values, emotional energy, and edge. With each element, participants write, share, and negotiate to a final group agreement.

One writing exercise is particularly powerful. Two-thirds of the way through a three-day workshop, every member of the team works for one hour on a journalistic article that puts his or her organization on the cover of an appropriate magazine — say *Fortune* magazine — written from the perspective of several years in the future and explaining how the organization achieved success. I

ask participants to write a narrative with lots of details. Inevitably, leaders provide very rich data as they articulate a lot of pieces that are just floating around in their heads. We usually have trouble stopping people at the end of an hour. Next, we ask each person to read his or her article to the entire group. Group members pull out the themes and then we go on to the next person. It is a very powerful way to get people in touch with the vision, as well as where they agree and disagree.

We asked New York City principals to prepare their articles as a cover story for *Time* or *Newsweek* describing what students, teachers, parents, and others were doing to make the school outstanding. Principals are asked to discuss test scores and other measures of learning and the interventions they and others used. Many principals apply the same process with their teachers.

USING STORIES

JSD: This brings us back to Virtuous Teaching Cycles. You recommend that leaders communicate their Teachable Points of View through "interactive teaching," a type of dialogue you emphasize is not the same as selling or telling. "Interactive teaching," you write, "occurs when the teacher respects the students and has a mindset that they probably know things that he or she doesn't, and when the students have the mindset that they have something to say and that the teacher would be interested in hearing it." You also advocate weaving a Teachable Point of View into a story "that people can understand, relate to, and remember."

Tichy: I was very influenced by Howard Gardner's book, *Leading Minds: An Anatomy of Leadership* (HarperCollins, 1996). He says great leaders lead through three kinds of stories. The first is the "who I am" story, which explains the leader's values and motivation. The second is "who we are," which gives the group a sense of identity. The third is a "where we are going and how we'll get there" story. It's important that school leaders be able to tell these three

NOEL TICHY

Position: Noel M. Tichy is a professor of organizational behavior and human resource management at the University of Michigan Stephen M. Ross School of Business, where he is the director of the Global Business Partnership.

For more than a decade, the partnership ran the Global Leadership Program, a 36-company consortium of Japanese, European, and North American companies who worked together to develop senior executives and conduct action research on globalization in China, India, Russia, and Brazil. He now heads the Global Leadership in Healthcare Program, working with CEOs and their senior teams from major medical centers in the U.S., along with teams in Europe and India. Tichy also conducts the Cycle of Leadership executive program at the University of Michigan. Most recently, he led the launch of the Global Corporate Citizenship Initiative in partnership with General Electric, Procter & Gamble, and 3M. The initiative was designed to create a national model for partnership opportunities between business and society, emphasizing free enterprise and democratic principles. Tichy consults widely in both the private and public sectors. He is a senior partner in Action Learning Associates.

Education: Tichy has a bachelor of arts degree in psychology from Colgate University and a doctorate in social psychology from Columbia University.

Professional history: In the mid-1980s, Tichy was head of GE's Leadership Center, where he led the transformation to a system of action learning at GE. From 1985 to 1987, Tichy was manager of management education for GE, where he directed its worldwide development efforts. Prior to joining the Michigan faculty, he served for nine years on the Columbia University Business School faculty.

Honors and awards: *BusinessWeek* rated Tichy one of the "Top 10 Management Gurus." He has served on the editorial boards of the *Academy of Management Review*, *Organizational Dynamics*, *Journal of Business Research*, and *Journal of Business Strategy*. He served as chairman of the Academy of Management's Organization and Management Theory Division and was a member of the board of governors of the American Society for Training and Development. He was named distinguished fellow by the National Academy of Human Resources in 1999, received the 1993 Best Practice Award from the American Society for Training and Development, and received the 1994 Sales and Marketing Executives International Educator of the Year Award.

Publications: Tichy is the author of numerous books and articles. His most recent book is *The Ethical Challenge: How to Lead With Unyielding Integrity* (with Andrew McGill, Jossey-Bass, 2003). He also authored *The Cycle of Leadership: How Great Leaders Teach Their Companies to Win* (with Nancy Cardwell, HarperBusiness, 2002) and *The Leadership Engine: How Winning Companies Build Leaders at Every Level* (with Eli Cohen, HarperCollins, 1997), which was named one of the top 10 business books in 1997 by *BusinessWeek*. He is co-author of *Every Business is a Growth Business* (with Ram Charan, Random House, 1998). In addition, Tichy is co-author of *Control Your Destiny or Someone Else Will* (with Stratford Sherman, HarperBusiness, 1994).

stories, that there is alignment among the stories, and that others sign up and mobilize around them. We often end the workshop by asking people to do a five-minute vision speech on video in which they weave together these stories. People don't think in PowerPoint; they think in and remember stories. Great leaders have always intuitively known that.

LEADERSHIP IS AUTOBIOGRAPHICAL

JSD: In *The Cycle of Leadership*, you note that good leaders are shaped by transformative events that define who they are as people.

Tichy: Leadership, in my view, is autobiographical. Who we are as leaders comes from the ups and downs of our life experience, not the books we have read or the courses we have taken. When people look back at what shaped them, inevitably it is the tough times. Really good leaders learn from those experiences.

To get at this, I ask participants in workshops to create a leadership journey line on a flipchart. They draw a graph with two axes. On the bottom is time. People can go back as far as they want; some go back all the way to birth or early childhood. The vertical axis has positive emotional energy at the top and negative emotional energy at the bottom. In the middle is neutral energy. I ask people to plot their life journey lines as their energy goes up and down. A variety of things may bring us down — the death of a loved one, getting fired at work, a crisis in the organization or community. These

things vary from person to person. People will self-edit so they don't share more than they're comfortable with.

John Chambers, the CEO of Cisco, is a good example. He had a learning disability as he was growing up in West Virginia. He was picked on and laughed at by other kids. A teacher even told him that he wouldn't graduate from high school. He says that today, the stock price falling rapidly at Cisco is nothing compared to being in 3rd grade and thinking you are dumb. Chambers ended up getting a law degree and an MBA, but he says that through his early experiences, he learned to treat people as he wanted to be treated, to stick with things through tough times, and to believe in the importance of a good education. That final area led to Cisco-sponsored programs for inner-city kids. You don't really understand John Chambers unless you understand the experiences that shaped him.

It's amazing how often people who've worked together for 20 years will do this exercise and afterward say something like, "I didn't know that about you. Now I understand." It's a very powerful exercise for leaders to do with their teams. It really gets participants thinking about who they are as leaders, and it helps team members understand one another in a very different way. I've done it with thousands of people, and it's a very powerful, positive exercise.

ABOUT THE AUTHOR

Dennis Sparks is executive director of the National Staff Development Council.

JSD, Spring 2005 (Vol. 26, No. 2)

Shared culture
A consensus of individual values

By Joan Richardson

Principals are the primary shapers of school culture, in both large and small ways. Principals send large cultural messages to staff and students with every decision regarding budgets, curriculum, instruction, as well as interactions with central office and community leaders. But principals also send hundreds of small cultural messages to students and teachers every day. In every interaction with a student or teacher, a principal telegraphs a message about his or her expectations for that school. That gives principals enormous opportunities to shape a school's culture — for good or ill.

Some principals provide cultural leadership intuitively, said Kent Peterson, professor of educational administration at the University of Wisconsin and co-author with Terrence Deal of *Shaping School Culture* (Jossey-Bass, 1999). But all principals can learn to consciously identify culture-making opportunities and use them to influence teachers, students, and parents to move in a new direction, he said.

Peterson recalled one principal who recognized that he did not intuitively know when a "cultural moment"

was presenting itself. So, using a 3x5 index card, he wrote down five elements of the school culture that he wanted to improve. He stuck the card in his shirt pocket and pulled it out throughout his day as a way to remind himself of questions he could ask.

"You can find ways to encourage yourself to be more conscious of this. Eventually, it becomes internalized," Peterson said.

Peterson also recalled shadowing a principal who found ways to blend administrative tasks with opportunities to influence attitudes in his building. This principal had to provide central office with the total number of ceiling tiles in his building. Rather than assign that task to a maintenance employee, the principal assumed the job himself. The principal's arrival in each classroom was, of course, a big event to both students and teachers. In each classroom, he asked what students were learning that day and asked to see student work — then he counted the ceiling tiles. He had taken responsibility for a mundane task because it allowed him to connect with every classroom in the building and to send a message about the importance of students' work.

Results, May 2001

Although principals are enormously influential, they alone cannot shape the culture of a school, Peterson said. "Culture is the accumulation of many individuals' values and norms. It is a consensus about what's important. It's the group's expectations, not just an individual's expectations. It's the way *everyone* does business," he said.

Teachers are especially important in influencing the direction of a school's culture. Teachers connect with other teachers, with their students, and with the parents of their students. When teachers are sending a shared cultural message, that message reverberates throughout the entire school community.

ONE SCHOOL'S STORY

Joan Vydra practically gushes about her school in suburban Chicago. "It's so awesome to walk in the door here," she said of Briar Glen School in Wheaton. The school with 480 students in grades K-5 is in Glen Ellyn Community Consolidated District 89.

As a veteran principal, Vydra believes no school can improve unless it has a culture that supports improvement and collaboration and a shared vision for what it wants to achieve. She also believes fervently that a school will improve only if it has a culture of caring. "If teachers don't feel cared about, they can't perform at optimum levels. If I care about the teachers, they will pass that on to the kids," she said.

When she arrived at Briar Glen five years ago, there was some tension in the school. Briar Glen, an award-winning school, had "wonderful teachers" who worked well within their teams, but spent most of their team time on organizational rather than instructional issues. Although wonderful things were happening in individual classrooms, there was little sense of an overall direction and no school improvement plan to guide their collective work. "There was no shared vision about what the school should be," she said.

Vydra began by telling the staff, "I'm going to walk in your shoes for a year. Then, whatever changes we make, we're going to make together." High on Vydra's agenda was ensuring that teachers could do the work they were hired to do.

"I don't want anything on a teacher's plate that doesn't belong there. I want them to focus on their students and on the goals of our school improvement plan."

For example, rather than overloading teachers with excessive testing data and expecting them to wade through it, Vydra winnows the data down to what each teacher needs to know. Then, when she meets with teachers, they are able to focus on individual children who need assistance, rather than swimming through irrelevant numbers.

When teachers agreed that they wanted parents to have a better understanding of what children are expected to know and be able to do, Vydra wrote a grant that would enable her to give teachers summer stipends to prepare standards-based newsletters for distribution during the school year. "If I'm asking them to improve their communication with parents, I want to remove obstacles that prevent them from doing that. Time is an obstacle and this was a way to work around that," she said.

LISTENING TO PARENTS

As she listened to teachers, Vydra also listened to parents. It was parents' perceptions that not enough teachers attended the parent-sponsored events. Vydra asked parents which events were most important for teacher attendance. From a long list, parents identified four significant events.

With that list, Vydra approached teachers and said, "You don't have to do this, but this is very important to our parents. If we're going to build our learning community, this is a good first step. If you'll try to attend these specific events, I'll tell parents that you won't be at all the other events and meetings."

Results, May 2001

At the same time, Vydra thanked the teachers for their willingness to attend events by informing them that she would not enforce previously mandatory starting and ending times for the work day. "I trust these teachers. They don't need to be told what time to get here or when they can leave. They're going to be here."

The teachers quickly responded to the request and have made teacher attendance at the identified events part of the cultural norm.

NOTHING IS PERFECT

During her five years at Briar Glen, Vydra admits to missteps along the way. An enthusiastic advocate for school and classroom newsletters, she announced in a faculty meeting during her second year at the school that she would be sharing teachers' classroom newsletters. "I found something good in every newsletter, but they hated it," she said. "Nobody wanted to be put out in front."

"We're more ready for that now. But I'm still careful to praise teams, not individuals," she said.

When personal praise is warranted, she writes personal notes instead of making a public statement. "In meetings, I might mention the example without mentioning the name," she said.

Vydra acknowledges that if she had entered a school with a "toxic culture," she would have responded differently. "If it's a broken school and kids are being hurt and there is low achievement, there have to be some top-down initiatives.

"Shaping a culture takes time. Anything that is top-down will last only as long as the leader stays in that office. Then those ideas will evaporate and everything will go right back to the way it was," Vydra said.

But culture stays. "Culture protects a school and teachers from willy-nilly fads and from leaders who think they own the day," she said.

ABOUT THE AUTHOR

Joan Richardson is publications director for the National Staff Development Council.

On the edge
Have the courage to lead with soul

By Parker J. Palmer

In December 2007, Parker Palmer spoke to attendees of NSDC's 39th Annual Conference in Dallas about the role of education leaders in changing today's educational culture. This article, adapted from his keynote speech, serves as a call to collective action for principals and other educators seeking the best outcomes for students.

Here is my challenge to school leaders, staff developers, and all who care about public education and the students it is meant to serve: We must go beyond helping educators become better at doing their jobs — as important as that is — and support them in becoming agents of institutional change. It is no longer enough for professionals to do their work well. Today's professionals have an ethical obligation to help transform the toxic settings in which their work is done.

A small story will help me make my point. The Center for Courage & Renewal, which I founded and am privileged to work with, offers long-term group retreats to help people in the serving professions (especially K-12 teachers) renew their professional integrity and rejoin "soul and role." In a moment of soul-searching at one of those retreats, a physician said, "The truth is that the health care system I work in has me right on the edge of violating my Hippocratic oath two or three times a week." Then he spoke again: "You know, I've never said that to another person." After a pause he added, "In fact, I've never said that to myself before."

In recent years, many educators have been hearing a persistent inner voice saying that the educational system has them on the edge of violating their ethical obligations to the young. And once you have heard that challenge from within, you know that it's not enough simply to become better at what you do, to become a more skillful leader or teacher in an institution that is morally as well as functionally flawed.

Our institutions too often become the worst enemies of their own missions, in part because they operate on signals from another planet. Too much of what goes on in health care is shaped by the insurance industry, not the values of doctors and nurses. Too much of what goes on in our schools is shaped by politicians who are more interested in winning elections than in winning good futures for our kids, who know that being tough but

JSD, Spring 2008 (Vol. 29, No. 2)

simplistic about "getting results" wins votes, whether or not it fosters learning.

The consequence is an educational culture that is mechanical, reductionist, competitive, focused on downloading information, and committed to forcing all children to measure up to the same standards regardless of their starting point, their special gifts, or the unique demands and dynamics of their lives. High-stakes testing does violence to the souls of the young, to say nothing of the souls of those who would teach deeply and well — just as the way we finance health care does violence to the sick and dying and those who would serve them well. How do we go beyond getting better at our jobs to challenge these deformations?

Movements for cultural change require two simple but demanding things. The first is personal moral agency — the human capacity for individual acts animated by intelligence, insight, wisdom, compassion, and courage. In a culture obsessed with external factors, we need to keep reminding ourselves that, in the absence of personal moral agency, there is no curriculum, no technique, no budget, no management strategy or governance system that will take us where we need to go.

Second, movements for cultural change require collegial community — the human capacity to come into relationships that support moral agency, that can inform, critique, inspire, amplify, and sustain acts of individual integrity. If collegial community is lacking, there is no way for individuals to make a difference. And in my experience, our institutions not only offer scant support for personal agency and collegial community, but often work actively to undermine them to protect themselves against challenge and change.

BUILD TRUST IN RELATIONSHIPS

These are not simply talking points for a sermon. We have empirical evidence that in the absence of moral agency and peer community, schools are less likely to

PARKER J. PALMER

Parker J. Palmer is founder and senior partner of the Center for Courage & Renewal. A writer, teacher, and activist, he is known for his work in education, spirituality, and social change.

His books include *A Hidden Wholeness: The Journey Toward an Undivided Life* (Jossey-Bass, 2004), *Let Your Life Speak: Listening for the Voice of Vocation* (Jossey-Bass, 2000), *The Courage to Teach: Exploring the Inner Landscape of a Teacher's Life* (Jossey-Bass, 1998), *The Active Life: A Spirituality of Work, Creativity, and Caring* (Jossey-Bass, 1999), *To Know as We Are Known: Education as a Spiritual Journey* (Harper San Francisco, 1983), *The Company of Strangers: Christians and the Renewal of America's Public Life* (Crossroad, 1983), and *The Promise of Paradox: A Celebration of Contradictions in the Christian Life* (Servant Leadership School, 1993).

He holds a Ph.D. from the University of California at Berkeley, and has been named one of the most influential senior leaders and agenda-setters in higher education.

Living the Questions: Essays Inspired by the Work and Life of Parker J. Palmer was published by Jossey-Bass in 2005.

The Center for Courage & Renewal offers "Courage to Teach" and "Courage to Lead" programs for the personal and professional renewal of public school teachers and leaders, programs designed to "reconnect who you are with what you do." Learn more at www.CourageRenewal.org.

grow their capacity to serve the young. Look, for example, at the study by Anthony Bryk and Barbara Schneider on school reform in Chicago during the 1990s (2002). The authors asked a simple question: Why did some Chicago schools get better at educating children during that decade, while others did not?

Bryk and Schneider looked at all of the usual suspects: curriculum, technique, professional development support, models of governance, and, of course, budgets. They found that none of those external variables had significant power to predict who would succeed and who would fail on behalf of kids. But they found one variable that made a huge difference, a variable they call "relational trust."

If your school had high levels of relational trust and/or leaders who cared about that factor, your chances of getting better at educating children were over 50%. But if your school had low levels of relational trust and/or leaders who did not regard trust as worth attending to, your chances of getting better at educating children were only one out of seven. Significantly, this correlation between relational trust and educational success held strong no matter what happened with those other, external variables: e.g. having the money to do what's needed does not overcome the distrust that keeps us from doing it.

And what lies behind relational trust? One answer is moral agency (e.g. the personal capacity to sideline one's ego for the sake of a larger good) and collegial community (e.g. the collective capacity to collaborate rather than compete). Bryk and Schneider's data suggest that these factors can make or break our capacity to serve children well, that the external variables that we obsess over may be less important than we think. Not that we shouldn't attend to external aspects like money; of course, we should. But when we fail to attend to what goes on within and between people, we're making a huge mistake, a mistake sanctioned by a culture that keeps insisting that we look "out there" for solutions.

FOUR PATHWAYS TO CHANGE

The great promise of staff development is this: It is the one function in schools where we can consistently

encourage both personal moral agency and collegial community. But even as I applaud staff developers and the school leaders who support them, I want to suggest four ways of deepening the staff development agenda, four ways to support educators in becoming internal agents of change, four ways to seed a movement in support of the true mission of education. I have written at length about these possibilities in my book, *A Hidden Wholeness: The Journey Toward an Undivided Life* (Jossey-Bass, 2004).

First, collegial communities cannot be built around work alone. They must also be built around honoring the selfhood of the people who do the work. There's a great wound in our culture. Many people feel that they are treated as means to ends in the workplace, not as ends in themselves, leading them to lose heart, to disengage, to withdraw. We must create teams in the workplace that not only employ the individual but honor the individual, teams that not only help people do a better job but empower the human spirit in the process.

How can we do this? There are a thousand ways, and here's a simple example: Invite more storytelling about people's lives. Start small-group meetings with an optional question that everyone gets two or three minutes to answer (but is always free to take a pass on): "Tell us about an elder who has been important in your life." "Tell us about the first dollar you ever earned." Tell us, that is, about something that helps us know you a little better and enhances your feeling of being known for who you are.

As we practice storytelling in workplaces — where we often spend years alongside each other while learning next to nothing about each other — a simple truth kicks in: The more you know about another person's journey, the less possible it is to distrust or dislike that person. Want to know how to build relational trust? Learn more about each other. Learn it through simple questions that can be tucked into the doing of work, creating workplaces that not only employ people but honor the soul in the process.

JSD, Spring 2008 (Vol. 29, No. 2)

This is how to weave a fabric of communal relationships that has resilience in times of crisis, resourcefulness in times of need. It's a fabric that must be woven before the need or the crisis arrives, when it's too late for community to emerge in the stress of the moment. So let's make sure, in our language and in our practice, that we're building collegial communities around persons as well as tasks, around souls as well as roles.

Second, we need to create teams and communities that support people not only in doing outer work — like mastering techniques, planning lessons, and solving problems — but in doing inner work as well.

Ask yourself once again, "What lies behind relational trust?"

Ultimately, it is not skills of the sort that we normally learn at workshops but the skills required to do "soul work." It's becoming aware enough of my own insecurities that I can hold my ego at bay and start relating to you as a colleague rather than a competitor. It's learning to do the hard work of forgiveness — of you for your failures and of myself for my own failures — without which all roads are dead-ends.

I call this kind of thing "the work before the work." Normally, we are fully focused on the task immediately at hand — producing the program, creating the curriculum, solving the problem. But if we want to do these things well, there's usually prior work to be done. It's personal inner work of the sort Montessori teachers do when, prior to entering a classroom, they find a quiet place to meditate for a few moments on the name of each child in their care. And it's collective inner work, as when a group of health care professionals makes "safe space," nonjudgmental space, for a physician to speak in front of colleagues about the threat to his Hippocratic oath. Whatever form it takes, it's work that builds the relational trust so critical to success in schools.

Third, in order to do inner work, we must go beyond data points, concepts, and theoretical constructs as the

foci of our conversations. We must learn to work with images, with metaphors, with poetry, with stories, with music, and with silence. We must tap into a deeper layer of human knowing than can be reached by the intellect alone, a layer evoked by intuition, emotion, aesthetics, and soul.

In summer 1964, Harvard psychiatrist Robert Coles was in Oxford, Ohio, as a group of young people got ready to go to Mississippi for what was to become the infamous Freedom Summer. Three of their number — James Chaney, Andrew Goodman, and Michael Schwerner — decided to go ahead of the others and were murdered by the Ku Klux Klan.

For several days, the young people back in Oxford grieved and agonized: Did they still have the courage to go ahead and make the witness to human equality they had intended to make? Coles reports that they found their courage not in the data of social science, not in nonviolent tactics and strategies, not in mutual exhortation and cheerleading. They found their courage in what Coles calls the "words and the music of social change." They read poetry, sang songs, and shared images and metaphors that touched, energized and empowered their hearts and connected them with one another (Coles, 1969).

The journey of change I'm talking about requires courage on the part of educators. It requires the courage of being champions for children in a way that may risk your reputation and even put your job on the line. To find that courage, we need to go to a deeper place in ourselves than data points and theories can take us, or than cheerleading for quick fixes can evoke.

Fourth, we must help people reclaim their soul-deep identities as educators as well as the courage to act from that place. As long as our identities are defined by the institutions we work for, we will be powerless to change those institutions, for whatever threatens business as usual in those institutions will threaten our identities, too. Like the doctor whose story I told, we need to find a place to stand outside the self-protective logic of institutions — not because we hate those institutions, but because we love them and their missions too much to let them sink to their lowest life form.

LIVE ON THE EDGE

Finding alternative ground to stand on is essentially a spiritual decision, and it is the starting point for all great movements for social change. Every movement I've studied is sparked by isolated individuals discovering their most fundamental commitments and convictions and deciding to live "divided no more" — deciding that they will no longer behave on the outside in a way that contradicts values and convictions they hold deeply on the inside — and then finding or creating communities, peer communities, collegial communities to support them in that witness.

The doctor who acknowledged that he was on the edge of violating his Hippocratic oath was on another edge as well, deciding whether to commit to an undivided life. Would he make that decision and create a peer community to help him hold and witness to it, or would he bury his own truth and return to business as usual?

That's a big edge to be on. But it's precisely the edge we need to be on if we want to transform the school culture into one that helps more and more young people become well-educated and whole. School leaders and staff developers need to help educators stand on that edge with minds and hearts prepared to take the next step.

REFERENCES

Bryk, A.S. & Schneider, B. (2002). *Trust in schools: A core resource for improvement.* New York: Russell Sage Foundation.

Coles, R. (1969). The words and music of social change. *Daedalus, 98*(3), 684-698.

Palmer, P. (2004). *A hidden wholeness: The journey toward an undivided life.* San Francisco: Jossey-Bass.

ABOUT THE AUTHOR

Parker J. Palmer is founder and senior partner of the Center for Courage & Renewal.

Leaders as creators of high-performance cultures

By Dennis Sparks

High-quality professional learning by all teachers is critically important if high quality teaching is to occur in every classroom. Such learning is ultimately based in and stimulated by a high-performance culture, the creation of which is a major and often-neglected role of school leaders.

A widely held view of instructional improvement is that good teaching is primarily an individual affair and that principals as instructional leaders will interact one-on-one with each teacher to strengthen his or her efforts in the classroom. The principal is like the hub of a wheel with teachers at the end of each spoke. Communication about instruction moves back and forth along the spoke to the hub but not around the circumference of the wheel.

NSDC's view, on the other hand, is that some of the most important forms of professional learning occur in daily interactions among teachers in which they assist one another in improving lessons, deepening understanding of the content they teach, analyzing student work, examining various types of

Principals are responsible for developing a high-performance culture in which productive relationships can thrive.

data on student performance, and solving the myriad of problems they face each day. From this perspective, sustained teacher-to-teacher communication about teaching and learning is one of the most powerful and underused sources of professional learning and instructional improvement. While the Council's view does not negate the value of principals' expertise and direct engagement in the improvement of instruction and student learning, it recognizes that it cannot be the exclusive or even the primary form of learning-oriented interactions among educators.

Consequently, one of the most important responsibilities of principals is the development of a high-performance culture in which productive relationships can thrive. Because culture is the sum total of interactions among community members and the beliefs that they bring to those interactions, the creation of such a culture means establishing norms and practices that lead to trust and mutual respect, continuous improvement, team-focused collaboration, clarity of thought, the candid expressions of views, and interpersonal accountability for the fulfillment of commitments. Because few principals have worked in such settings or have been formally prepared to assume this role, it is essential that preparation programs and leadership development efforts for practicing principals teach these skills and provide one-on-one support as they are implemented in the complex interpersonal environment of the schoolhouse.

A skeptic may read the previous paragraph and wonder what long-term culture-building skills have to do with the pressing issue of improving test scores in reading and math, a priority which consumes a great deal of principals' day-to-day attention. Perhaps nothing, if a school's dominant goal is nudging up test scores to satisfy externally imposed demands. A common human response to such a situation is to do that which is most familiar, especially if in the short run it will likely produce the desired result. And for many school leaders, what is familiar is command and control procedures — define the problem, prescribe solutions, issue directives, monitor compliance, and use carrots and sticks to motivate performance, methods which are hardly the substance of a high-performance culture.

While I understand why principals may default to such actions — even when they are against their better judgment — over the long term these methods will not produce quality teaching in every classroom nor schools in which teachers and students alike experience success, joy, and satisfaction each day. Such schools are grounded in relationships and intellectual tasks that honor and challenge every member of the community to more fully development his or her talents to serve both individual and collective purposes. Those are the schools to which we would all happily send our own children.

ABOUT THE AUTHOR

Dennis Sparks is executive director of the National Staff Development Council.

Results, November 2003

What leaders need to know about school culture

By Joye Hall Norris

By understanding the culture existing in school, linking with the cultural network, meeting teachers' needs and continually modeling and articulating the emerging vision of the school, leaders can shape the school culture toward continuous improvement.

A school is more than a building — it is a society and a culture that shapes the learning of staff and students alike. Because that fact is too often ignored, national and state reform efforts have left schools fundamentally unchanged.

For the most part, teachers are doing their best under increasingly difficult circumstances, yet their individual best is no longer good enough. All educators need to understand the cultural constraints that may lead to low performance to examine ways to maximize staff involvement in sustained change. To address these issues, this article provides an overview of school culture, descriptions of school cultures, and seven mechanisms leaders may use to affect the culture of a school.

SCHOOL CULTURE

In a general sense, culture refers to the dynamics of a social group and includes the beliefs, values, and practices accepted by the group members. The group operates within a common set of assumptions about the way things are done. Because the culture actually defines what is possible and not possible (Erickson, 1987), people within a culture tend to view issues in a similar manner.

This is as true in schools as it is in society at large. As new teachers become socialized into a school setting, they adopt the common practices of the school.

SCHOOLS AS LOOSELY-COUPLED SYSTEMS

Some organizational cultures are, by nature, strongly binding. These cultures are characterized by a single purpose and, to a great extent, standardized procedures. School cultures, however, have been described as loosely-coupled systems, (Weick, 1982) forged in part by teachers' isolation from their peers. Weick (1982) describe loosely-coupled systems as, "more elusive, less tangible and harder to grasp," than other organizations (p. 675).

Journal of Staff Development, Spring 1994 (Vol. 15, No. 2)

Teachers are professionals with recognized subject expertise, which results in different forms of expert power within the school setting. Consequently, administrative practices which are directive in nature or contrary to teachers' beliefs will have little impact on classroom practices, and it is unlikely that meaningful change can be accomplished through administrative command or fiat (Purkey & Smith, 1983).

CONTRASTING SCHOOL CULTURES

While the culture of schools in general may be defined as loosely coupled, this does not describe the culture of all schools. Many schooling practices are unique and reflect differences in community expectation, beliefs of the founding faculty, and administrative preferences. Often these differences are apparent even to a casual observer. Rosenholtz (1989) found that school cultures varied from building to building and can be placed on a continuum from the highly cohesive "forward-moving" school on one end to "stuck" schools on the other end, in which teacher isolation and estrangement are the norm.

FORWARD-MOVING SCHOOLS

Forward-moving schools have growth-oriented values and beliefs supported by all the teachers in the building. These values become the guiding principles used to made decisions and determine educationally-appropriate action. In this healthy system, communication is open as information is shared among all participants, and there is a high level of trust.

Rosenholtz (1989) found that healthy schools are also high-consensus schools and that teacher concern for student academic progress is the focus that prompts teachers to work together, share instructional strategies, and engage in continuous improvement. Teachers in high-consensus schools put aside petty differences to accomplish the goals of the school.

Research describing effective schools (Kritek, 1986) delineates the characteristics of some cohesive, forward-moving schools. These schools were generally characterized by principal leadership which focuses on instruction, a safe and orderly environment, high expectations of students, clearly articulated instructional goals, and monitoring of student progress (Edmonds, 1982).

However, there is a key element missing from the literature: descriptions of the ways the schools achieved these qualities. Lambert (1988) speculates that the correlates of effective schools are merely the "tip of the iceberg" and that the correlate of a "safe and orderly environment," for instance, describes what the school has but that "isn't what makes the school effective" (p. 55). Lambert states:

A school in which the staff, working together, examines itself and decides that the reading ability of the students is within their power to change and sets about to design a program to do just that is undoubtedly an effective school. Not because of a strong reading program, but because they possess a set of beliefs that causes them to value the following ideas: self-examination, nondefensiveness, working together, power to effect change, unwillingness to believe that certain students can't learn, effective program design and implementation, continued evaluation, the expectation that their program will work but may need changes along the way, willingness to work through problems, and staff leadership (p. 55).

If healthy school cultures are the key to school success (Lambert, 1988; Rosenholtz, 1989), then faculty consensus and support are instruments of effective cultures and school improvement. The challenge for school leaders is forging a common vision which often requires changing educators' underlying beliefs and attitudes (Purkey & Smith, 1983).

STUCK SCHOOLS

According to Rosenholtz, stuck schools are characterized by a lack of consensus on educational

Journal of Staff Development, Spring 1994 (Vol. 15, No. 2)

TOOL 3.4

goals, teacher isolation, and contrived collegiality. Because education is complex and lacks clear boundaries, there is professional latitude regarding what constitutes teaching and learning. When teachers within a given school are free to define teaching as each sees fit, then they may choose goals which meet their personal needs and preference (Rosenholtz, 1989). Lack of consensus may also result in competing factions within the school, and groups of teachers may form cliques which engage in ongoing power struggles.

Teacher isolation also creates barriers to a healthy school culture. Since isolated teachers perceive others to be self-reliant, they are reluctant to ask for help. Isolation from others increases uncertainty as teachers feel that they alone are experiencing the doubts and frustrations teaching. This perception increases the need to avoid self-disclosure. Fullan and Hargreaves (1990) relate teachers' isolation to feelings of powerlessness as teachers strive for safe, risk-free conditions. They describe the situation as follows:

When teachers are afraid to share their ideas and successes for fear of being perceived as blowing their own horns; when teachers are reluctant to tell others of a new idea on the grounds that others might steal it or take credit for it (or on that they did); when teachers, young or old, are afraid to ask for help because they might be perceived as less than competent; when a teacher uses the same approach year after year even though it is not working — all these tendencies shore up the walls of privatism. They limit growth and improvement quite fundamentally, because they limit access to ideas and practices that might offer better ways of doing things. They institutionalize conservatism (pp. 39-40).

While teacher isolation and conservatism hamper improvement, another situation called "contrived collegiality" (Hargreaves & Dawe, 1990) can have a similar impact. Contrived collegiality occurs when teachers are placed in a collaborative situation by administrative design for the purpose of implementing

standardized processes. Within this context, standardized and centralized school improvement does not allow teachers' voices to be heard. The result is that teachers work together to learn and implement a program with little or no opportunity to discuss the validity or utility of the program within the existing school culture. According to Hargreaves and Dawe (1990):

Cooperative learning, active learning, inductive teaching … are not merely different technical procedures to be selected according to their proven efficiency or inefficiency. They embody particular and disputable educational purposes, they suit teachers with particular kinds of personality and educational beliefs, and they are more appropriate for some contexts than for others. To suppress discussion of these things by drawing in the boundaries of the debate at an early stage and reducing possible disputes about ends to technical discussion over means is to create the conditions for private withdrawal and submerged resistance at a later stage. No amount of standardization will eradicate the meaning and purpose of teaching from those who practice the craft: It will simply drive them underground (p. 236).

CULTURAL CHANGE

Realistically, how can change be approached in schools when frequently, if not always, the existing culture does not support change? While some educators deal with new initiatives by taking early retirement, others retire-on-the-job, and still others choose to fight change. Leaders often become fearful and protective of their domains, or stand back and take a disengaged, wait-and-see posture.

MECHANISMS FOR SHAPING SCHOOL CULTURE

School leaders can approach school improvement through cultural change by becoming familiar with the values and beliefs embedded in the school and by shaping the culture in new directions. This is a lengthy process which takes understanding, patience, human relations skills, and the ability to communicate. Changing the culture involves changing habits of mind, body, and spirit and involves the following processes:

1. *Learn the existing culture.* Study the culture of a school in terms of heroes and heroines, areas of pride, rituals, ceremonies, and cultural networks (Deal & Kennedy, 1982). Heroes and heroines are persons revered for their accomplishments and contributions to the school and exemplify the values of the school. Rituals are the routines of school life that establish boundaries of acceptable behavior and ceremonies provide concrete examples of what is valued. In order to enter the cultural network, learn the role that various people play in shaping, interpreting, and supporting the culture of the organization. To learn about the culture and key people, ask questions about the meanings behind event and why things are done the way they are.

   Deal and Kennedy (1982) recommend asking people who relate stories about the organization for the names of others who could share additional information. Establish a relationship with the key people who can explain events and provide insights. Get the storyteller's perspectives on past change initiatives, a description of the change process, level of success, and current feeling regarding the changes. These stories are likely to provide insight into areas where change approaches have caused institutional resistance.

   Learning the culture of the school is learning how things are done, why they are done in that way, and what happened to the people and institution in the process. Allowing people to share their stories and historical insights provides them with a chance to get feelings and even hostilities out in the open.

2. *Establish communication linkages.* Tapping into the formal and informal communication system of the organization provides understanding of the current culture and can help create new cultural realities. Feel the pulse of the organization through informal conversations, feedback surveys, suggestion boxes, spontaneous interviews, and an open-door policy. People at all levels of the organization can be key players in providing communication linkages to the broader community.

3. *Meet teacher needs.* Because of the complex, non-routine nature of teaching, teacher social and psychological well-being is often threatened by change (Rosenholtz, 1989). To combat this, leaders can provide teachers with a sense of achievement by documenting the accomplishments of the school. One leadership team begins each school year describing the history of the school improvement efforts from inception. This allows participants to reflect and appreciate their progress.

   One principal enhances teacher self-esteem by providing the resources and encouragement necessary for every teacher to be the in-house expert on a facet of education. Teachers need to know that their efforts are noticed and appreciated by other (Rosenholtz, 1989). Simple acknowledgements can go a long way toward making staff feel valued. Rewarding faculty activities compatible with the vision for the school provides incentives to continue.

4. *Create opportunities for renewal.* A learning organization is possible only when its individual members are learners (Senge, 1990). Leaders who create opportunities for individual growth recognize that teachers' well-being and learning have a direct bearing on student learning. Enlarging the role of professional development to encompass areas of personal renewal and reflection shows respect for teachers and promotes good mental health, which is essential in healthy organizations.

Journal of Staff Development, Spring 1994 (Vol. 15, No. 2)

TOOL 3.4

Encouraging teachers to accept challenges such as teaching a different grade or course, teaching other teachers, organizing staff development programs, or seeking external funding for their ideas creates avenues for growth and self-actualization. Little (1990) supports the concept of "joint work" which allows teachers to work together on common problems related to their jobs. Through truly collaborate ventures, teachers can gain technical knowledge, appreciate the complexity of the job as others share their problems, and increase their esprit de corps.

5. *Practice leadership.* The role of leadership is to build a strong culture which is open to self-examination and innovation. Promoting a learning community where the principal is the No. 1 learner can set the stage. One principal, for example, might buy 10 copies of educationally-relevant books for teachers to read and host after school meetings to discuss the new ideas. The constant infusion of ideas and opportunity to share insights with peers can change the belief system of a school.

   A leader needs to question current practice and determine if there are more creative ways to approach the issue. The leaders of forward-moving organizations are risk takers, open to the ideas of others, willing to admit to mistakes, trust others to do their jobs, have a sense of humor, energize other, and believe in continuous improvement.

6. *Model desired behaviors.* School leaders model the vision that they have for the school. If the vision includes teachers sharing power with students and parents, then leaders must be willing to share power with teachers. If the vision includes a learning environment for all persons involved with education, then principals must focus on adult learning as well as student learning.

7. *Hire the right people.* As school leadership has the opportunity to hire new faculty, a match between school vision and individual philosophy is critical (Purkey & Smith, 1983; Rosenholtz, 1989). Schools with a well articulated set of beliefs must recruit people who support this orientation or the school will not move forward. Districts need to pay attention to teacher recruitment and the selection process. Last minute or hurried hiring practices need to be replaced by screening processes which assess the values and educational beliefs of candidates as well as their teaching skills. The school must determine if the candidate can work with others to create a community of learners, is flexible, views issues through multiple perspectives, deals with ambiguity, and sees his or her own learning as lifelong.

CONCLUSION

The culture of schools greatly influences what types of changes and the degree to which change may occur within a given school. Leaders need to be aware of pervasive cultural aspects of schools, such as lack of consensus, teacher isolation, and contrived collegiality, that are barriers to school improvement.

Leaders need to understand that they are shapers of school culture. By understanding the existing culture, linking with the cultural network, meeting teachers' needs, and continually modeling and articulating the emerging vision of the school, leaders can shape the school culture toward continuous improvement.

REFERENCES

Deal, T.E. & Kennedy, A.A. (1982). *Corporate cultures.* Reading, MA: Addison-Wesley.

Edmonds, R.R. (1982). Programs for school improvement: An overview. *Phi Delta Kappan, 64*(4), 4-11.

Erickson, F. (1987). Conceptions of school culture: An overview. *Educational Administration Quarterly*, *23*(4), 11-24.

Fullan, M.G. & Hargreaves, A. (1990). *What's worth fighting for? Working together for your school.* Andover, MA: The Regional Laboratory for Education Improvement of the Northwest and Islands.

Hargreaves, A. & Dawe, R. (1990). Paths of professional development: Contrived collegiality, collaborative culture, and the case of peer coaching. *Teaching & Teacher Education*, *6*(3), 227-241.

Kritek, W.J. (1986, April). *School culture and school improvement.* Paper presented at the annual meeting of the American Educational Research Association, San Francisco, CA.

Lambert, L.G. (1988). Building school culture: An open letter to principals. *NASSP Bulletin*, *72*(506), 54-62.

Little, J.W. (1990). The persistence of privacy: Autonomy and initiative in teachers' professional relations. *Teachers College Record*, *91*(4), 509-536.

Purkey, S.C. & Smith, M.S. (1983). Effective schools: A review. *The Elementary School Journal*, *83*(4), 427-452.

Rosenholtz, S.J. (1989). *Teachers' workplace.* New York: Longman.

Senge, P.M. (1990). *The fifth discipline: The art and practice of the learning organization.* New York: Doubleday/Currency.

Weick, K.E. (1982). Administering education in loosely coupled schools. *Phi Delta Kappan*, *63*(10), 673-676.

ABOUT THE AUTHOR

Joye Hall Norris is an assistant professor, Arizona State University West, Department of Educational Leadership, P.O. Box 37100, Phoenix, AZ 85069-7100, (602) 543-6370.

Journal of Staff Development, Spring 1994 (Vol. 15, No. 2)

If we are to call ourselves professionals, we are obligated to use the best practices
Anything less is unacceptable

By Rick DuFour

Highly regarded organizations such as the National Staff Development Council, National Association of Elementary School Principals, and American Association of School Administrators have called on educational leaders to develop their schools and districts as "professional" learning organizations. But what is a profession, and what can leaders do to promote professionalism? Have we used the term so loosely that it has lost its meaning?

In the past, we were able to draw sharp distinctions between amateurs and professionals. Amateurs pursued an activity as an unpaid avocation, while professionals were compensated for their efforts. For example, an Olympic athlete was an amateur, while a member of the New York Knicks or Toronto Maple Leafs was a professional. That distinction has been blurred as professional athletes compete in the Olympics and amateur athletes receive lucrative compensation for endorsements.
In the past, when an individual chose a profession, he or she selected from medicine, law, or education. Today, people in virtually every occupation — flight attendants, masseuses, bartenders — refer to themselves as professionals. What does the term mean?

One characterization describes a professional as someone with expertise in a specialized field, an individual who not only has pursued advanced training to enter the field, but who also is expected to remain current in its evolving knowledge base. According to this definition, members of a profession assume a personal responsibility to seek and implement the best practices in their field. They are not expected to embrace every new hypothesis or careen wildly from one fad or trend to the next. When, however, the field evolves to the point that there is consensus regarding best practice, the professionals within that field are expected to become familiar with and to use that practice. In fact, to disregard best practice would be considered a dereliction of their responsibilities, or unprofessional.

For example, my sister decided 15 years ago to seek corrective eye surgery to cure her myopia and eliminate her reliance on contact lenses. Her doctor performed radial keratotomy on her left eye. While she was under heavy anesthesia, he used a razor to cut tiny slits in that eye. He then reshaped the cornea and placed a heavy bandage over the eye. Medication kept her semiconscious for two days as an antidote to the intense pain that resulted from the surgery. After several weeks, the patch was removed. Over several months as the eye healed, her vision improved, and after six months she was sufficiently recovered to repeat the procedure with her right eye.

Three years ago, I decided to have corrective eye surgery to address my own double-digit myopia that left me legally blind without corrective lenses. The Lasik surgery took less than 10 minutes. The doctor advised me to go home and sleep for the rest of the day. Within several days, I had 20-20 vision in both eyes.

The field of eye surgery had evolved dramatically during the years that separated our surgeries. The best practice of the 1980s had given way to a far superior procedure by 2000. Now imagine that when I went to my doctor, he opted to ignore the breakthroughs in his field and instead performed the same radial keratotomy my sister endured years earlier. He could have offered several reasons for refusing to learn and implement the procedure that was now universally regarded as best practice in his field. "Radial keratotomy has always worked for my patients in the past." "I haven't had time to learn the new procedures because I have been too busy slicing eyeballs." "I have invested heavily in razor blades, and I don't want to waste them." I would not have considered any of those explanations a compelling argument for behavior that at best would be considered unprofessional, if not malpractice.

A PROFESSIONAL OBLIGATION

If one characteristic of a professional is to engage in a continuous process of seeking and implementing best practices in the field, it follows that educational leaders have an obligation to align the practices of their schools and districts with what we know to be the most effective strategies to achieve the fundamental purpose of our profession — high levels of learning for all students.

There is clear consensus among leading educational researchers as to the best practices for improving

schools. When staff work together as a professional learning community — when they work together to clarify purpose and priorities, establish and contribute to collaborative teams, participate in continuous improvement cycles of gathering data on student achievement, identify areas of concern, generate strategies for improving student performance, support each other as they implement those strategies, and gather new data to assess the impact of their collective efforts — and when they are relentless in their efforts to improve achievement for all students, they increase the likelihood of sustained, substantive school improvement. The research is clear and compelling on this point. In fact, I am unaware of any credible research that suggests the best strategy for school improvement is to ensure each teacher works in isolation.

I also know intuitively, as well as from my own experience, that school structures and cultures that celebrate working in isolation are unlikely to result in significantly higher levels of achievement. Early in my educational career, I was one of four individuals in my school teaching U.S. history to the junior class. The only thing our courses had in common was the title. On my own, I determined what I felt was important about U.S. history and what I was interested in teaching. I decided how to sequence and pace the content to cover what I felt was important. I chose supplementary materials and determined the best instructional strategies for each lesson. I created the assessments to determine the levels of learning of my students. And when, at the end of this process, I found that students had failed to learn, I was expected to figure out what went wrong and to rectify the situation.

The problem, of course, was that on my own, it was unlikely I would find a solution. I had just taught what I thought was the most important content, in the most logical sequence, using what I felt were the best materials and instructional techniques. I had used what I

TOOL 3.5

considered to be a valid assessment of student mastery. If students had not learned, it was not due to a lack of effort on my part. I had done my best, and if I were simply left to my own devices, to what I knew or did not know, there was little reason to believe that, on my own, I could help students achieve at higher levels.

This troubled me when I was teaching more than 30 years ago. What troubles me even more today is that my experience continues to characterize teaching throughout North America, despite the widespread knowledge that best practice, the best hope for helping all students learn, is to have teachers working together in a collaborative culture.

Educational leaders have a professional obligation to align the practices of their school with the best thinking in the field, and there is virtually no justification for not fulfilling this obligation. We should be just as intolerant of educators' inattention to best practices as we would be of the eye surgeon.

Those who argue that a professional operates with a minimum of supervision, enjoys a high degree of autonomy, and exercises judgment based on the situation are correct. Powerful concepts such as teacher empowerment, academic freedom, and site-based management are based on the premise that professionals need and benefit from a degree of discretion in carrying out their duties. But advocating autonomy for individual teachers and schools should not extend to ignoring what we know about what works when it comes to student learning. School leaders who align the workings of their schools and classrooms with the knowledge base regarding best practice enhance their profession. Those who allow misalignment to go unaddressed diminish the profession.

It is time for school leaders to stop making excuses for their failure to implement what we know about improving schools. Superintendents are not justified in giving schools the autonomy to continue bad practice in the name of site-based management. Principals are not justified in allowing teachers to work in isolation in the guise of teacher empowerment. Teachers are not justified in going it alone under the pretext of academic freedom. Either we are a profession, or we are not.

ABOUT THE AUTHOR

Rick DuFour is an educational consultant.

One clear voice is needed in the din
Define priorities, concentrate efforts, and stay the course

By Rick DuFour

What is the primary task of leaders in contemporary organizations? Consider the responses of some of the nation's leading thinkers on the subject:

- Developing the structures and culture that encourage continuous learning (Peter Senge).
- Creating a clear and compelling vision (Warren Bennis).
- Serving others (Robert Greenleaf).
- Shaping culture (James Heskett).
- Defining the future and aligning people to achieve that future (James Kotter).
- Clarifying organizational values (Tom Peters and Robert Waterman).

Contemporary leadership is so complex that it is neither possible nor desirable to define it in terms of a single focus. Today's effective leader must tend to all of the above issues and myriad others. But, at the risk of oversimplifying, I contend the primary responsibility of educational leaders is creating and communicating the school's purpose and priorities in a way that connects with, and gives clear direction to, those in it. And this responsibility can be fulfilled only if the leader demonstrates a sustained, enthusiastic commitment to the direction in which the school is headed.

Educators have been bombarded with countless (and often conflicting) images and ideas of how schools should function and the purposes they should serve. Legislative initiatives wash upon us in waves. The business community calls on us to raise standards. Advocates for special education demand we accommodate the unique needs of every student. Parents, who often have widely differing views on schooling, demand a larger say in their children's education. The debates never seem to get resolved: back to basics vs. higher order thinking; phonics vs. whole language; cultural literacy vs. learning to learn; content vs. process.

The cacophony of mixed signals swirling around schools is tantamount to the discordant noise as scores of individual musicians in the orchestra tune up before a concert. It takes someone to step up to the podium to provide the focus that translates random noise into music. School leaders certainly must be willing to collaborate with others and delegate authority. They certainly must be willing to build consensus rather than impose their will. But the pendulum has swung too far. While we can caution against autocratic leadership and endorse shared

Journal of Staff Development, Spring 2002 (Vol. 23, No. 2)

decision making, we should not replace John Wayne with George Gallup. Schools need more than someone who polls the group on every question or leans whichever way the wind blows. It is difficult to look up to a leader who always has his ear to the ground.

Schools stumble when their leaders cannot identify priorities, or when they seem to say, "Pay attention to everything; everything is important." Schools will never have a widely shared sense of purpose and priorities until their leaders can help the educators within them cut through the noise and clarify "this is what is important, this is what we stand for, this is what we strive toward." While leaders can defer to others on the question of the best strategies to accomplish the organization's fundamental purpose, they must be responsible for defining that purpose clearly enough to give direction to the day-to-day decisions of every staff member in the school. School leaders must also acknowledge that the disconnected, fragmented change initiatives that have characterized school improvement efforts cannot be attributed solely to external forces. Educators must accept some responsibility for the fact that schools seem to pursue the latest fads so indiscriminately.

Many school leaders seem to embrace virtually every innovation available to educators in order to demonstrate their personal enthusiasm for change. They lose sight of the fact that it is the quality of a change initiative rather than the number of initiatives a staff is pursuing that is likely to bring about meaningful change. There is no prize for having the most innovations. Five new projects are not better than two. Six school improvement goals are not better than one. Meaningful, substantive changes in schools occur through focused, concentrated efforts.

It is equally important that educational leaders acknowledge that real change is real hard, an effort that will demand sustained commitment over an extended period of time. Why do leaders so often embrace new ideas with initial enthusiasm, only to abandon them a short time later? I contend that it is because leaders persist in their quest for the quick and easy solution to the complex challenges facing schools. Thus, when the inevitable difficulties of implementation occur, when the going gets tough and things get messy, they tend to quit and search anew for the quick and easy answer.

This tendency to bail out at the first sign of difficulty has at least two serious consequences. First, it is in working through the unavoidable mess of a profound change process that a school staff develops the capacity to improve. Retreat robs a staff of an opportunity to learn. Second, teachers who have been tossed first in one direction and then another have been conditioned to respond to calls for yet another new project or program with jaded resignation, the assumption that "this too shall pass." As Phil Schlechty observed, "Nothing is more destructive to the cause of school change than the tendency of schools to move by fits and starts, to reverse direction, to behave in generally erratic ways."

It has been said that the first rule of leadership is simple: There is no leader without followers. If school leaders will help clarify purpose and priorities, if they will concentrate precious resources of time, money, and energy on the core purpose and resist the temptation to be pulled in too many directions at once, and if they will stay the course when buffeted by ill winds, they will increase the likelihood not only of having followers, but also of helping them reach a better destination.

ABOUT THE AUTHOR

Rick DuFour is an educational consultant.

In the right context
The effective leader concentrates on a foundation of programs, procedures, beliefs, expectations, and habits

By Rick DuFour

An old story says Ralph Waldo Emerson often began conversations with acquaintances he had not seen in some time by posing the question: "What has become more clear to you since last we met?"

The *Journal of Staff Development* presented me with a similar challenge when it asked that I reflect upon an article I co-authored five years ago titled, "The Principal as Staff Developer" (Berkey & DuFour, 1995).

While I am relieved to conclude the ideas in that article have held up well, some things principals must do to fulfill their responsibilities as staff development leaders have become much clearer to me.

IMPORTANCE OF CONTEXT

Shortly after my article was published, the National Staff Development Council identified professional development standards to help schools and districts assess their programs. Content standards articulated the what of professional development — the knowledge and skills staff members should have. Process standards addressed how professional development should be delivered.

Although both the content and process of professional development are significant issues worthy of a principal's attention, I have come to understand the most significant contribution a principal can make to developing others is creating an appropriate context for adult learning. It is context — the programs, procedures, beliefs, expectations, and habits that constitute the norm for a given school — that plays the largest role in determining whether professional development efforts will have an impact on that school.

In the right school context, even flawed professional development activities (such as the much-maligned single-session workshop) can serve as a catalyst for professional growth. Conversely, in the wrong school context, even programs with solid content and powerful training strategies are unlikely to be effective (DuFour, 1998).

When principals recognize how critical school context is to the effectiveness of professional development, important shifts begin. The primary arena for professional development moves from workshops to the workplace. Emphasis shifts from finding the right trainers or speakers to creating opportunities for staff to work together,

Journal of Staff Development, Winter 2001 (Vol. 22, No. 1)

engage in collective inquiry, and learn from one another. The artificial distinction between teacher work and teacher learning that exists in most schools is eliminated. Opportunities for learning and growth are structured into routine practices. I am convinced the single most effective way in which principals can function as staff development leaders is providing a school context that fosters job-embedded professional development.

I have also come to understand that the context principals should strive to create in their schools is the collaborative culture of a professional learning community. Creating a collaborative culture has been described as "the single most important factor" for successful school improvement initiatives, "the first order of business" for those seeking to enhance their schools' effectiveness, an essential requirement of improving schools, the critical element in reform efforts, and the most promising strategy for sustained, substantive school improvement (Eastwood & Louis, 1992; Fullan, 1993; Newmann & Wehlage, 1995; McLaughlin, 1995).

But if principals are to create this context of a collaborative culture in their schools, they must do more than encourage teachers to work together. The tradition of teacher isolation is too deep to be uprooted simply by offering opportunities for collegial endeavors. Collaboration by invitation never works. Principals who function as staff development leaders embed collaboration in the structure and culture of their schools. Teachers' work is specifically designed to ensure that every staff member is a contributing member of a collaborative team. Creating an appropriate structure for teacher collaboration is vitally important, but also insufficient. Principals must do more than organize teacher teams and hope for the best. They must provide the focus, parameters, and support to help teams function

effectively. More specifically, principals who are staff development leaders must:

1. Provide time for collaboration in the school day and school year. Providing time for teachers to work together does not require keeping students at home and/or an infusion of new resources. Principals as staff development leaders work with staff to identify no-cost strategies that enable teachers to work together on a regular basis while students are on campus.

2. Identify critical questions to guide the work of collaborative teams. The impact of providing time for teachers to engage in collective inquiry will be determined to a great extent by the nature of the questions teachers are considering. Principals must help teams frame questions that focus on critical issues of teaching and learning.

3. Ask teams to create products as a result of their collaboration. The best way to help teachers use their collaborative time productively is to ask them to produce and present artifacts in response to the critical questions they are considering. Examples might include statements of student outcomes by units of instruction, development of new units to address gaps between state standards and local curriculum, creation of common assessments and rubrics, articulation of team protocols or norms to guide the interactions of team members, or formulation of improvement plans based on analysis of student achievement data.

4. Insist that teams identify and pursue specific student achievement goals. The driving force behind the effort to create a collaborative culture must be improved results. Principals foster improved results when they ask teaching teams to identify and pursue specific, measurable student achievement goals.

5. Provide teams with relevant data and information. When every teacher has access to information on his or her students' performance in meeting agreed upon standards, on valid assessments, in comparison to other students trying to achieve the same standards, both individual teachers and teams improve their effectiveness.

Simply put, when teachers operate within the context of a learning community, they are more likely to develop professional competence. And it is principals who play the critical role in forging conditions that give rise to the growth of professional communities in schools (Louis, Kruse, & Raywid, 1996).

RESULTS-DRIVEN LEARNING

Some principals continue to cling to the notion that they function as staff development leaders when they offer a potpourri of professional development opportunities for staff. These peripatetic principals strive to expose their staff to every new educational fad in order to keep their schools on the "cutting edge." This eagerness to pursue change and embrace every "new thing" results in what has been referred to as the "Christmas tree" school. Programs, training, and initiatives are simply hung on the existing structure and culture of the school like the ornaments on a Christmas tree. Like ornaments, they never become truly organic or part of the tree. They dangle fragilely without ever being absorbed into the school's culture.

Principals who function as staff development leaders recognize that professional development is a means to an end — improved student achievement. They work with faculty to identify the specific competencies that are most critical in helping staff achieve that end; they design purposeful, goal-oriented strategies and programs to develop those competencies; and they sustain the commitment to those strategies and programs until staff acquire and use the intended knowledge and skills. They assess the impact of professional development not on the basis of the number of offerings or initial enthusiasm for the offerings, but on the basis of improved results.

The emphasis on results also means that building the group's collective capacity to achieve schoolwide goals must become a higher priority than the individual's independent learning. The traditional structure of schools has emphasized developing individual knowledge and skills. Each staff member has been provided incentives to take courses from a myriad of universities or to attend random conferences and workshops based upon personal interests. But it is time for a profession that has been fiercely protective of individual autonomy to acknowledge that individual development does not ensure organizational development. The random learnings of staff members may contribute little to a school's ability to solve its problems.

A famous symphony conductor once commented that while he wanted each violin player in the orchestra to work at becoming a better violin player, developing individual skills did not result in a great orchestra. He also had to help each section of the orchestra develop its ability to work together as a section. Finally, he had to ensure that each member and each section heard the music the same way, that they had a common sense of what they were trying to accomplish. Principals who function as staff development leaders function in much the same way. They want each 3rd grade teacher to work at becoming a better teacher, but they realize a focus on individual development will not create a great school. They must also help the 3rd grade team learn to function in ways that strengthen the entire 3rd grade. Most importantly, they must keep everyone in the school committed to a shared vision of improved learning for all.

Journal of Staff Development, Winter 2001 (Vol. 22, No. 1)

TOOL 3.7

MODELING

Principals who hope to encourage others to continue to grow and learn professionally must remember the words of Albert Schweitzer: "Example isn't the best way to influence others — it's the only way." When principals model a commitment to their own ongoing professional development, when they demonstrate openness to new experiences and ideas, when they are willing to pose questions and engage in action research, they increase the likelihood that others on the staff will make a similar commitment.

No principal could ever hope to know enough to be a resource in every content area for everyone in the school. Therefore, principals must identify areas for their own professional development that offer the most powerful leverage points for advancing the school toward its goals.

Because the fundamental purpose of school is learning, principals must become students of the teaching-learning process. Because learning communities require shared vision and collective commitments, principals must become skilled in building consensus and resolving conflict.

Because clarity of communication helps signal priorities and focus improvement efforts, principals must develop powerful strategies for communicating effectively. Because learning communities are results-oriented and committed to continuous improvement, principals must become proficient in gathering and reporting data in ways that are meaningful to teachers. Because the transformation of traditional school cultures into professional learning communities is a difficult task replete with obstacles, frustrations, and setbacks, principals must learn how to encourage the hearts of those with whom they work. This is by no means an exhaustive list. It is, however, representative of the kind of professional development principals could pursue to help those within a school accomplish their collective goals.

How can principals develop these skills? Read voraciously, secure a mentor, participate in a principal network, create a guiding coalition within the school to help generate, assess, and refine improvement strategies. Most importantly, look continuously for experiences that offer an opportunity for professional growth. There is much wisdom in the adage, "Leadership cannot be taught, but it can be learned."

There are those who contend that school improvement initiatives have suffered because schools are too dependent upon their principals, that the influence of the principal must be lessened in order for schools to function as learning communities. I do not subscribe to that theory. In fact, I believe schools need strong, effective leadership from principals more than ever. But the nature of that leadership is not the autocratic "my-way-or-the-highway" model of the past. Principals who embrace their role as staff development leaders act in accordance with the tenets of servant-leadership. As Robert Greenleaf (1990) described this model of leadership:

The servant-leader is servant first. … It begins with the natural feeling that one wants to serve, to serve first. Then conscious choice brings one to aspire to lead. … The best test and the most difficult to administer, is: Do those served grow as persons? Do they become healthier, wiser, freer, more autonomous, more likely themselves to become servants? (p. 7).

When principals focus on creating an environment in which people are working toward a shared vision and honoring collective commitments to one another, an environment in which all staff are provided with structures and supports that foster collaborative efforts and continuous professional growth, an environment in which each teacher has someone to turn to and talk to when confronted with challenges, they address one of the deepest yearnings in the hearts of most teachers: To

Journal of Staff Development, Winter 2001 (Vol. 22, No. 1)

make a positive difference in the lives of their students. And in helping teachers address that fundamental need, they increase the likelihood that teachers will themselves become servant-leaders to their students. And that is what the principal as staff development leader is all about.

REFERENCES

Berkey, T. & DuFour, R. (1995). The principal as staff developer. *Journal of Staff Development, 16*(4), 2-6.

DuFour, R. (1998). Why look elsewhere: Improving schools from within. *The School Administrator, 2*(55), 24-28.

Eastwood, K. & Louis, K. (1992). Restructuring that lasts: Managing the performance dip. *Journal of School Leadership, 2*(2), 213-224.

Fullan, M. (1993). *Change forces: Probing the depths of educational reform.* London: Falmer Press.

Greenleaf, R. (1990). *The servant as leader.* Indianapolis, IN: Robert Greenleaf Center for Servant Leadership.

Louis, K., Kruse, S., & Raywid, M.A. (1996). Putting teachers at the center of reform. *NASSP Bulletin, 80*(580), 9-21.

McLaughlin, M. (1995). Creating professional learning communities. Keynote address at the National Staff Development Council Annual Conference.

Newmann, F. & Wehlage, G. (1995). Successful school restructuring. Madison, WI: University of Wisconsin.

ABOUT THE AUTHOR

Rick DuFour is an educational consultant.

The principal shares leadership

CREATE A LEARNING ENVIRONMENT

The teacher's principal
Collegiality instead of control is one thing teachers appreciate in a leader

By Jo and Joseph Blasé

hat does effective instructional leadership look like? How can a principal improve teaching? How do teachers' views of leaders affect what they do in the classroom?

There has been little research into what teachers think makes an effective leader. And there have been few practical guides for leaders to become more effective. This article describes the everyday strategies of principals practicing exemplary instructional leadership and how these principals influenced teachers.

In our study of 809 teachers from public elementary, middle, and high schools in diverse regions of the United States, teachers used open-ended questionnaires to describe the characteristics of their principals (strategies, behaviors, attitudes, and goals) that influence their classroom instruction. Teachers also described their thoughts, behaviors, and feelings. All retained their anonymity.

Our research shows what teachers define as the characteristics of effective leaders, paving the way for professional development to help leaders become more effective.

Effective leaders:

- Avoid restrictive and intimidating approaches to teachers, as well as approaches that elicit "dog and pony shows" based on narrow definitions of teaching. Administrative control gives way to collegiality.
- Believe in teacher choice and discretion. Teachers are not criticized or forced to teach in limited ways.
- Integrate collaboration, peer coaching, inquiry, collegial study groups, and reflective discussion to promote professional dialogue.
- Embrace growth and change. These leaders believe change is a journey of learning and risk taking.
- Respect teachers' knowledge and abilities, seeing the teacher as "intellectual rather than teacher as technician" (Little, 1993, p. 129).
- Are committed not only to enacting school improvement and reform, but also to enhancing professional community in schools (Louis & Kruse, 1996).

In addition, instructional leadership is embedded in school culture; it is expected and routinely delivered.

We found that in effective principal-teacher interaction about instruction, the result is inquiry,

Journal of Staff Development, Winter 2001 (Vol. 22, No. 1)

reflection, exploration, and experimentation. Teachers build repertoires of flexible alternatives rather than rigid teaching procedures and methods.

THEMES

There are two major themes that principals exhibit in effective instructional leadership: Talking with teachers to promote reflection and promoting professional growth.

Principals whom teachers say are effective leaders use a range of strategies described here, and use them frequently.

Talking with teachers to promote reflection

Effective principals value dialogue that encourages teachers to reflect on their learning and practice. The study revealed five primary talking strategies:

1. **Make suggestions.** Do this during post-observation conferences and informally, day to day. Suggestions

The collegial school leader

School leaders work for a culture of individual and shared critical examination that leads to instructional improvement. Educational leaders should:

Talk about instruction with teachers frequently.

This requires skills, knowledge, attitudes, and personal characteristics different from those routinely taught and developed in many traditional educational leadership programs (Murphy, 1992). Specifically, make suggestions, give feedback, and solicit teachers' advice and opinions about instruction in an inquiry-oriented approach. Strive to develop cooperative, non-threatening teacher-supervisor partnerships — characterized by trust, openness, and the freedom to make mistakes — that are crucial to analyzing teaching and its effects (Cangelosi, 1991). As instructional leaders, emphasize studying teaching and learning, and be prepared and willing to model effective teaching.

Support collaborative efforts by supporting the development of coaching skills and reflective conversations.

Provide time and opportunities for peer connections. This will send two powerful messages to teachers: that you realize that collaborative processes (in contrast to a principal's authoritarian approach) elevate teachers as thoughtful,

responsible, growing professionals, and that you believe growth and development are most likely to occur with open, mutual, critical dialogue, rather than with judgmental, evaluative criticism (see Freire's (1985) argument on this point).

Develop a structure (e.g., provide resources and support to redesign programs, apply the principles of adult growth to staff development programs and activities) and core resources (e.g., promote positive school climate and group development, teamwork, collaboration, innovation and continual growth, trust in staff and students, and caring and respect to enhance teacher efficacy (Blasé & Blasé, 1997, 2000; Hipp, 1995).

Enhance these by inspiring group purpose and providing rewards such as praise.

De-emphasize competition among teachers. Professional development programs should teach practicing and aspiring principals how to develop professional dialogue and collegiality among educators. The anchors for such programs should be training in group development, theories of teaching and learning (vis-à-vis both adults and children), action research methods, change, and reflective practice.

Journal of Staff Development, Winter 2001 (Vol. 22, No. 1)

must be purposeful, appropriate, and non-threatening. Principals should listen carefully, share their own experiences, use examples and demonstrations, give teachers choices, contradict outdated or destructive policies, encourage risk taking, offer professional literature, recognize teachers' strengths, and focus on improving instruction.

2. **Give feedback.** Effective principals "hold up a mirror," serve as "another set of eyes," and are "critical friends" to teachers. Feedback focuses on observed classroom behavior, is specific, expresses caring and interest, provides praise, is problem solving, responds to concerns about students, and stresses the principal's availability for follow-up talk.

3. **Model.** Demonstrate teaching techniques in classrooms and during conferences. Model positive interactions with students. Teachers viewed these forms of modeling as impressive examples of instructional leadership.

4. **Use inquiry and solicit advice/opinions.** Question teachers and solicit their advice about instruction.

5. **Praise.** Focus on specific and concrete teaching behaviors.

As a result of leaders who used these strategies, teachers reflected more and used a greater variety of teaching strategies, responded to student diversity, planned more carefully, and took more risks. Teachers reported positive effects on their motivation, satisfaction, self-esteem, efficacy, sense of security, and feelings of support.

In addition to the strategies discussed above, principals enhanced teacher reflective behavior by distributing professional literature, encouraging teachers to attend workshops and conferences, and encouraging reflective discussions and collaboration with others.

Promoting professional growth

Effective instructional leaders use six strategies to promote teachers' professional development:

1. **Emphasize the study of teaching and learning.** Provide staff development opportunities that address emergent needs. Encourage teacher input, allow discretion in attending, and support innovation. Principals who were identified as effective leaders in the study often participated in staff development sessions.

2. **Support collaboration among educators.** Networks are essential for successful teaching and learning. Model teamwork, provide time for collaborative work, and advocate sharing and peer observation. Encourage teachers to visit other teachers, even in other schools, to observe classrooms and programs.

3. **Develop coaching relationships.** Encourage teachers to become peer coaches. Based on two decades of research, Joyce and Showers (1995) concluded training is effective only when it includes peer coaching in the classroom.

4. **Encourage and support program redesign.** Encourage teachers to redesign instructional programs and support diverse approaches to teaching and learning. Be flexible on grouping and strategies. Provide resources to support program redesign when possible.

5. **Apply principles of adult learning, growth, and development to staff development.** Create cultures of collaboration, inquiry, lifelong learning, experimentation, and reflection consistent with the principles of adult learning and an understanding of teachers' life cycles, roles, and motivation (see for example, Glickman, Gordon, & Ross-Gordon, 1998).

6. **Implement action research to inform instructional decision making.** Use action research. Effective principals in the study are working to conduct staff development as a large-scale action research project, although the efforts are not yet extensive. This is consistent with Calhoun's (1994) thesis that without class and school-based data about learning, teachers

cannot determine the effects of what they do in the classroom.

These six strategies resulted in increased teacher innovation/creativity, risk taking, instructional focus, and reflection, as well as positive effects on teachers' motivation, sense of efficacy, and self-esteem.

Overall, our data indicate that each of the instructional leadership strategies enhances teachers' well-being, emotionally, cognitively, and behaviorally.

Today's successful schools have increasingly become centers of shared inquiry and decision making. In such schools, instructional leadership is shared with teachers, and in its most progressive forms is being cast as coaching, reflection, collegial investigation, study teams, explorations into uncertain matters, and problem solving (Glanz & Neville, 1997). Discussions of alternatives, not directives or criticism, are the focus, and administrators and teachers are working together as "communities of learners" engaged in professional and moral service to students. By making this happen, principals have a direct effect on teachers and classroom instruction (cf. Sheppard, 1996).

REFERENCES

Blasé, J. & Blasé, J. (2000). *Empowering teachers: What successful principals do* (2nd. ed.). Thousand Oaks, CA: Corwin Press.

Blasé, J.R. & Blasé, J. (1997). *The fire is back: Principals sharing school governance.* Thousand Oaks, CA: Corwin Press.

Calhoun, E. (1994). *How to use action research in the self-renewing school.* Alexandria, VA: ASCD.

Cangelosi, J.S. (1991). *Evaluating classroom instruction.* New York: Longman.

Freire, P. (1985). *The politics of education: Culture, power, and liberation.* Hadley, MA: Bergin & Garvey.

Glanz, J. & Neville, R.F. (1997). *Educational supervision: Perspectives, issues, and controversies.* Norwood, MA: Christopher-Gordon Publishers.

Glickman, C.D., Gordon, S.P., & Ross-Gordon, J.M. (1998). *Supervision of instruction: A developmental approach* (4th ed.). Needham Heights, MA: Allyn & Bacon.

Hipp, K.A. (1995). Exploring the relationship between principals' leadership behaviors and teachers' sense of efficacy in Wisconsin middle schools. Unpublished doctoral dissertation, University of Wisconsin, Madison, WI.

Joyce, B.R. & Showers, B. (1995). *Student achievement through staff development: Fundamentals of school renewal* (2nd ed.). New York: Longman.

Little, J.W. (1993). Teachers' professional development in a climate of educational reform. *Educational Evaluation and Policy Analysis, 15*(2), 129-151.

Louis, K.S. & Kruse, S.D. (1996). Teachers' professional community in restructuring schools. *American Educational Research Journal, 33*(4), 757-798.

Murphy, J. (1992). *The landscape of leadership preparation: Reframing the education of school administrators.* Thousand Oaks, CA: Corwin Press.

Sheppard, B. (1996). Exploring the transformational nature of instructional leadership. *Alberta Journal of Educational Research, 42*(4), 325-344.

ABOUT THE AUTHORS

Jo Blasé and Joseph Blasé are professors of educational leadership at the University of Georgia, Athens.

Principals partner with supervisors, teacher leaders

By Dennis Sparks

"Everyone in the organization is expected to be constantly in a teaching and learning mode. … [T]rue learning takes place only when the leader/teacher invests the time and emotional energy to engage those around him or her in a dialogue that produces mutual understanding."

— Noel Tichy

L eadership of the complex social organization of the modern school is far too demanding to be the work of just one individual. Therefore, successful principals invest energy in developing both their supervisors and teacher leaders through dialogue and other means to continuously improve teaching and learning.

Successful principals "develop up" on the organizational chart by skillfully and persistently educating district leaders about high-quality professional learning and advocating for the policies, data, tools, resources, and other forms of support that are essential in their schools. They ask their supervisors to evaluate them based on the quality of professional learning and the culture of their schools as well as on more traditional

areas. They request regularly-scheduled meetings to discuss goals and assess progress using various sources of evidence. These principals tap supervisors' thinking about educational issues and enlist district administrators as allies and partners in the continuous improvement of their schools.

Successful principals develop the leadership talents of teachers by delegating increasingly more complex responsibilities to them and nurturing the knowledge and skills to successfully fulfill those responsibilities. They do so by arranging formal learning experiences for teacher leaders and aspiring administrators and by engaging teachers in more sophisticated and demanding leadership tasks. They also provide generous amounts of one-on-one time with teacher leaders that enables them to reflect on and extract lessons from their experiences and to create plans for future learning and work.

An important way in which principals distribute leadership within schools is to recruit, develop, and support teachers to serve in special assignments within their schools. These individuals may function as team leaders or committee chairs, as full- or part-time instructional coaches, or as mentors for beginning

Results, December 2004/January 2005

teachers or veteran teachers who are struggling with their assignments. As a result of principals' efforts, teacher leaders feel well trained for their new roles and perceive that they and their principals are functioning as a team to improve the quality of teaching, learning, and job satisfaction in their schools.

Developing and distributing leadership within the school requires that principals be well grounded in instruction, curriculum, assessment, and professional development. While they do not have to know as much as teachers do about the fine-grained details of curriculum, instruction, and assessment, it is important that principals know enough to engage in deep and extended growth-promoting conversations with teachers about issues of teaching and learning.

Expanding the leadership capacity of others in the organization also requires sophisticated interpersonal skills. Successful principals are clear about their values and intentions, know how to succinctly and powerfully express their views, engage in dialogue to penetrate more deeply into the heart of issues, make requests for what they want, and act with integrity. They also know how to listen deeply and to honor the perspectives of others, even though they may not agree with them.

Principals who successfully promote high levels of learning in their schools know that they cannot do it by themselves. They understand the value of strong partnerships with their supervisors and teacher leaders. Most importantly, they know such partnerships are too important to be left to chance.

ABOUT THE AUTHOR

Dennis Sparks is executive director of the National Staff Development Council.

Bring the whole staff on board
Make everyone a part owner of the school's success

By Rick DuFour

One of the most formidable obstacles in school improvement is unwillingness to accept responsibility for student learning (Newmann & Wehlage, 1995). Tracy Kidder presents a classic illustration of that obstacle in *Among School Children* (Houghton Mifflin, 1989). Upon learning that the school, once again, was one of the lowest-performing schools in the state, the principal tells the staff:

"I don't want to hear about test scores anymore. I know what kids we got here. We can't bring them up to grade level no matter what we do. But can we improve instruction here? You bet we can. And we're doin' a good job. We really are" (p. 199).

The principal's response is telling. He asserts that the causes of learning lie outside the sphere of influence of the staff and that nothing can be done to help their kind of students achieve standards. He exonerates himself and the staff and makes it clear there is no reason to expect better results in the future.

This principal failed to fulfill one of the most fundamental obligations of leadership — holding oneself accountable for results. As John Gardner (1990) wrote,

"The willingness to accept responsibility is at the very heart of leadership." In contrast, low-performing schools typically blame lack of student achievement on external factors. Something or someone else is always the problem.

Improvement initiatives are unlikely to have a positive impact on student achievement if the leader of the school refuses to acknowledge responsibility for student learning. But, while the leader's willingness to accept personal responsibility for results is essential for school improvement, it is not sufficient. The larger challenge is building a collective sense of responsibility among the entire staff.

What can school leaders do to foster collective responsibility for student learning?

1. Insist staff work together in collaborative teams that focus on student learning, and then provide the time, support, and parameters that promote team success. When teachers work together to clarify the essential outcomes of each course, grade level, or unit of instruction, they can become more focused (and thus more effective) in their instruction. When they move beyond the pleasant affirmation that "all kids can learn" to clarify specifically what each student should know and be

Journal of Staff Development, Summer 2002 (Vol. 23, No. 3)

able to do as a result of instruction, they are more likely to accept responsibility for achieving those outcomes. When they work together to develop common assessments and to analyze results, they approach the question, "How do we know whether students are learning?" with greater confidence. When they can work together to identify areas of concerns regarding student performance, to develop strategies for addressing those concerns, and to support one another as they implement the strategies, they are more likely to feel the self-efficacy essential to responsibility.

2. Insist that teaching teams establish SMART goals.
When teaching teams establish specific standards or targets that demonstrate mastery, students are more likely to achieve at high levels. SMART goals are:

S - Strategic and specific

M - Measurable

A - Attainable

R - Results-oriented

T - Time bound

A team that states "By the end of the semester, all students will meet the mastery standard of 70% or higher on each subtest of essential knowledge and skills" is more likely to focus on results than teachers who teach, test, and hope for the best. Schools will not become more results-oriented unless they foster results-oriented teams whose members work together to establish and achieve goals that are specific, strategic, measurable, attainable, and time bound.

3. Provide individual teachers and teams with relevant feedback that identifies the levels of mastery of each student and informs teacher practice.
When schools have systems that provide each teacher with timely information on the extent to which students have met established standards on valid assessments in comparison with all the students attempting to meet

the standard, three things can happen. First, individual students who are having difficulty can be identified and given additional time and support. Second, each teacher can assess strengths and weaknesses in the learning of his or her students compared with the total group of students, and can then seek the assistance of teammates for addressing areas of concern.

Finally, the team can focus on the performance of the entire group of students and develop strategies to improve that performance. As the team becomes more effective in helping all students master the intended outcomes, the team becomes more confident about its ability to help all students learn.

4. Celebrate improvements.
It has been said that the culture of an organization is found in the stories it tells about itself. Leaders who hope to foster a sense of collective responsibility for learning must engage in a never-ending process of articulating stories that convey the message, "We have the capacity to help all kids achieve at high levels."

For example, for the past 15 years, Adlai Stevenson High School has devoted a portion of every faculty meeting to stories celebrating the commitment and accomplishments of individual teachers, teacher teams, and the entire staff. Typically, the principal presents accounts of teachers who helped students establish new levels of achievement in a particular course. Some meetings are devoted to sharing good news about the collective accomplishments of the student body. Other meetings provide teachers with opportunities to share stories of colleagues who have helped or inspired them. At every meeting, however, staff members are presented with meaningful illustrations of the impact teachers are having on student learning. They hear a consistent, persistent message: "We can and do make a difference in student achievement."

Journal of Staff Development, Summer 2002 (Vol. 23, No. 3)

CONCLUSION

If accepting responsibility is at the very heart of leadership, then principals must embed leadership throughout the school. Even the most passionate principal cannot improve a school single-handedly. School improvement may begin when a principal accepts responsibility for student learning, but it is only when the entire staff embraces that responsibility that sustained school improvement takes place.

REFERENCES

Gardner, J. (1990). *On leadership.* New York: Free Press.

Kidder, T. (1989). *Among school children.* Boston: Houghton Mifflin.

Newmann, F. & Wehlage, G. (1995). *Successful school restructuring: A report to the public and educators by the Center for Restructuring Schools.* Madison, WI: University of Wisconsin.

ABOUT THE AUTHOR

Rick DuFour is superintendent of Adlai Stevenson High School District 125.

The principal's role in community building through staff development

By Raymond L. Calabrese

Community, an environment in which everyone feels he or she belongs, is a key component to effective education. The school, as a community, is composed of members with different roles who come together for a common purpose. Like any community, the school organization's success is often based on how effectively the various groups unite to meet common goals. Thus, a school community should be aware of subgroup needs, individual needs, and the entire school community's needs. The principals may promote an effective community by using staff development to unite the school's various subgroups.

Schools that lack community often promote distress and conflict. In effect, faculty members and administrators wrestle for control (Truesdell, 1985). Members of both groups complain of burnout, bureaucratic obstructions, and lack of funding. Enthusiasm for education diminishes without a sense of community. This may result in a climate where the principal players disengage from their common mission: providing quality education.

The frequently reported friction between regular classroom teachers and special education teachers provides an example of the lack of community. Many regular classroom teachers believe that children with learning problems should be taught by those with special skills, whereas many special education teachers see their function as providing support to regular classroom teachers as they teach mainstreamed children (McAfee, 1987). Rather than seeking common ground, both groups stake out diverse positions. A win-lose philosophy forces principals to choose between these groups.

Disharmony among school groups need not exist. Community is enhanced when the organization is inclusive and its members accept each other's uniqueness (Peck, 1987). The principal, as the key player, may alter this situation by introducing a staff development model that focuses on building school community through a policy of inclusion. In this approach, the principal, rather than building coalitions, seeks to incorporate all groups. Thus, the principal, teachers, and students benefit by mutually developing an environment where all members feel included. Such a policy unites the school's divergent groups around common themes such as discipline,

Journal of Staff Development, Winter 1989 (Vol. 10, No. 1)

parental assistance, or curriculum. The following model has proven to be effective in building community in school organizations.

A COMMUNITY-BUILDING MODEL

There are two dimensions to community-building: preparing the environment for community and building an educational community.

Preparing the environment for community

When preparing the environment for community, the principal cares about individuals and initiates a process that stimulates community growth.

The principal cares about individuals. The principal who builds community forms caring relationships with staff members; the principal is concerned with each staff member's personal and professional growth. There is a recognition that organizational needs cannot be addressed until personal needs are met. One way to nurture this environment is to ensure that staff development is beneficial to all members of the school community by combining personal with organizational needs.

The principal stimulates community growth through communication and common goals. The principal achieves a sense of unity by focusing on community. Traditional models tend to focus on staff development as a means of meeting organizational needs, i.e., programs are designed to overcome perceived teacher inadequacies or upgrade teacher competencies (Showers, Joyce, & Bennett, 1987). In effect, organizational needs become paramount and people are viewed as resources to meet those needs.

The principal should nurture community by building an environment where communication among groups is a major priority. The organization, by communicating with its constituents, generates a feeling that they are working for common goals.

The principal initiates a process that stimulates community growth. Because community building can be

a tedious process, effective principals rely on patience and perseverance to accomplish this task.

This process of stimulating community growth has seven components. First, the principal recognizes that each teacher is unique. Second, principals assist teachers to fully develop as human beings. Third, principals determine, with the teacher, the personal, organizational, and professional barriers that prevent growth. Fourth, the principal initiates a process that unifies diverse groups and sustains unity. Fifth, the principal communicates a vision of empowerment. Sixth, the principal allocates organizational resources to staff development programs that focus primarily on building community. And seventh, the principal leads by example through interaction with faculty members to synthesize common themes to unify.

Building an educational community

The second dimension of community building unites the faculty and principal into a community. As a community, the principal and faculty rediscover the reasons they entered teaching, identify the roadblocks that have dampened their initial enthusiasm for education and inhibited collegial relationships, and develop a renewed sense of personal and professional joy.

The principal can use the following six-step staff development model at a faculty retreat to unite individual and organizational needs as a means of contributing to the growth of community.

Plan and conduct a faculty retreat. A community-building retreat renews and rekindles the human spirit. The principal's major goal is to rejuvenate the career goals and dreams of administrators and teachers. It is a time to reflect upon why one entered education and to plan how to unite one's idealism with the reality of the work place. The retreat process should take place away from the school setting and be scheduled minimally for an entire day. The principal or trained facilitator can lead the retreat. In any event, the principal and faculty are co-participants. There

Journal of Staff Development, Winter 1989 (Vol. 10, No. 1)

are no group or status advantages in the retreat process. The retreat is designed to renew participants through the discovery of illusionary barriers and the elimination of isolation. It breaks down the barriers that prevent subgroups from cooperating.

Have teachers reflect on reasons for entering the education profession. Most teachers and administrators entered teaching with a strong desire to make a difference in the lives of young people. Over time, this goal often loses its priority as teachers and administrators have battled with paperwork, mandated programs, and lack of resources (Calabrese, 1987). At the retreat, the principal assists faculty members in recalling their sense of idealism. Ironically, as administrators and teachers share their reasons for entering teaching, they often discover commonalities in their idealism.

One effective activity to assist participants in reflecting on why they entered education is to ask them to write a letter to a college student who is considering education as a career. This letter, to a fictitious person, describes the participant's feelings when he or she first entered the education profession. This letter, when shared with the other group members, builds a feeling of solidarity and that one's career is important.

Determine barriers to success. Once the group has conceptualized their reasons for entering the education profession, participants in large and small groups at the retreat identify the barriers that have prevented them from maintaining their initial enthusiasm. Participants usually find that similar barriers confront teachers and administrators.

The interaction between small and large groups accomplishes two major goals. First, participants recognize that they are not confronting unique obstacles. And second, many important issues surface that frequently block important school initiatives. In effect, this activity exposes the underlying reasons that prevent participants from achieving their potential.

Determine real versus perceived barriers. The principal then helps teachers determine which barriers can be eliminated and which are beyond their control. Too often, faculty and administrators resign themselves to living with perceived barriers rather than focusing on the reduction or elimination of those barriers. This step is a form of empowerment that increases the control teachers and administrators feel over their professional lives. The principal assists participants in prioritizing the barriers and then works with teachers to humanize the work place and to nurture a sense of community.

This activity can have profound effects. One group of teachers, for example, believed that their environment was too hostile and that they were wasting their time trying to change things. Once they were able to review these barriers, however, they realized that they could alter all but six. The group requested that this list of barriers, over which they had control, be posted in the teachers' room.

Develop long- and short-range plans. At the retreat, participants next develop a prioritized list of the barriers that they believe can be altered. The principal then facilitates a planning process to overcome those barriers. In essence, this listing becomes a staff development plan that balances personal and organizational needs. The plans are developed through small and large group interaction; each small group shares its plan with the larger group. A community feeling is developed as groups interact to accomplish common goals and recognize that there is more than one possible solution.

Develop commitment. The principal assists participants in developing both a personal and group commitment to the success of each plan developed in step five. Each individual's personal commitment is shared with their group, helping develop a sense of trust and intimacy.

CONCLUSION

The bonds formed by the retreat process are maintained when the principal uses his or her leadership to make sure that each group implements its plans. The retreat process should be a yearly activity and be a time to reflect, rejuvenate, and rebuild.

The principal is the major player because faculty members traditionally look to the principal as a leader. If the principal uses this two-phase approach, the faculty and administrator will form bonds that result in effective staff development, high morale, and improved student learning.

REFERENCES

Calabrese, R.L. (1987). The effect of the school environment on female teachers. *Education, 108*(2), 228-232.

McAfee, J.K. (1987). Integrating therapy services in the school: A model for training educators, administrators, and therapists. *Topics in Early Childhood Special Education, 7*(3), 116-126.

Peck, M.S. (1987). *The different drum: Community making and peace.* New York: Simon & Schuster.

Showers, B., Joyce, B., & Bennett, B. (1987). A synthesis of research on staff development: A framework for future study and a state of the art analysis. *Educational Leadership, 45*(3), 77-81.

Truesdell, L. (1985). Assessing the quality of inservice training for special education. *Teacher Education and Special Education, 8*(4), 25-32.

ABOUT THE AUTHOR

Raymond L. Calabrese is associate professor and department chairperson, Educational Administration, Eastern Illinois University.

Moving another big desk

By Gay Fawcett

It was my first day on the new job. I should have been excited, but for some reason, I felt out of sorts. "What's wrong with you?" I scolded myself as I unpacked paper clips, scissors, pencils, and tape. "You've got your own private office — with windows — a secretary, a staff of 10, a Ph.D. posted on the wall, and a big desk." The BIG DESK! As the realization hit me, I dropped into the oversized leather chair that my predecessor had left behind. "BIG DESK," I said aloud. Did I have what it would take to move another one?

Years before as a classroom teacher, I had sat at a big desk, hiding behind my bulletin board punch outs, resource files, teacher manuals, smiley stickers, and ego. There I sat planning how I would control those people sitting at little desks. My intentions were sincere; I was a "good" teacher. But I did not trust my students to make wise choices for their own learning. I believed they lacked the maturity and wisdom of one who sits at a big desk.

Moving that big teacher desk to the back of the room in order to make way for the people who sat at little desks was a slow and painful process. It had been hard for me to relinquish control and to trust children to direct their own learning (Fawcett, 1992), and the big desk was still not totally out of the way when I decided to leave the classroom to become a language-arts consultant for a county school system.

In the new role, I told my big desk story to teacher after teacher. I encouraged them to trust children, and I helped them move their own big desks. Looking back now, I realize I had become almost smug about the big desk. It was easy to offer advice. As a consultant, I was no longer in a position where I had to share decision making beyond a surface level. (What topic shall we cover in the next workshop, and who would like to lead the next discussion group?) Now I had a new job as director of curriculum and instruction with a staff of seven consultants and three secretaries, and I was once again sitting at a big desk, the symbol of organizations designed to control.

FACING THE HYPOCRITE IN THE MIRROR

For the first few weeks, I sat uncomfortably at the big desk, taking care of tasks that a "boss" must take care

Journal of Staff Development, Winter 1996 (Vol. 17, No. 1)

of — signing forms, balancing budgets, and scheduling meetings. It felt very much like my former big desk classroom days of writing lesson plans, grading papers, and gathering materials with little input from the people who sat at little desks. The reluctance of my co-workers to interrupt was almost palpable. Although my door was never closed, they would knock on the door frame or stand outside the doorway and clear their throats until I invited them in. The big desk created a distance between us that conveyed a message of rank and control.

As I looked around my office, the excuses came easily: The desk is too heavy; I can't move it. There is no place to put it anyway; it will have to stay there. The department has a good reputation; great things have been accomplished under the direction of former big desk bosses — why change? Organizations are different than classrooms; children are different than adults. I am expected to make the decisions; that's what I'm getting paid to do. My intentions are sincere; I'm a "good" boss.

Giving control to children was difficult, but there was comfort in knowing that as the older and stronger adult, I could always go back if it did not work. But could I extend such trust to adults? If things did not work out the way I wanted them to, it would be much harder to regain control. Facing the hypocrite in the mirror was most disconcerting.

LOOKING TO THE EXPERTS

Years earlier, when I did not know what to do with students, I went to the professional literature and read what the experts on children's learning had to say. Now, once again, I found myself in the professional literature looking for answers. I read what experts in the field of leadership had to say. Senge (1990; Interview, 1993), Sergiovanni (1990, 1992, 1994), Barth (1990, cited in Sparks, 1993), and Drucker (1992) insisted that people in organizations should share responsibility and power.

They said that open communication is essential and that trust makes it possible. They wrote about the importance of building a sense of community where people share values and ideas about human nature and schooling. They said that good bosses "… lead by following. They lead by serving. They lead by inviting others to share in the burdens of leadership" (Sergiovanni, 1994, p. xix). Once again, the message was clear — get out from behind that big desk!

MOVING THE BIG DESK

With excitement and remembrances of my old desk-moving days, I looked around my office. Because of bookshelves and windows, there was simply no other place for the big desk. It would have to stay in the center of the room even though it looked so daunting. There was nothing requiring me to sit at it, however. The first move I made was to sit at a small table beside the door. I still had forms to sign and budgets to balance, but now I could see co-workers as they approached the door. The symbol of power and control was behind us, not between us.

Next, I moved away from the table and into workshops that my co-workers were teaching. I made it clear that I was not attending as their "boss" but as a workshop participant. If they felt uneasy at first, they soon realized that my participation was an acknowledgement of their expertise. My teaching background was language arts. I had no idea what one could do with a graphing calculator, I didn't know how to integrate high school biology with chemistry, and I couldn't even remember the details of the Northwest Ordinance, let alone give teachers suggestions on how to teach it from a constructivist perspective.

Finally, members of our department together moved as far away from the big desk as we could. We began meeting once a month during the work week at one another's homes to "struggle with such issues as who (we) are, what (we) hope to become for the students (we) serve, and how (we) will decide, organize, teach, learn, and live together" (Sergiovanni, 1994, p. xv). Our calendar on those days indicated that we were attending a "hopes and dreams" meeting.

Through dialogue we learned to trust one another, communicate honestly, and share responsibility. We moved away from big-desk leadership and began acknowledging the fluidity of leadership that exists among members of a group committed to its hopes and dreams. Through our conversations, we learned who among us had expertise to inform us about certain situations, who had passion to drive us when we got tired, who could listen and objectively reflect back what we said, and who could ask the hard questions to help us clarify our thinking. We began to think about leadership in new ways.

NEW WAYS OF THINKING ABOUT LEADERSHIP

Pajak (1993) examined educational leadership over the last 50 years and concluded, "We sorely need new ways of thinking about educational supervision and leadership as we confront the technological, social, political, and moral issues of today" (p. 159). Telecommunication is leading to an increasingly sophisticated global economy, tyranny is threatened by easy access to information, and social and moral realities are being transformed daily as knowledge and the ability to use it increases political and economic power.

How is leadership defined, then, in the face of such daunting changes? Citing a recent issue of *Fortune* magazine, Pajak (1993) said, "The most successful corporation of the 1990s will be something called a learning organization that is capable of adapting quickly in a rapidly changing environment" (p. 173). Senge (Interview, 1993) described the role of leaders in such organizations when he said, "Leaders in learning organizations are responsible for building organizations where people are continually expanding their capabilities to shape their future — that is, leaders are responsible for learning" (p. 9). The images of leaders as top-down change agents or as corporate visionaries must be replaced by the notion of leaders as democratic teachers (Pajak, 1993).

ESTABLISHING A CLIMATE OF TRUST

Senge (Interview, 1993) maintains that while human beings are born to learn, human organizations are made to control. Traditionally, our organizations have been run by leaders who make and monitor rules and regulations, review and make final decisions on proposals made by subordinates, and control budgetary and personnel hiring and firings. In other words, our leaders have sat at the metaphorical big desk — certainly a far cry from the image of a democratic teacher! Before new ways of thinking about leadership can begin, the old notions must be dispelled. This can only begin within a climate of trust.

Leaders must make symbolic gestures that encourage trust. In our department, it started with a physical move away from the big desk that sent the message, "You can approach me." Trust is also established when those who are at the top of hierarchically organized institutions openly acknowledge that they do not know all the answers. We made small steps in that direction as I attended inservice sessions the consultants presented, not to evaluate them but to learn from them.

DEVELOPING PERSONAL VISIONS

Before we could develop a vision of what our role in education should be, we needed to be consciously aware of and be able to clearly articulate our own personal vision — what Senge (1990) called our "mental pictures … of how the world works" (p. 12). However, because all the members of our department are products of structured hierarchical schooling, we were not accustomed to such conversations. We began, therefore, by taking turns seeking out provocative articles to serve as springboards to discussion at our hopes and dreams meetings.

We started with Frank Smith's (1993) essay, "Politics of Ignorance." In that essay, Smith maintains that there are two kinds of ignorance: soft core (in which we believe someone else has all the answers for us) and hard core (in which we believe we are the ones who have all the answers). We agonized over who plays what role in education and over what role most of us were playing! We read James Clavell's (1963) *The Children's Story: But Not Just for Children,* the story of a teacher who brainwashed her elementary students in less than half an hour. We hotly debated whether students can so easily be manipulated and whether teachers themselves are simply pawns of a high-order establishment. We watched a video ("Peter Senge," 1993) of Peter Senge and read many other articles. We are currently discussing Wheatley's (1992) astounding book, *Leadership and the New Science,* which is forcing us to struggle with issues that trouble us: order and chaos, autonomy and control, structure and flexibility, and planning and innovation.

We are certainly not yet where we need to be, but each discussion leads us farther away from the big desk and closer to a learning organization and shared leadership. There are days when we wonder if we're doing the right thing; removing the big desk requires a "vulnerability that does not always feel comfortable" (Lee, 1993). Senge (Interview, 1993) said, "The more progress any organization makes, I guarantee you, the more it will see its inadequacy. That is the fundamental characteristic of learning" (p. 18).

IMPLICATIONS FOR SCHOOLS

New ways of thinking about leadership require that leaders move their big desks and establish environments that encourage trust and open communication. Time must be provided for teachers to share their own hopes and dreams for themselves and their students. This will not be easy in a profession that has come to expect quick fixes from hard core ignorance.

As teachers are treated democratically as leaders, however, classrooms will also become democratic learning organizations. As Glickman (1992) observes,

In time, they (will) learn that the independence from hierarchical authority they have achieved needs to be reflected in their relationships and activities with students. This is the only way educators can come to understand democratic participation as an educative process for all who live in schools. (p. 27).

For leaders, the choice should be clear; we can no longer hide behind forms, budgets, schedules, and egos. We must trust our colleagues to make wise choices. Only then will we stop seeing ourselves as "workers, bosses, and executives and see (ourselves) as teachers again" (Coulter, cited in Sergiovanni, 1994, p. 101).

REFERENCES

Barth, R. (1990). *Improving schools from within.* San Francisco, CA: Jossey-Bass.

Clavell, J. (1963). *The children's story: But not just for children.* New York: Dell.

Drucker, P.F. (1992). The new society of organizations. *Harvard Business Review, 70*(1), 95-103.

Fawcett, G. (1992). Moving the big desk. *Language Arts, 69,* 183-185.

Glickman, C.D. (1992). The essence of school renewal: The prose has begun. *Educational Leadership, 50*(1), 24-27.

Interview: Peter Senge. (1993, March/April). *Business Ethics,* 17-20.

Lee, G.V. (1993). New images of school leadership: Implications for professional development. *Journal of Staff Development, 14*(1), 2-5.

Pajak, E. (1993). Change and continuity in supervision and leadership. In G. Cawelti (Ed.), *Challenges and achievements of American education* (pp.

TOOL 3.8

158-186). Alexandria, VA: Association for Supervision and Curriculum Development.

Senge, P.M. (1990). The leader's new work: Building learning organizations. *Sloan Management Review, 22*(1), 7-23.

Senge, P.M. (December 10, 1993). Corners of the learning organization (Live Video Conference). Available from the PBS Adult Learning Satellite Service and the AED Foundation.

Sergiovanni, T.J. (1990). *Value-added leadership.* Orlando, FL: Harcourt Brace, Jovanovich.

Sergiovanni, T.J. (1992). *Moral leadership.* San Francisco, CA: Jossey-Bass.

Sergiovanni, T.J. (1994). *Building community in schools.* San Francisco, CA: Jossey-Bass.

Smith, F. (1983). *Essays into literacy.* Exeter, NH: Heinemann.

Sparks, D. (1993). The professional development of principals: A conversation with Roland Barth. *Journal of Staff Development, 14*(1), 18-21.

Wheatley, M.J. (1992). *Leadership and the new science.* San Francisco, CA: Berrett-Koehler.

ABOUT THE AUTHOR

Gay Fawcett is director of curriculum and instruction, Summit County Educational Service Center, Cuyahoga Falls, Ohio.

Making the leap to shared leadership

By Suzette D. Lovely

"Surround yourself with the best people you can find, delegate authority, and don't interfere."
— *Ronald Reagan*

Great sports heroes recognize the power of teamwork. Take former Boston Celtics star Bill Russell. Russell measured his success on the basketball court not by his own play, but rather by how he made his teammates play. According to Russell, "Our performance depended on both individual excellence and how well we worked together. None of us had to strain to understand that we had to complement each other's specialties; it was a simple fact. We all tried to figure out ways to make our combination more effective" (Senge, 1990, p. 233). This synergy propelled the Celtics to 11 NBA championships in 13 years. No other team in the history of the league has come close to matching this dynasty.

When shared responsibility flows through the arteries of a school, the wisdom of working as a whole supersedes any desire for individual triumph. Teachers understand what is necessary to bring out the best in students, and principals recognize what they must do to bring out the best in teachers. In championship schools, everyone is in sync.

The concept of shared leadership is one of the most neglected elements of professional development for administrators and teachers. Educators tolerate a degree of adult dysfunction and denial because they lack the appropriate strategies for working together (Lambert, 2003). Without conditioning and intervention, efforts to design a school of leaders are likely to be unfocused, inconsistent, or ineffective.

DELEGATION WITHOUT GUILT

As I listened to staff discuss questions like "Should we close the parking lot at 2:30 to keep parents out?" "Who will have recess duty when it rains?" "Is $25 too much for the coffee fund?," I wondered how I was going to make instructional leadership the priority of my day. After awhile, I realized there were certain things I had to do myself and other things I could delegate. Empowering others to make the decisions about rainy day schedules, coffee funds, and parking lots brought me good will.

— A new principal (Pruitt, 2003)

JSD, Spring 2005 (Vol. 26, No. 2) © Suzette D. Lovely. Used with permission.

TOOL 3.9

In schools, if others aren't entrusted to act, the principal's successes are limited to only those tasks he can complete on his own. This is not only unreasonable, it's physically impossible. With student achievement at the forefront of every district's mission, principals must learn to delegate without guilt. If they don't, they'll labor just to complete assignments they're good at with consistency.

Because teachers are the largest, most influential group in a school, they should assume the majority of responsibility (Lambert, 2003). This doesn't mean that each teacher is expected to contribute in exactly the same way. Some may assume more modest roles than others. For example, a first-year math teacher probably isn't the right choice to chair the committee to develop the algebra curriculum map, yet she may be ideal for coordinating Family Math Night. An exceptionally organized teacher might be enlisted to facilitate Student Study Team meetings.

In other words, teacher leaders need to be cultivated in accordance with their talents and interests. Finding tasks that suit each individual best allows every member of a faculty to experience a sense of accomplishment. Although most principals are aware that a "tell and command" approach suppresses shared leadership, some still fear that relying too heavily on teachers will cause them to lose control, be viewed as a sign of weakness, or reflect poorly on them if teachers make mistakes. Such misconceptions trick principals into thinking they hold a license on knowledge and expertise that others don't. Dismissing teachers' capabilities in such a way is not only demeaning, it's counterproductive.

Delegation is an ethical responsibility principals owe to themselves, their staff, and the organization itself. For the principal, delegating provides more time for planning, engenders trust, and facilitates open communication. For teachers, it builds self-esteem, fosters creativity, and offers training in skillful leadership. For the school as a whole,

delegation increases productivity, stimulates learning, and promotes a positive climate.

Delegating isn't about giving people more to do or assigning all the unpleasant duties to someone else. That's called dumping. Instead, delegating is about prompting others to get involved by capitalizing on the vast knowledge of a group. When principals activate team talents through delegation, teachers grow personally and professionally and their confidence as leaders soars.

CREATING A CHAMPIONSHIP SCHOOL

So how do principals get teachers past the confines of individualism to create a championship school? What approaches might be used to deal with teachers who just "want to do their own thing" or are "too busy" to plan with colleagues? First, principals have to start funneling more of their work to others. In doing so, they must also accept the fact that others may make mistakes or things might not be done all the time as they would do them. The alternative — trying to do it all themselves — reinforces isolation, creates overload, and prevents teachers from stepping up to the plate.

Carolyn Williams, a principal in the Capistrano Unified School District in Orange County, Calif., offers a poignant illustration of how delegation is applied to harvest a school of leaders. In 2001, Williams became the fifth principal assigned to Dana Hills High School in less than a decade. With 30 years of history and many original staff members still on board, it was important that Williams chart a slow but steady course toward improvement. Her goal: to get teachers to work collaboratively and develop common assessments in every discipline. Using the slogan "It's All About You," Williams told the staff that it was up to them to align the school's academic experiences for students. However, recognizing this was a tall order, she further explained her role as cheerleader and coach to assure their success.

JSD, Spring 2005 (Vol. 26, No. 2) © Suzette D. Lovely. Used with permission.

After attending a summer institute at Adlai Stevenson High School in suburban Chicago, Williams modeled her game plan after the pillars of a professional learning community. Conversations were framed around three correlating questions (DuFour & Eaker, 1998):

- What is it we want students to learn?
- How will we know if they've learned it?
- What will we do when they don't learn it?

Knowing that change wouldn't happen overnight, Williams sketched out a four-year game plan. After all, getting 122 strong-willed, loosely connected individuals to the championship takes persistence and plenty of practice.

In the first year, the staff focused on what the students should be learning. Using the California content standards, each department created curriculum maps. Williams assigned each of her six co-administrators a different discipline, and they were to lead discussions and insightfully examine concerns that were an outgrowth of the mapping process. As a former English teacher, Williams linked up with the English department. She observed group dynamics in meetings, redirected people when necessary, and followed up with reticent teachers who opted out of planning sessions. Realizing that collaboration by invitation didn't work, Williams also went before the District Restructuring Council to seek approval for six late start days. These late starts along with a fall professional growth day built into the collective bargaining agreement provided structured opportunities throughout the year for teachers to reflect on their practice. As a result, teacher collaboration throughout the school started to become a routine obligation rather than a random choice.

During the second year, respected teacher leaders and administrators accompanied Williams on a two-day retreat with an outside consultant to learn more about the inner workings of a professional learning community. Williams fostered confidence and enthusiasm by capitalizing on the group's talents. At the conclusion of the training, she asked, "What can we do to bring your colleagues along?" Aware that the leadership team had to provide purposeful guidance without appearing condescending or superior to peers, the principal steered them away from micromanaging the effort. Instead, she offered strategies the group could use to facilitate dialogue and build internal capacity. Her suggestions were tailored to address the varied styles and needs of the eight different high school departments. She reminded the leadership cadre that an important function was to ensure nonmembers' views were heard and respected. Without Williams' sustained coaching and encouragement, the leadership group would not have had the momentum to bring others along.

The English department group agreed that a subcommittee would draft assessments for each level (English I, II, and III) and then the collective group would fine-tune the assessments. The group developed a question bank and scoring rubric to assess writing conventions. When committee members complained about not having enough time to finish their drafts, Williams quickly eliminated the obstacle by delegating the typing to a secretary. In a professional learning community, the principal orchestrates the abandonment or redistribution of tasks that pose an impediment to achieving schoolwide goals.

In the third year, teachers were ready to start using the assessments. Williams layered the learning in the English department by meeting one-on-one with the more than 20 faculty members and setting individual performance goals aligned with the content standards. In this way, teachers' performance goals and final evaluations were linked to student data gleaned from the curriculum maps and common assessments. Once the assessments

JSD, Spring 2005 (Vol. 26, No. 2) © Suzette D. Lovely. Used with permission.

HOW TO ACHIEVE SYNERGY

Synergy develops when leaders mine the culture to reveal what really exists and matters in a school. Capacity-building leaders work to make the strengths of employees productive and their weaknesses inconsequential.

To establish a framework for shared leadership, staff members first are taught to examine complex issues in an insightful, honest manner. Small grade-level or interdisciplinary groups are an ideal venue for leaders to facilitate this learning. In this more intimate setting, hard questions can be posed to surface conflict or obstacles. Such questions might include:

- What is bothering us about this program, requirement, or situation?
- Is this the real issue or is there more to the concern?
- Why do we think this is happening?
- What evidence validates our assumptions?
- What can we do about it?

The bottom line: Without in-depth probing and dialogue, weaknesses are camouflaged, mistakes are covered up, and assumptions rule the day.

As a team prepares for its season, skills and conditioning are built as players get out on the court and start practicing. Court time for distributed leadership requires principals to activate team talents. If structured activities are missing from the game plan, teachers will continue to roam their campuses as free agents. Leaders must:

1. **Layer the learning.**

   Introduce new information in bite-size pieces so teachers don't feel overwhelmed.

2. **Promote social interaction.**

   Plan socialization activities outside the work day to help teachers get to know one another on a personal level. When people like each other, they perform better together.

3. **Spotlight success.**

   Applaud individuals and/or teams publicly for their accomplishments. If faculty members hear about colleagues' achievements, they feel connected, valued, and proud.

4. **Ink practice sessions into the weekly schedule.**

   Have teachers read and reflect on a journal article during a staff meeting. Give grade levels/departments a snippet of assessment data, demographic information, or student work and ask them to share their questions or findings with the rest of the faculty. Present the leadership team with a problem that needs to be solved. Have the team present its conclusions and proposed solutions to the entire faculty.

5. **Use "us" language.**

   Rather than I, my, and them, use language like us, we, and our. Talk about "our" staff, not "my" staff, and "It's up to us to make this better," not "up to them."

6. **It's not a choice.**

   Don't let collaboration be an option. Confront individuals who don't adhere to the commitments endorsed by the team by asking: "How is your refusal to work/collaborate with Ms. XYZ helping Johnny's learning?"

7. **Dare to delegate.**

   Muster the courage to delegate duties to others. Asking subordinates to get involved in decisions and projects raises the bar on their level of commitment toward the institution.

JSD, Spring 2005 (Vol. 26, No. 2) © Suzette D. Lovely. Used with permission.

were administered, teacher leaders convened subject-area meetings to analyze the information and identify strengths, gaps, and trends. A natural outgrowth of this reflection was to question what to do about the students who weren't learning. Various teachers were assigned follow-up tasks such as putting the data on a spreadsheet, talking to the students' academic advisers, and researching interventions being used at the other district high schools. By fall, a tutorial period was added to the master schedule to further assist students.

The assistant principals watched Williams in action and replicated the process in the other disciplines. Throughout the journey, the administrative team recognized group accomplishments both publicly and privately. And what does this principal/coach plan for year four? Vertical teaming.

Although Williams is the first to admit that being a high school principal can be overwhelming and fraught with challenges, she is able to focus her priorities on student learning by relying on others to collect data, complete projects, and make decisions. By establishing a climate of true — rather than contrived — collegiality, Williams is able to show teachers that alone they can do a few things, but together they can do anything.

CONCLUSION: SPIN A WEB OF LEADERSHIP

In high-achieving schools, the functions of leadership resemble a web, with principals in the center. The web is a nonhierarchical structure of authority and control. If the principal falls, she is supported. In this environment, administrators are keenly aware that leadership is learned and shared, not a birthright or enthroned. Therefore, they work to ensure every staff member is involved in the drive toward excellence.

To become the architect of a school with one principal but many leaders, use the checklist (p. 20). By homing in on areas of need, principals can find better ways to manage

delegated tasks and get commitments from others to do what they say. Without establishing an understanding that everyone is part of the team whether they like it or not, principals will continue to be daunted by assignments. Although delegation doesn't eliminate work in schools or diminish accountability, it does create a multiplier effect. The time spent on a single project is instead devoted to numerous people spending time on many projects.

There's plenty of work to be done in schools. Delegation affords a larger number of teachers the chance to assume formal leadership roles, permits several assignments to be done simultaneously, and increases the quality of the end result. Principals who activate team talents and delegate without guilt are able to distribute responsibility equitably — not equally — among those with a vested interest in increased student learning. They are sure to see changes rivaling the Boston Celtics. The act of delegating combats employee isolation, reduces job overload, and lessens the chance for burnout. What better way to keep both principals and teachers from spreading themselves too thin?

REFERENCES

DuFour, R. & Eaker, R. (1998). *Professional learning communities at work: Best practice for enhancing student achievement.* Bloomington, IN: Solution Tree.

Lambert, L. (2003). *Leadership capacity for lasting school improvement.* Alexandria, VA: ASCD.

Pruitt, L. (2003, Fall). From a new principal's perspective. *New Teacher Center Reflections, 6*(3), 11.

Senge, P. (1990). *The fifth discipline: The art & practice of the learning organization.* New York: Doubleday.

ABOUT THE AUTHOR

Suzette D. Lovely has worked as a principal and director of elementary school operations. Currently she is deputy superintendent for personnel services for the Capistrano Unified School District.

JSD, Spring 2005 (Vol. 26, No. 2) © Suzette D. Lovely. Used with permission.

TOOL 3.10

theme / LEADERSHIP AT THE SCHOOL LEVEL

D A R E   T O   D E L E G A T E *CHECKLIST*

Many school leaders have difficulty delegating responsibility. Complete the checklist to determine areas you need to focus on to improve your delegation skills.

	ALWAYS	SOMETIMES	NEVER
1. Do you decide what you can delegate?			
2. Do you break the task into the smallest pieces possible?			
3. Do you form a mental picture of each completed task?			
4. Do you select the tasks you must do yourself?			
5. Do you assess the skills of the people to whom you will delegate tasks?			
6. Do you assess the interests of these people?			
7. Do you assign the tasks based on skills and interests?			
8. Do you assign the authority and limits of discretion so the task can be completed?			
9. Do you identify who will do the task?			
10. Are you specific about what you want done?			
11. Do you determine why you want this person to do the task?			
12. Do you decide when the task must be completed?			
13. Do you explain what the completed task will look like?			
14. Do you ask questions to ensure understanding?			
15. Do you inform others who need to know about the assignment?			
16. Are you enthusiastic about the duties you delegate?			
17. Do you monitor the progress of each task at regular intervals?			
18. Do you require feedback?			
19. Do you provide feedback?			
20. Do you reward others for a job well done?			

SCORING GUIDE: Give yourself 2 points for every Always response, 1 point for Sometimes, and 0 for Never.

30-40 POINTS: A DARING DELEGATOR. You consistently and expertly adhere to the principles of delegation. These skills maximize your effectiveness and help you develop the full potential of your staff. You demonstrate confidence as a leader.

20-29 POINTS: A PROGRESSING DELEGATOR. Morale and efficiency are good, but could be even better if you were more conscientious in assigning and following up with delegated tasks. Even though you may be able to perform a task better or faster, you are aware that delegation allows others to grow personally and professionally.

10-19 POINTS: A RELUCTANT DELEGATOR. You have a hard time figuring out when and what to delegate. You worry that assigning tasks to others will lead to a loss of authority or control. It's time to re-evaluate your priorities and recognize that if a task doesn't involve privileged information or setting policies, you probably can delegate it.

9 AND BELOW: A GUILT-RIDDEN DELEGATOR. You struggle to complete tasks on time and feel overwhelmed at work. Your lack of mental discipline keeps you spiraling from one activity to the next. You need to take a step back and look in the mirror. Consider what the worst and best outcomes are if you start allowing others to help.

© Suzette D. Lovely. Used with permission.

A leadership conundrum

By Pat Roy

The principal is crucial in developing a climate that encourages continuous growth for teachers and students. But the principal can't do it alone.

The Innovation Configuration maps for the NSDC Standards for Staff Development clarify that principals "promote a school culture that supports ongoing team learning and improvement" (NSDC, 2003). Reculturing schools is critical to maximizing the instructional expertise of staff. But the principal cannot be the school's cultural architect without the conscious and deliberate involvement of teachers. In a review of teacher leadership, York-Barr and Duke (2004) found that teachers are "central to the process of 'reculturing' schools."

Others argue that principals are not the only instructional leaders. Instructional leadership "must come from teachers if schools are to improve and teaching is to achieve professional status" (Pellicer & Anderson).

Leadership:
Staff development that improves the learning of all students requires skillful school and district leaders who guide continuous instructional improvement.

Indeed, this work suggests principals are critical to developing teacher leadership. Principals had to encourage it; better — they had to actively support the development of teacher leaders who joined in creating a shared vision and new cultural norms. Principals cannot be threatened by growing other leaders within the school. The principal becomes a leader of leaders.

In the past, teacher leadership was viewed as serving in formal roles such as mentor, grade-level leader, or instructional coaches. Current work suggests teachers can serve as leaders by:
- Asking thoughtful questions at staff meetings;
- Expressing a different perspective during faculty discussions;
- Sharing classroom practices and challenges with peers;
- Initiating new methods and procedures for accomplishing learning tasks;
- Solving problems rather than assigning blame;
- Volunteering to address issues;
- Admitting mistakes and asking for assistance;

Results, March 2005

- Identifying unsolved instructional issues and asking for assistance;
- Discussing students in ways that demonstrate a belief that all children can learn; and
- Modeling skills of listening, paraphrasing, and inquiry (Lambert, 2003).

There are many challenges to the development of teacher leadership. One is a norm of egalitarianism — a belief of equal treatment and rights without regard for social status or role — or more vividly, the "crab bucket culture" (York-Barr & Duke, 2004). Crabs in a bucket will hold back any that rise to the top. This is parallel to teachers who discourage colleagues from functioning as leaders rather than supporting and inspiring them. The growth of professional learning communities and collegiality should inhibit this "crab bucket" effect. Teacher leaders must develop trusting and collaborative relationships with colleagues before they can influence their peers (York-Barr & Duke, 2004).

This research presents numerous challenges to teachers and principals. First, teachers need to believe that everyone can be a leader. They demonstrate this belief through interactions with peers to reduce isolation, reinforce new practices (such as examining student work), and develop a new vision of conducting school to benefit all students. Second, principals need to honestly examine their leadership style and beliefs. Do they believe there can be only "one leader" in the school or do they believe they can lead a community of leaders?

We cannot accomplish the lofty goals of educating all children well until we accept that leadership is a set of actions taken by many to influence the organization's vision and norms of operation.

REFERENCES

Lambert, L. (2003). *Leadership capacity for lasting school improvement.* Alexandria, VA: ASCD.

National Staff Development Council. (2003). *Moving NSDC's staff development standards into practice: Innovation configurations.* Oxford, OH: Author.

Pellicer, L. & Anderson, L. (1995). *A handbook for teacher leaders.* Thousand Oaks, CA: Corwin Press.

York-Barr, J. & Duke, K. (2004). What do we know about teacher leadership? Findings from two decades of scholarship. *Review of Educational Research, 74*(3), 255-316.

ABOUT THE AUTHOR

*Pat Roy is co-author of **Moving NSDC's Staff Development Standards into Practice: Innovation Configurations** (NSDC, 2003).*

CONTENT
PROCESS
CONTEXT

LEARNING COMMUNITIES

The Principal

DESIRED OUTCOME 1.1: Prepares teachers for skillful collaboration.

LEVEL 1	LEVEL 2	LEVEL 3	LEVEL 4	LEVEL 5	LEVEL 6
Ensures that the role of group facilitator becomes the responsibility of everyone and rotates as the skill level of group members increases. Provides training and support to develop faculty members to serve as skilled facilitators who provide support during whole school and learning team meetings.	Provides training and support to develop faculty members to serve as skilled facilitators who provide support during whole school and learning team meetings.	Provides opportunities for team leaders to learn about group process, group dynamics, the stages of group development, and group decision-making. Schedules multiple sessions throughout the year as well as coaching experiences.	Provides support to learning teams and/or whole school meetings throughout the stages of group development by supplying a skilled group facilitator.	Does not provide teachers professional development to build collaboration skills.	

DESIRED OUTCOME 1.2: Creates an organizational structure that supports collegial learning.

LEVEL 1	LEVEL 2	LEVEL 3	LEVEL 4	LEVEL 5	LEVEL 6
Persists with a regular schedule for collegial interaction in the face of resistance. Structures time for teacher reflection about their learning. Monitors to ensure the time is used well.	Structures the daily/weekly schedule for regular meeting times during the school day for collegial interaction. Monitors to ensure the time is used well.	Uses staff meetings for collegial interaction and sharing. Grade level and content area groups meet throughout the year with the goal of sharing ideas, resources, and curricula.	Does not adapt the structure of the school to accommodate collegial learning.		

60   National Staff Development Council   •   www.nsdc.org   •   *Moving NSDC's Staff Development Standards into Practice: Innovation Configurations*

www.nsdc.org   Professional Learning for School LEADERS ■ 149

TOOL 3.12

LEARNING COMMUNITIES: THE PRINCIPAL

DESIRED OUTCOME 1.3: Understands and implements an incentive system that ensures collaborative work.

LEVEL 1	LEVEL 2	LEVEL 3	LEVEL 4	LEVEL 5	LEVEL 6
Works with teachers to create and implement an incentive system for learning teams. Recognizes and rewards joint work that results in student gains and accomplishes school goals.	Recognizes and rewards teams for working together to accomplish school goals and increase student learning.	Creates structures and processes to ensure there is mutual support among teachers while expecting each person to focus work on school goals and outcomes.	Requests that faculty members cooperate with each other.	Does not implement a support system for collaborative work.	

DESIRED OUTCOME 1.4: Creates and maintains a learning community to support teacher and student learning.

LEVEL 1	LEVEL 2	LEVEL 3	LEVEL 4	LEVEL 5	LEVEL 6
Builds a culture that respects risk-taking, encourages collegial exchange, identifies and resolves conflict, sustains trust, and engages the whole staff as a learning community to improve the learning of all students.	Works with faculty to create a variety of learning teams to attain different goals. Facilitates conflict resolution among group members. Supports learning teams by providing articles, videos, and other activities for use during team time.	Works with faculty to create learning teams with clear goals, outcomes, and results outlined in writing. Expects and reviews team logs each month in order to coordinate activities within and among the teams.	Creates ad hoc study teams without clear direction or accountability.	Does not create learning teams.	

DESIRED OUTCOME 1.5: Participates with other administrators in one or more learning communities.

LEVEL 1	LEVEL 2	LEVEL 3	LEVEL 4	LEVEL 5	LEVEL 6
Attends regularly learning community meetings organized at the district, regional, state, and/or national level to identify and solve school challenges, as well as to learn together.	Meets regularly with a district learning team to solve school challenges and learn together.	Meets informally with administrative colleagues to discuss school challenges.	Provides support to learning teams and/or whole school meetings throughout the stages of group development by supplying a skilled group facilitator.	Does not participate in any learning community.	

Moving NSDC's Staff Development Standards into Practice Innovation Configurations • www.nsdc.org • National Staff Development Council

61

LEADERSHIP

The Principal

CONTENT

PROCESS

CONTEXT

DESIRED OUTCOME 2.1: Promotes a school culture that supports ongoing team learning and improvement.

LEVEL 1	LEVEL 2	LEVEL 3	LEVEL 4	LEVEL 5	LEVEL 6
Recognizes and rewards the accomplishments of teams and improvement efforts. Builds a plan with the faculty to support ongoing team learning and improvement. Recognizes the value of team learning and improvement, and discusses improvement activities in staff meetings. Conducts conversations, dialogues, and discussions within the school community until team learning and improvement become a shared goal.	Builds a plan with the faculty to support ongoing team learning and improvement. Recognizes the value of team learning and continuous improvement, and discusses improvement activities in staff meetings. Conducts conversations, dialogues, and discussions within the school community until team learning and improvement become a shared goal.	Recognizes the value of team learning, models continuous improvement, and discusses improvement activities in staff meetings. Conducts conversations, dialogues, and discussions within the school community until team learning and improvement become a shared goal.	Conducts conversations, dialogues, and discussions within the school community until team learning and improvement become a shared goal. Communicates that team learning and improvement are essential processes of the school at faculty meetings.	Communicates that team learning and improvement are essential processes of the school at faculty meetings, during evaluations, and with parents and students.	Does not address team learning and improvement.

TOOL 3.12

LEADERSHIP: THE PRINCIPAL

DESIRED OUTCOME 2.2: Creates a school culture that supports continuous improvement.

LEVEL 1	LEVEL 2	LEVEL 3	LEVEL 4	LEVEL 5	LEVEL 6
Expects and recognizes team members for their efforts to implement new instructional procedures and share student results. Provides models in which teams review their students' achievement results, identify high-priority learning goals, and identify new instructional procedures that result in increased learning. Models continuous improvement during staff meetings by discussing current schoolwide results and identifying new processes that result in improvements. Assesses and diagnoses the current school culture to determine which aspects support continuous improvement.	Provides models in which teams review student achievement results, identify high-priority learning goals, and identify new instructional procedures that result in increased learning. Models continuous improvement during staff meetings by discussing current schoolwide results and identifying new processes that result in improvements. Assesses and diagnoses the current school culture to determine which aspects support continuous improvement.	Models continuous improvement during staff meetings by discussing current schoolwide results and identifying new processes that result in improvements. Assesses and diagnoses the current school culture to determine which aspects support continuous improvement.	Uses staff meetings to discuss and identify the schoolwide results and to create new procedures that result in improvements. Assesses and diagnoses the current school culture to determine which aspects support continuous improvement.	Assesses and diagnoses the current school culture to determine which aspects support continuous improvement.	Does not address cultural conditions that support continuous improvement.

DESIRED OUTCOME 2.3: Creates experiences for teachers to serve as instructional leaders within the school.

LEVEL 1	LEVEL 2	LEVEL 3	LEVEL 4	LEVEL 5	LEVEL 6
Creates experiences for teachers to lead schoolwide committees that make decisions about curriculum, instruction, resources, and professional development. Establishes school guidelines that support these practices. Creates experiences for teachers to serve as mentors, master teachers, and instructional coaches.	Creates experiences for teachers to serve as mentors, master teachers, and instructional coaches.	Creates experiences for teachers to lead grade level/subject matter meetings.	Does not create experiences for teachers to serve in instructional leadership roles.		

Moving NSDC's Staff Development Standards into Practice Innovation Configurations • www.nsdc.org • National Staff Development Council

LEADERSHIP: THE PRINCIPAL

DESIRED OUTCOME 2.4: Involves the faculty in planning and implementing high-quality professional learning for the school.

LEVEL 1	LEVEL 2	LEVEL 3	LEVEL 4	LEVEL 5	LEVEL 6
Monitors implementation of professional development programs to ensure student learning results. States clear expectations for faculty implementation of new strategies while creating a system of follow-up to support implementation of new strategies. Works with the faculty to create a schedule that allows for additional time within the calendar for professional learning. Works with the faculty and staff developers to design and implement an ongoing staff development program based on assessed student and teacher needs.	States clear expectations for faculty implementation of new strategies while creating a system of follow-up to support implementation of new strategies. Works with the faculty to create a schedule that allows for additional time within the calendar for professional learning. Works with the faculty and staff developers to design and implement an ongoing staff development program based on assessed student and teacher needs.	Works with the faculty to create a schedule that allows for additional time within the calendar for professional learning. Works with the faculty and staff developers to design and implement an ongoing staff development program based on assessed student and teacher needs.	Works with the faculty to schedule staff development activities for designated days in the calendar.	Does not solicit input from the staff when designing professional learning for the school.	

DESIRED OUTCOME 2.5: Models continuous improvement and professional learning.

LEVEL 1	LEVEL 2	LEVEL 3	LEVEL 4	LEVEL 5	LEVEL 6
Persists with the same learning goals through implementation and mastery. States publicly personal professional learning goals, practices new strategies, and asks for feedback from the faculty.	States publicly personal professional learning goals, practices new strategies, and asks for feedback from the faculty.	Participates in a variety of professional development activities (e.g., reads articles, attends professional conferences, and uses technology to learn about new practices.)	Does not participate in personal professional learning activities.		

66   National Staff Development Council   •   www.nsdc.org   •   *Moving NSDC's Staff Development Standards into Practice: Innovation Configurations*

www.nsdc.org   Professional Learning for School LEADERS ■ 153

TOOL 3.12

LEADERSHIP: THE PRINCIPAL

DESIRED OUTCOME 2.6: Articulates the intended results of school-based staff development.

LEVEL 1	LEVEL 2	LEVEL 3	LEVEL 4	LEVEL 5	LEVEL 6
Provides specific, expected student learning outcomes and a descriptive rubric of expected classroom practices connected to school-based staff development.	Creates a clear description of expected classroom practices that result from school-based professional development.	Describes general student learning outcomes and explains how school-based staff development supports the school improvement goals.	Schedules professional development events but does not articulate the rationale or expected results of the staff development.		

DESIRED OUTCOME 2.7: Advocates for high-quality school-based professional learning.

LEVEL 1	LEVEL 2	LEVEL 3	LEVEL 4	LEVEL 5	LEVEL 6
Advocates with school board members, community members, community partnerships, colleagues, and central office administration for high-quality, school-based professional learning.	Advocates with colleagues and central office administration for high-quality, school-based professional learning.	Advocates with colleagues for high-quality, school-based professional learning.	Advocates for high-quality, school-based professional learning.	Does not support school-based professional learning.	

DESIRED OUTCOME 2.8: Participates in professional learning to become a more effective instructional leader.

LEVEL 1	LEVEL 2	LEVEL 3	LEVEL 4	LEVEL 5	LEVEL 6
Participates in facilitated learning teams that problem solve and learn together. Participates in extensive, ongoing learning activities that include hands-on, problem-based, and multiple practice opportunities. Allocates time to explore and practice specific behaviors and strategies and receive feedback on the implementation of new skills.	Participates in learning activities that occur over a two-year period and include hands-on, problem-based, and multiple practice opportunities. Participates in follow-up, coaching, and feedback. Allocates time to practice specific behaviors and strategies and receive feedback on the implementation of new skills.	Participates in a series of short-term sessions on instructional leadership and plans to apply new knowledge, skills, and practices during the workday.	Reads articles about instructional leadership.	Does not participate in professional learning experiences related to instructional leadership.	

Moving NSDC's Staff Development Standards into Practice: Innovation Configurations • www.nsdc.org • National Staff Development Council

67

RESOURCES

CONTENT

PROCESS

CONTEXT

The Principal

DESIRED OUTCOME 3.1: Allocates resources to support job-embedded professional development in the school.

LEVEL 1	LEVEL 2	LEVEL 3	LEVEL 4	LEVEL 5	LEVEL 6
Allocates resources to create a system of both formal and informal interactions that support professional learning so that faculty spends 25% of its time during the workweek in learning and collaboration with colleagues.	Allocates resources to support school-based staff development that include regular time within the school day for the grade level or content area teams to discuss instruction, curriculum, and assessment.	Allocates resources to support time during the workday for the whole faculty to reflect on student achievement and identify areas of teacher learning needs.	Makes teachers aware of district professional development calendars, courses, and workshops that require no school resources.		

DESIRED OUTCOME 3.2: Focuses resources on a small number of high-priority goals.

LEVEL 1	LEVEL 2	LEVEL 3	LEVEL 4	LEVEL 5	LEVEL 6
Works with faculty to focus on a small number of high-priority goals and provides resources to support their accomplishment. Ensures resources are not diverted to other competing issues.	Identifies a small number of goals but does not dedicate school resources to these goals.	Identifies a large number of competing goals, which results in a lack of sufficient resources to accomplish goals.	Does not prioritize goals from among school, district, state, and national goals.		

70   National Staff Development Council   •   www.nsdc.org   •   *Moving NSDC's Staff Development Standards into Practice: Innovation Configurations*

www.nsdc.org   Professional Learning for School LEADERS ■ 155

TOOL 3.12

RESOURCES: THE PRINCIPAL

DESIRED OUTCOME 3.3: Allocates resources to provide for continuous improvement of school staff.

LEVEL 1	LEVEL 2	LEVEL 3	LEVEL 4	LEVEL 5	LEVEL 6
Works with faculty to create a learning community so that teachers are supported in their use of new instructional, curricular, and assessment strategies. Supports this program with adequate resources such as time, space, materials, schedules, and funding. Allocates resources to support master teachers, mentors, and instructional coaches who work with teachers and learning teams to use new instructional, curricular, or assessment strategies.	Allocates resources to support master teachers, mentors, and instructional coaches who work with teachers and learning teams to use new instructional, curricular, or assessment strategies. Accesses resources (time and funding) to support the use of external instructional coaches or experts to work with teachers in their classrooms.	Allocates resources (time and funding) to support the use of external instructional coaches or experts to work with teachers in their classrooms to improve instruction or focus on school improvement activities.	Allocates resources to support teacher professional development that consists of attendance at workshops that provide experiences for participant practice with feedback.	Allocates resources to support teacher professional development that consists primarily of attendance at workshops that provide awareness-level information about new programs and practices.	

DESIRED OUTCOME 3.4: Allocates resources so technology supports student learning.

LEVEL 1	LEVEL 2	LEVEL 3	LEVEL 4	LEVEL 5	LEVEL 6
Allocates resources to support differentiated staff development activities in technology application focused on increasing student learning and devotes 30% of the technology budget to this goal.	Allocates resources to support multiple experiences with classroom coaching in which teachers practice using technology that increases student learning. Expects teachers to create lessons/units that integrate technology during the training sessions and receive feedback on those lessons that target student learning. Allocates resources to support multiple professional development sessions scheduled over time, with expectations for implementation between sessions.	Expects teachers to create lessons/units that integrate technology during the training sessions and receive feedback on those lessons that target student learning. Allocates technology resources to support multiple professional development sessions scheduled over time, with expectations for implementation between sessions.	Allocates technology resources to support multiple professional development sessions scheduled over time, with expectations for implementation between sessions.	Allocates resources to support "one shot" professional development sessions related to the use of electronic technologies.	Does not provide learning experiences related to electronic technologies.

Moving NSDC's Staff Development Standards into Practice: Innovation Configurations • www.nsdc.org • National Staff Development Council

DATA-DRIVEN

The Principal

CONTENT

PROCESS

CONTEXT

DESIRED OUTCOME 4.1: Analyzes with the faculty disaggregated student data to determine school improvement/professional development goals.

LEVEL 1	LEVEL 2	LEVEL 3	LEVEL 4	LEVEL 5	LEVEL 6
Works with the whole faculty to analyze a variety of disaggregated student learning results to determine school improvement goals, plus student and adult learning needs.	Works with a representative group of faculty members to analyze disaggregated student achievement data to determine school improvement goals, plus student and adult learning needs.	Analyzes disaggregated student data alone and informs the faculty of the results and needs.	Uses personal experience and opinion to determine school improvement and staff development goals.		

DESIRED OUTCOME 4.2: Analyzes a variety of disaggregated data to identify school improvement/professional development goals.

LEVEL 1	LEVEL 2	LEVEL 3	LEVEL 4	LEVEL 5	LEVEL 6
Analyzes a variety of student achievement/learning results, as well as other data including discipline referrals, grade retention, high school completion, and enrollment in advanced courses, to determine school improvement/ staff development goals. Ensures that data are disaggregated by race, gender, SES, and special needs.	Analyzes a variety of student learning results such as norm-referenced tests, student work samples, student portfolios, and district-design tests to determine school improvement/staff development goals. Ensures that data are disaggregated by race, gender, SES, and special needs.	Analyzes student achievement results (norm-referenced and criterion-referenced) to determine school improvement/staff development goals.	Refrains from analyzing any data to determine school improvement/staff development goals.		

74   National Staff Development Council   •   www.nsdc.org   •   *Moving NSDC's Staff Development Standards into Practice: Innovation Configurations*

TOOL 3.12

DATA-DRIVEN: THE PRINCIPAL

DESIRED OUTCOME 4.3: Engages teachers, parents, and community members in data-driven decisionmaking.

LEVEL I	LEVEL 2	LEVEL 3	LEVEL 4	LEVEL 5	LEVEL 6
Works with parents, community members, and the whole faculty to make decisions about the focus of schoolwide work.	Works with the whole faculty to make decisions about the focus of schoolwide work.	Works with a representative teacher group to make decisions about the focus of schoolwide work.	Consults with selected teachers and/or community members before making decisions about the focus of schoolwide work.	Works alone to make decisions about the focus of schoolwide improvement work.	

DESIRED OUTCOME 4.4: Analyzes relevant staff data to design teacher professional development.

LEVEL I	LEVEL 2	LEVEL 3	LEVEL 4	LEVEL 5	LEVEL 6
Collects and uses data from teacher concern surveys, classroom observations, walk-throughs, and informal conversations with the staff to influence the design of teacher professional development experiences.	Collects and uses data from classroom observations, walk-throughs, and informal conversations with the staff to influence the design of teacher professional development experiences.	Collects and uses data from informal conversations with staff to influence the design of teacher professional development experiences.	Does not collect or use data to influence the design of teacher professional development experiences.		

DESIRED OUTCOME 4.5: Collects, uses, and disseminates data that monitor the accomplishment of schoolwide goals.

LEVEL I	LEVEL 2	LEVEL 3	LEVEL 4	LEVEL 5	LEVEL 6
Collects and analyzes student and teacher data at least four times a year to monitor the accomplishment of schoolwide goals. Uses baseline data to monitor improvements within the school year. Celebrates improvements and accomplishments based on data. Reports results to parents and the community throughout the year, as well as results required by the state or district.	Collects and analyzes student and teacher data at the beginning and end of the school year to monitor the accomplishment of schoolwide goals. Reports results to parents and the community throughout the year, as well as results required by the state or district.	Collects and analyzes student and teacher data at the end of the year to monitor the accomplishment of schoolwide goals. Reports results as required by the state or district.	Does not collect or use student and teacher data to monitor the accomplishment of schoolwide goals.		

Moving NSDC's Staff Development Standards into Practice: Innovation Configurations • www.nsdc.org • National Staff Development Council

EVALUATION

The Principal

CONTENT

PROCESS

CONTEXT

DESIRED OUTCOME 5.1: Develops a comprehensive plan for conducting ongoing evaluation of staff development programs.

LEVEL 1	LEVEL 2	LEVEL 3	LEVEL 4	LEVEL 5	LEVEL 6
Develops a comprehensive plan for the evaluation of a staff development program that specifies the evaluation question(s), multiple data sources, data collection methodology, data analysis, interpretation, dissemination, and evaluation of the evaluation to assess the impact of the staff development program on student achievement.	Develops a comprehensive plan for the evaluation of a staff development program that specifies the evaluation question(s), multiple data sources, data collection methodology, data analysis processes, and data interpretation to assess the impact of staff development on student achievement.	Develops a plan for the evaluation of a staff development program that specifies the evaluation question(s), data sources, data collection methodology, and data analysis processes.	Develops a plan to evaluate participant reaction to staff development events.	Develops tools to evaluate staff development events.	

78   National Staff Development Council   •   www.nsdc.org   •   *Moving NSDC's Staff Development Standards into Practice: Innovation Configurations*

www.nsdc.org   Professional Learning for School LEADERS ■ 159

TOOL 3.12

EVALUATION: THE PRINCIPAL

DESIRED OUTCOME 5.2: Evaluates school-based staff development programs using a variety of data.

LEVEL 1	LEVEL 2	LEVEL 3	LEVEL 4	LEVEL 5	LEVEL 6
Arranges for the collection of student data (test scores, student surveys, and interviews) and classroom observations to determine changes in student learning and behaviors. Arranges for teacher surveys, interviews, and observations to identify changes in classroom practices. Assesses the extent to which school culture and organizational structures, policies, and processes have changed. Identifies the changes in teacher knowledge and skills that resulted from participation in staff development. Collects information on participant satisfaction for each professional development session.	Arranges for teacher surveys, interviews, and observations to identify changes in classroom practices. Assesses the extent to which school culture and organizational structures, policies, and processes have changed. Identifies the changes in teacher knowledge and skills that resulted from participation in staff development. Collects information on participant satisfaction for each professional development session.	Assesses the extent to which school culture and organizational structures, policies, and processes have changed. Identifies the changes in teacher knowledge and skills that resulted from participation in staff development. Collects information on participant satisfaction for each professional development session.	Identifies the changes in teacher knowledge and skills that resulted from participation in staff development. Collects information on participant satisfaction for each professional development session.		

DESIRED OUTCOME 5.3: Designs formative and summative evaluations of school-based professional development.

LEVEL 1	LEVEL 2	LEVEL 3	LEVEL 4	LEVEL 5	LEVEL 6
Conducts both formative and summative evaluations of professional development. Uses results to improve the quality of the program as well as to identify the impact on teacher practices and student learning.	Develops a summative evaluation at the end of the three-to-five-year professional development program to identify the impact on teacher practices and student learning.	Develops an ongoing formative evaluation of professional development. Uses results to improve the quality of the program.	Establishes baseline information about professional development and student learning that is used to compare beginning-of-year results to end-of-year results.	Collects end-of-year data about professional development (i.e., the number of hours, sessions, and teachers involved).	Does not collect evaluative information concerning staff development.

Moving NSDC's Staff Development Standards into Practice: Innovation Configurations • www.nsdc.org • National Staff Development Council

79

RESEARCH-BASED

The Principal

CONTENT
PROCESS
CONTEXT

DESIRED OUTCOME 6.1: Reads and interprets educational research.

LEVEL 1	LEVEL 2	LEVEL 3	LEVEL 4	LEVEL 5	LEVEL 6
Demonstrates advanced skills in determining appropriate research design, interpreting research results, and determining whether results can be generalized.	Demonstrates modest skills in reading and interpreting educational research (validity and reliability, matching populations, and interpreting effect-size measures).	Demonstrates little skill in reading and interpreting educational research.	Does not recognize the need to read and interpret educational research.		

DESIRED OUTCOME 6.2: Develops staff and community capacity to analyze research that supports schoolwide instructional decisions.

LEVEL 1	LEVEL 2	LEVEL 3	LEVEL 4	LEVEL 5	LEVEL 6
Ensures that teachers and community members learn to use educational research.	Creates opportunities for teacher committees to learn to use educational research.	Creates opportunities for facilitators of learning teams to learn to use educational research.	Creates opportunities for a few, select teachers to learn to use educational research.	Does not create opportunities for staff or community to learn to use educational research.	

82   National Staff Development Council   •   www.nsdc.org   •   Moving NSDC's Staff Development Standards into Practice: Innovation Configurations

RESEARCH-BASED: THE PRINCIPAL

DESIRED OUTCOME 6.3: Uses educational research when adopting staff development/school improvement approaches.

LEVEL 1	LEVEL 2	LEVEL 3	LEVEL 4	LEVEL 5	LEVEL 6
Works with teachers to conduct an extensive review of all pertinent research studies to ensure a good match with populations and outcomes before adopting staff development/school improvement approaches.	Works with teachers to conduct an extensive review of all pertinent research studies—both positive and negative—when adopting staff development/school improvement approaches.	Uses research studies when adopting staff development/school improvement approaches. Understands what constitutes reliable and valid research. Knows how to interpret results.	Uses professional journals that summarize research (not actual research studies) when adopting staff development/school improvement approaches.	Does not use educational research when adopting staff development/school improvement goals.	

DESIRED OUTCOME 6.4: Involves faculty and the community in analyzing research to make informed instructional decisions.

LEVEL 1	LEVEL 2	LEVEL 3	LEVEL 4	LEVEL 5	LEVEL 6
Works with parents, community members, and the entire faculty to analyze research when making schoolwide instructional decisions.	Works with whole faculty to analyze research when making schoolwide instructional decisions.	Works with the school improvement team and elected teacher representatives to analyze research when making schoolwide instructional decisions.	Works with the school improvement team to analyze research when making schoolwide instructional decisions.	Works alone to analyze research when making schoolwide instructional decisions	

83

Moving NSDC's Staff Development Standards into Practice: Innovation Configurations • www.nsdc.org • National Staff Development Council

162 ■ Professional Learning for School LEADERS

National Staff Development Council

DESIGN

The Principal

CONTENT

PROCESS

CONTEXT

DESIRED OUTCOME 7.1: Ensures that staff development designs align with expected outcomes.

LEVEL 1	LEVEL 2	LEVEL 3	LEVEL 4	LEVEL 5	LEVEL 6
Advocates for collaborative interaction as a major component of professional development. Provides training in a variety of collaborative activities that are aligned with expected outcomes (e.g., collaborative lesson design, professional networks, analyzing student work, problem solving sessions, curriculum development, etc.). Aligns a variety of staff development designs with expected adult learning outcomes.	Provides a variety of staff development designs aligned with expected adult learning outcomes (e.g., use of study groups to create new knowledge, learning teams for planning lessons, networks for problem solving and reflection).	Provides workshops to inform participants about new program and classroom coaching to assist with implementation of new strategies and activities.	Provides a single model or inappropriate models of professional development not aligned with expected adult learning outcomes.		

86   National Staff Development Council   •   www.nsdc.org   •   *Moving NSDC's Staff Development Standards into Practice: Innovation Configurations*

www.nsdc.org   Professional Learning for School LEADERS ■ 163

TOOL 3.12

DESIGN: THE PRINCIPAL

DESIRED OUTCOME 7.2: Provides long-term, in-depth, sustained staff development efforts.

LEVEL 1	LEVEL 2	LEVEL 3	LEVEL 4	LEVEL 5	LEVEL 6
Ensures that staff development provides extensive support over a two-to-three-year period, including celebrations of effort and progress. Provides multiple classroom coaching experiences to assist with the implementation of new instructional practices, as well as multiple sessions on the same topic that are scheduled throughout the school year with expectations for implementation between sessions.	Provides multiple classroom coaching experiences to assist with the implementation of new instructional practices, as well as multiple sessions on the same topic that are scheduled throughout the school year with expectations for implementation between sessions.	Provides staff development as multiple sessions on the same topic scheduled throughout the school year, with expectations for implementation between sessions. Expects participants to practice new instructional strategies during the sessions and receive feedback.	Provides staff development as single, stand-alone events.		

DESIRED OUTCOME 7.3: Establishes expectations for implementation of new classroom practices.

LEVEL 1	LEVEL 2	LEVEL 3	LEVEL 4	LEVEL 5	LEVEL 6
Works with staff to create rubrics that clearly describe expected classroom practices. Communicates how those practices connect to ongoing school improvement programs and communicates expectations for implementation of new classroom practices.	Provides a rubric that clearly describes expected classroom practices. Communicates how those practices connect to ongoing school improvement programs and communicates expectations for implementation of new classroom practices.	Communicates broad expectations for implementation of new classroom practices and how those practices connect to ongoing school improvement programs (e.g., to increase student achievement in mathematics).	Articulates the learning goal of each staff development event but does not discuss expectations for implementation.	Does not articulate the rationale or establish expectations for implementation of new classroom practices.	

DESIRED OUTCOME 7.4: Promotes technology as a staff development tool.

LEVEL 1	LEVEL 2	LEVEL 3	LEVEL 4	LEVEL 5	LEVEL 6
Structures collegial exchange among teachers that is facilitated through technology (e.g., online subject area networks, courses, action research studies, problem solving, or lesson sharing among teachers.)	Provides CD-ROMs, e-mail, the Internet, and distance learning to support professional learning.	Provides electronic resources to support independent research.	Uses technology as a management tool only.		

87

Moving NSDC's Staff Development Standards into Practice: Innovation Configurations • www.nsdc.org • National Staff Development Council

164 ■ Professional Learning for School LEADERS

National Staff Development Council

LEARNING

The Principal

CONTENT
PROCESS
CONTEXT

DESIRED OUTCOME 8.1: Applies knowledge about the change process when planning and implementing school-based professional learning.

LEVEL 1	LEVEL 2	LEVEL 3	LEVEL 4	LEVEL 5	LEVEL 6
Builds capacity of school-based staff to apply information about individual and organizational change processes. Coaches internal facilitators to support individuals as they move through changes in school and classroom practices.	Plans school-based staff development using research concerning organization change processes (i.e., Three I's, RPTIM). Plans school-based staff development using research about how individuals experience the change process.	Plans school-based staff development using research about how individuals experience the change process (i.e., CBAM: SoC-LoU).	Does not apply research concerning the individual and organizational change process. Uses past experience as the primary source of information for planning.		

DESIRED OUTCOME 8.2: Ensures that school-based staff development develops teachers' deep understanding.

LEVEL 1	LEVEL 2	LEVEL 3	LEVEL 4	LEVEL 5	LEVEL 6
Provides experiences that deepen understanding and meaning of new concepts/strategies and enable educators to problem solve and adapt new strategies to match classroom and student circumstances. Provides programs to address content knowledge and underlying concepts as well as the use of new curriculum materials, assessment practices, and instructional practices.	Provides experiences that address content knowledge and underlying concepts that teachers need to enable students to achieve high standards. Provides programs to address the use of new curriculum materials, assessment practices, and instructional practices.	Provides experiences that address the use of new curriculum materials, assessment practices, and new instructional programs. Provides sessions that focus on procedural learning—"how to do it"—rather than on developing underlying concepts and understandings.	Provides sessions that address regulations, procedures, and policies.		

90   National Staff Development Council   •   www.nsdc.org   •   *Moving NSDC's Staff Development Standards into Practice: Innovation Configurations*

www.nsdc.org   Professional Learning for School LEADERS ■ 165

TOOL 3.12

LEARNING: THE PRINCIPAL

DESIRED OUTCOME 8.3: Provides professional development experiences appropriate to career stages.

LEVEL 1	LEVEL 2	LEVEL 3	LEVEL 4	LEVEL 5	LEVEL 6
Provides differentiated professional development experiences that reflect various career stage needs and interests, including mentoring, leading learning teams, utilizing technology, coaching, and curriculum writing. Provides specialized staff development for new teachers and mentor teachers.	Provides some staff development experiences for teacher leaders and teacher trainers. Provides some specialized staff development for new teachers and mentor teachers.	Provides some specialized staff development for new and mentor teachers.	Provides the same learning activities for all staff development participants.		

DESIRED OUTCOME 8.4: Considers staff feelings and concerns when designing staff development experiences.

LEVEL 1	LEVEL 2	LEVEL 3	LEVEL 4	LEVEL 5	LEVEL 6
Solicits staff feelings and concerns, and designs staff development to address and alleviate those concerns.	Solicits staff feelings and concerns, and directs staff members to resources that will resolve those concerns.	Solicits staff feelings and concerns but does not systematically use these data when planning staff development.	Does not solicit staff feelings and concerns when designing staff development.		

Moving NSDC's Staff Development Standards into Practice: Innovation Configurations • www.nsdc.org • National Staff Development Council

CONTENT

PROCESS

CONTEXT

COLLABORATION

The Principal

DESIRED OUTCOME 9.1: Builds a school culture that is characterized by trust.

LEVEL 1	LEVEL 2	LEVEL 3	LEVEL 4	LEVEL 5	LEVEL 6
Makes decisions putting the interests of students above personal and political interests. Keeps his or her word. Believes in teacher ability and willingness to fulfill their responsibilities effectively. Addresses incompetence fairly and firmly. Communicates a strong vision for the school and clearly defines expectations that are upheld for all faculty members. Talks and listens to staff members with respect and courtesy. Encourages staff to disagree effectively without retribution. Takes an interest in the personal and professional well-being of faculty members.	Believes in teacher ability and willingness to fulfill their responsibilities effectively. Addresses incompetence fairly and firmly. Communicates a strong vision for the school and clearly defines expectations that are upheld for all faculty members. Talks and listens to staff members with respect and courtesy. Encourages staff to disagree effectively without retribution. Takes an interest in the personal and professional well-being of faculty members.	Communicates a strong vision for the school and clearly defines expectations that are upheld for all faculty members. Talks and listens to staff members with respect and courtesy. Encourages staff to disagree effectively without retribution. Takes an interest in the personal and professional well-being of faculty members.	Talks and listens to staff members with respect and courtesy. Encourages staff to disagree effectively without retribution. Takes an interest in the personal and professional well-being of faculty members.	Takes an interest in the personal and professional well-being of faculty members.	Does not address issues related to building trust within the school.

94   National Staff Development Council • www.nsdc.org • *Moving NSDC's Staff Development Standards into Practice: Innovation Configurations*

www.nsdc.org   Professional Learning for School LEADERS ■   167

TOOL 3.12

COLLABORATION: THE PRINCIPAL

DESIRED OUTCOME 9.2: Builds a school culture that is characterized by collective responsibility for student learning.

LEVEL 1	LEVEL 2	LEVEL 3	LEVEL 4	LEVEL 5	LEVEL 6
Creates expectations and supports all teachers being responsible for whole school academic learning.	Creates expectations and supports grade level or content area teams to be responsible for all their students' academic learning.	Expects teachers to assume responsibility for their own students' academic learning.	Does not address collective responsibility for student learning.		

DESIRED OUTCOME 9.3: Assists teachers in learning how to work successfully with colleagues.

LEVEL 1	LEVEL 2	LEVEL 3	LEVEL 4	LEVEL 5	LEVEL 6
Assists teachers to apply trust building and group decision-making skills, cooperative group structures, effective conflict resolution skills; and group development to the classroom and school improvement work.	Helps teachers gain and use knowledge and skills related to monitoring and adjusting group interaction to improve effectiveness, group decision-making, group structures, group development, and effective interaction skills.	Offers experiences for teachers to gain and use knowledge and skills related to group decision-making, group structures, group development, and effective interaction skills.	Offers opportunities for teachers to gain knowledge of the stages of group development and effective interaction skills.	Does not offer opportunities to learn how to work successfully with colleagues.	

DESIRED OUTCOME 9.4: Models the use of effective collaboration skills when working with faculty.

LEVEL 1	LEVEL 2	LEVEL 3	LEVEL 4	LEVEL 5	LEVEL 6
Participates in decision-making committees as "another member of the group," and encourages others to take leadership roles during meetings.	Asks a skillful teacher to act as facilitator for the group to ensure that the group makes collective decisions rather than merely "rubber stamping" ideas. Alters group process based on the stages of group development. Provides an external expert to facilitate difficult decisions.	Alters group process based on the stages of group development. Provides an external expert to facilitate difficult decisions.	Forms committees but still views role as "selling" ideas to the committee.	Does not use effective collaboration skills.	

Moving NSDC's Staff Development Standards into Practice: Innovation Configurations • www.nsdc.org • National Staff Development Council

95

COLLABORATION: THE PRINCIPAL

DESIRED OUTCOME 9.5: Assists team members in learning effective conflict management skills.

LEVEL I	LEVEL 2	LEVEL 3	LEVEL 4	LEVEL 5	LEVEL 6
Encourages the use of conflict resolution skills within the learning team and in grade level and whole school meetings. Provides coaching, observation, and feedback sessions to reinforce the use of new skills. Provides learning opportunities that use simulations, case studies, and role-playing. Offers opportunities to gain and use knowledge and skills related to personal conflict management strategies and effective conflict resolution behaviors and skills.	Provides coaching, observation, and feedback sessions to reinforce the use of new skills. Provides learning opportunities that use simulations, case studies, and role-playing. Offers opportunities to gain and use knowledge and skills related to personal conflict management strategies and effective conflict resolution behaviors and skills.	Offers opportunities to gain and use knowledge and skills related to personal conflict management strategies and effective conflict resolution behaviors and skills.	Provides opportunities to gain knowledge about personal conflict management strategies.	Does not provide any learning opportunities related to conflict management.	

DESIRED OUTCOME 9.6: Uses effective conflict management skills with staff and colleagues.

LEVEL I	LEVEL 2	LEVEL 3	LEVEL 4	LEVEL 5	LEVEL 6
Serves as a role model for the school in how to address conflicts productively. Uses conflict management skills effectively with other district administrative staff.	Demonstrates mastery of conflict management skills and can discuss conflicts with any member of the faculty or staff.	Practices effective conflict management with faculty with whom trust has been established.	Practices conflict resolution on a limited basis with staff and colleagues.	Does not use effective conflict management skills and is unaware of or frightened by conflicts within the organization.	

96   National Staff Development Council • www.nsdc.org • *Moving NSDC's Staff Development Standards into Practice: Innovation Configurations*

www.nsdc.org   Professional Learning for School LEADERS ■ 169

TOOL 3.12

COLLABORATION: THE PRINCIPAL

DESIRED OUTCOME 9.7: Encourages and provides technology to support collegial interactions.

LEVEL 1	LEVEL 2	LEVEL 3	LEVEL 4	LEVEL 5	LEVEL 6
Seeks resources to provide technology and encourages staff to participate in subject area networks, action research studies, and share lessons with their colleagues. Encourages staff to participate in and distributes information about available online discussion forums, web sites, and e-mail that support collegial interaction. Supports and provides e-mail and access to chat rooms to support collegial interaction.	Encourages staff to participate in and distributes information about available online discussion forums, web sites, and e-mail that support collegial interaction. Supports and provides e-mail and access to chat rooms to support collegial interaction.	Supports and provides e-mail and access to chat rooms to support collegial interaction.	Does not encourage or provide technology for collegial interaction among teachers.		

Moving NSDC's Staff Development Standards into Practice: Innovation Configurations • www.nsdc.org • National Staff Development Council

EQUITY

CONTENT

PROCESS

CONTEXT

The Principal

DESIRED OUTCOME 10.1: Communicates high expectations for self and for all teachers and students.

LEVEL 1	LEVEL 2	LEVEL 3	LEVEL 4	LEVEL 5	LEVEL 6
Accepts no excuses for the lack of achievement by subgroups of students. Changes school schedules, curriculum, and use of staff time to support learning of struggling students. Expects teachers to change classroom practices to support the learning of struggling students. Encourages respectful dialogue among faculty regarding their role in helping all students learn. Emphasizes developing student effort, persistence, and resiliency. Challenges educators' underlying assumptions concerning the role of parents, SES, race, and background in student learning. Provides an ongoing system of staff development to enhance teacher skills and knowledge about teaching struggling students.	Encourages respectful dialogue among faculty regarding their role in helping all students learn. Emphasizes developing student effort, persistence, and resiliency. Challenges educators' underlying assumptions concerning the role of parents, SES, race, and background in student learning. Provides an ongoing system of staff development to enhance teacher skills and knowledge about teaching struggling students.	Challenges educators' underlying assumptions concerning the role of parents, SES, race, and background in student learning. Provides an ongoing system of staff development to enhance teacher skills and knowledge about teaching struggling students.	Provides an ongoing system of staff development to enhance teacher skills and knowledge about teaching struggling students.	Asserts publicly that "all children can learn" but makes no substantive changes in schedule, curriculum, or use of staff to support learning for students who are struggling.	Believes all children are not capable of learning at high levels.

100   National Staff Development Council   •   www.nsdc.org   •   *Moving NSDC's Staff Development Standards into Practice Innovation Configurations*

www.nsdc.org

Professional Learning for School LEADERS ■ 171

TOOL 3.12

EQUITY: THE PRINCIPAL

DESIRED OUTCOME 10.2: Works with staff to understand the impact of attitudes on instruction and to modify classroom practices.

LEVEL 1	LEVEL 2	LEVEL 3	LEVEL 4	LEVEL 5	LEVEL 6
Schedules classroom coaching and follow-up discussions to ensure behaviors that communicate high expectations become part of daily practice. Supports development of new skills and attitudes related to holding high expectations for all students. Arranges for observation of classroom practices regarding how expectations are communicated to students. Provides learning opportunities to identify how educator attitudes, background, culture, and social class impact the teaching and learning process.	Supports development of new skills and attitudes related to holding high expectations for all students. Arranges for observation of classroom practices regarding how expectations are communicated to students. Provides learning opportunities to identify how educator attitudes, background, culture, and social class impact the teaching and learning process.	Arranges for observation of classroom practices regarding how expectations are communicated to students. Provides learning opportunities to identify how educator attitudes, background, culture, and social class impact the teaching and learning process.	Provides learning opportunities to identify how educator attitudes, background, culture, and social class impact the teaching and learning process.	Does not consider how educator attitude, background, culture, and social class impacts the teaching and learning process.	

Moving NSDC's Staff Development Standards into Practice: Innovation Configurations • www.nsdc.org • National Staff Development Council

101

EQUITY: THE PRINCIPAL

DESIRED OUTCOME 10.3: Establishes a school environment that is emotionally and physically safe for teachers and students.

LEVEL 1	LEVEL 2	LEVEL 3	LEVEL 4	LEVEL 5	LEVEL 6
Develops student and faculty responsibility for reinforcing positive behaviors within the school. Supports schoolwide themes of respect, caring, and safety, and ensures those themes are taught, reinforced, celebrated, and publicized in the classroom and in the school. Confronts both students and teachers who violate norms of respect, caring and safety.	Empowers teachers to teach and reinforce school rules that promote emotional and physical safety. Confronts both students and teachers who violate norms of respect, caring, and safety.	Establishes a school environment that meets district expectations for ensuring student safety and focuses on maintaining order.	Establishes a school environment that focuses on maintaining order.		

DESIRED OUTCOME 10.4: Demonstrates respect and appreciation for students and families and for their cultural backgrounds.

LEVEL 1	LEVEL 2	LEVEL 3	LEVEL 4	LEVEL 5	LEVEL 6
Involves families and community in creating schoolwide activities related to the contribution and traditions of their cultures. Assists teachers in developing schoolwide investigations, curriculum units, and other activities that recognize the contributions of various cultures.	Participates with teachers to develop schoolwide investigations, curriculum units, and other activities that recognize the contributions of various cultures.	States publicly an appreciation for different cultural backgrounds of students and staff. Supports the celebration of holidays related to cultural backgrounds of students.	Demonstrates no understanding or appreciation for the cultural backgrounds of students and staff.		

102   National Staff Development Council   •   www.nsdc.org   •   *Moving NSDC's Staff Development Standards into Practice: Innovation Configurations*

TOOL 3.12

QUALITY TEACHING

The Principal

CONTENT

PROCESS

CONTEXT

DESIRED OUTCOME 11.1: Promotes educators' deep understanding of content knowledge and the use of research-based instructional strategies as a high priority in the school.

LEVEL 1	LEVEL 2	LEVEL 3	LEVEL 4	LEVEL 5	LEVEL 6
Persists with the goal of deep content knowledge and use of research-based instructional strategies when challenged either internally or externally to alter that goal. Promotes the development of content knowledge and use of research-based instructional strategies through the allocation of resources, formal evaluations, and public recognition of teacher efforts. Models the use and importance of deep understanding of content knowledge and research-based instructional strategies at staff meetings, committee meetings, and schoolwide events. Emphasizes content knowledge and research-based instructional strategies in classroom observations and conversations with faculty. Provides the time needed to develop the use of deep understanding of content knowledge and use of research-based instructional strategies. Encourages staff to participate in ongoing, intensive district-based professional learning experiences that build content knowledge and use of research-based instructional strategies.	Promotes the development of content knowledge and use of research-based instructional strategies through the allocation of resources, formal evaluations, and public recognition of teacher efforts. Models the use and importance of deep understanding of content knowledge and use of research-based instructional strategies at staff meetings, committee meetings, and schoolwide events. Emphasizes content knowledge and research-based instructional strategies in classroom observations and conversations with faculty. Provides the time needed to develop the use of deep understanding of content knowledge and research-based instructional strategies. Encourages staff to participate in ongoing, intensive district-based professional learning experiences that build content knowledge and use of research-based instructional strategies.	Models the use and importance of deep understanding of content knowledge and use of research-based instructional strategies at staff meetings, committee meetings, and schoolwide events. Emphasizes content knowledge and research-based instructional strategies in classroom observations and conversations with faculty. Provides the time needed to develop the use of deep understanding of content knowledge and use of research-based instructional strategies. Encourages staff to participate in ongoing, intensive district-based professional learning experiences that build content knowledge and use of research-based instructional strategies.	Follows up with staff members who participate in deepening content knowledge and using research-based instructional strategies. Encourages staff to participate in ongoing, intensive district-based professional learning experiences that build content knowledge and use of research-based instructional strategies.	Encourages staff to participate in ongoing, intensive district-based professional learning experiences that build content knowledge and use of research-based instructional strategies.	Hires best qualified teacher for each position and assumes they will develop any necessary skills and knowledge to teach the subject area.

QUALITY TEACHING: THE PRINCIPAL

DESIRED OUTCOME 11.2: : Promotes the use of a variety of classroom assessments as a high priority in the school.

LEVEL 1	LEVEL 2	LEVEL 3	LEVEL 4	LEVEL 5	LEVEL 6
Persists with the goal of the use of a variety of classroom assessments when challenged, either internally or externally, to alter that goal. Promotes the use of classroom assessment strategies through allocation of resources to support implementation, formal evaluations, public recognition, formal recognition for implementation efforts, and supporting initial practice of new strategies. Models the use and stresses the importance of a variety of classroom assessment strategies at staff meetings, committee meetings, and schoolwide events. Emphasizes the importance of using a variety of classroom assessment strategies during classroom observations and conversations with faculty. Provides time to develop a variety of classroom assessment strategies. Provides an ongoing, differentiated staff development program focused on the development and application of a variety of classroom assessment strategies.	Promotes the use of classroom assessment strategies through allocation of resources to support implementation, formal evaluations, public recognition for implementation efforts, and supporting initial practice of new strategies. Models the use and stresses the importance of a variety of classroom assessment strategies at staff meetings, committee meetings, and schoolwide events. Emphasizes the importance of using a variety of classroom assessment strategies during classroom observations and conversations with faculty. Provides time to develop a variety of classroom assessment strategies. Provides an ongoing, differentiated staff development program focused on the development and application of a variety of classroom assessment strategies.	Models the use and stresses the importance of a variety of classroom assessment strategies at staff meetings, committee meetings, and schoolwide events. Emphasizes the importance of using a variety of classroom assessment strategies during classroom observations and conversations with faculty. Provides time to develop a variety of classroom assessment strategies. Provides an ongoing, differentiated staff development program focused on the development and application of a variety of classroom assessment strategies.	Provides ongoing staff development focused on the use of a variety of classroom assessment strategies. Provides time to develop a variety of classroom assessment strategies.	Explains at staff meetings, committee meetings, and schoolwide events the importance of the use of a variety of classroom assessment strategies.	

Moving NSDC's Staff Development Standards into Practice: Innovation Configurations ● www.nsdc.org ● National Staff Development Council

QUALITY TEACHING: THE PRINCIPAL

DESIRED OUTCOME 11.3: Creates work schedules that support professional learning and collaboration about quality teaching.

LEVEL 1	LEVEL 2	LEVEL 3	LEVEL 4	LEVEL 5	LEVEL 6
Maintains the schedule despite challenges from faculty, staff, and community. Alters weekly schedule to allow for regular collegial meetings of the entire professional staff during the school day. Monitors this time to ensure it is used productively.	Alters weekly schedule to allow for regular collegial meetings of the entire professional staff during the school day. Monitors this time to ensure it is used productively.	Uses staff meetings for collegial interaction and sharing. Creates grade level and content area groups that meet throughout the year to learn together.	Maintains working conditions that result in teacher isolation and individual practice. Views collegial interactions as unimportant to the school.		

DESIRED OUTCOME 11.4: Promotes a culture of innovation that continuously improves teaching.

LEVEL 1	LEVEL 2	LEVEL 3	LEVEL 4	LEVEL 5	LEVEL 6
Creates an environment of trust, risk-taking, and support in which staff members who implement innovative strategies are encouraged, protected, and supported to learn from implementation mistakes.	Creates an environment of risk-taking and trust in which staff members who implement innovative strategies are encouraged, protected, and provided additional support.	Creates an environment of risk-taking and trust in which staff members who experiment with innovative strategies are protected.	Creates an environment of trust in which both successes and failures are shared, and expressions of opinions and feelings are welcomed.	Creates an environment that is open to new ideas and practices that can improve teaching and learning. Allows anyone within the school community to offer new ideas and practices.	Maintains an environment that is satisfied with current practices and procedures. Does not express a need for new practices and procedures.

CONTENT

PROCESS

CONTEXT

FAMILY INVOLVEMENT

The Principal

DESIRED OUTCOME 12.1: Develops partnerships among teachers, families, and community stakeholders.

LEVEL I	LEVEL 2	LEVEL 3	LEVEL 4	LEVEL 5	LEVEL 6
Offers after-school programs for students with support from community businesses, agencies, or volunteers. Organizes the faculty to create community service programs conducted by students. Works with local businesses, industries, and community organizations to develop programs that enhance student skills and talents. Disseminates information about community activities that link to student learning skills and talents. Develops an ongoing school committee that focuses on family and community partnerships.	Works with the school–community partnership committee and local businesses, industries, and community organizations to develop programs that enhance student skills and talents. Disseminates information about community activities that link to student learning skills and talents. Develops an ongoing school committee that focuses on family and community partnerships.	Disseminates information about community activities that link to student learning skills and talents. Develops an ongoing school committee that focuses on family and community partnerships.	Develops an ongoing school committee that focuses on family and community partnerships.	Does not develop any activities in collaboration with parents or other community stakeholders.	

108   National Staff Development Council   •   www.nsdc.org   •   *Moving NSDC's Staff Development Standards into Practice: Innovation Configurations*

www.nsdc.org   Professional Learning for School LEADERS ■ 177

FAMILY INVOLVEMENT: THE PRINCIPAL

DESIRED OUTCOME 12.2: Implements strategies to increase family involvement.

LEVEL 1	LEVEL 2	LEVEL 3	LEVEL 4	LEVEL 5	LEVEL 6
Sponsors parent education workshops on child development and home conditions that support learning. Educates families about strategies that support student learning at home. Communicates with families about school programs and student progress such as information about report cards, grading practices, school events, student work, and homework.	Educates families about strategies that support student learning at home. Communicates with families about school programs and student progress such as information about report cards, grading practices, school events, student work, and homework.	Communicates with families about school programs and student progress such as information about report cards, grading practices, school events, student work, and homework.	Encourages families to attend school functions, yearly conferences, and school performances.		

DESIRED OUTCOME 12.3: Uses technology to increase family involvement.

LEVEL 1	LEVEL 2	LEVEL 3	LEVEL 4	LEVEL 5	LEVEL 6
Provides an interactive web site where families and educators can discuss instructional issues. Uses e-mail or voice mail to communicate with families. Develops a homework hotline. Ensures all teachers have easy access to telephones in order to communicate with parents during and after school. Works with external organizations to provide families with access to computers and the Internet to support family involvement.	Provides a web site where families can view school news, special notices, tips on parenting, and reading lists. Uses e-mail or voice mail to communicate with families. Develops a homework hotline. Ensures all teachers have easy access to telephones in order to communicate with parents during and after school. Works with external organizations to provide families with access to computers and the Internet to support family involvement.	Uses e-mail or voice mail to communicate with families. Develops a homework hotline. Ensures all teachers have easy access to telephones in order to communicate with parents during and after school. Works with external organizations to provide families with access to computers and the Internet to support family involvement.	Ensures all teachers have easy access to telephones in order to communicate with parents during and after school. Works with external organizations to provide families with access to computers and the Internet to support family involvement.	Does not use technology to communicate with families.	

Moving NSDC's Staff Development Standards into Practice: Innovation Configurations • www.nsdc.org • National Staff Development Council

109

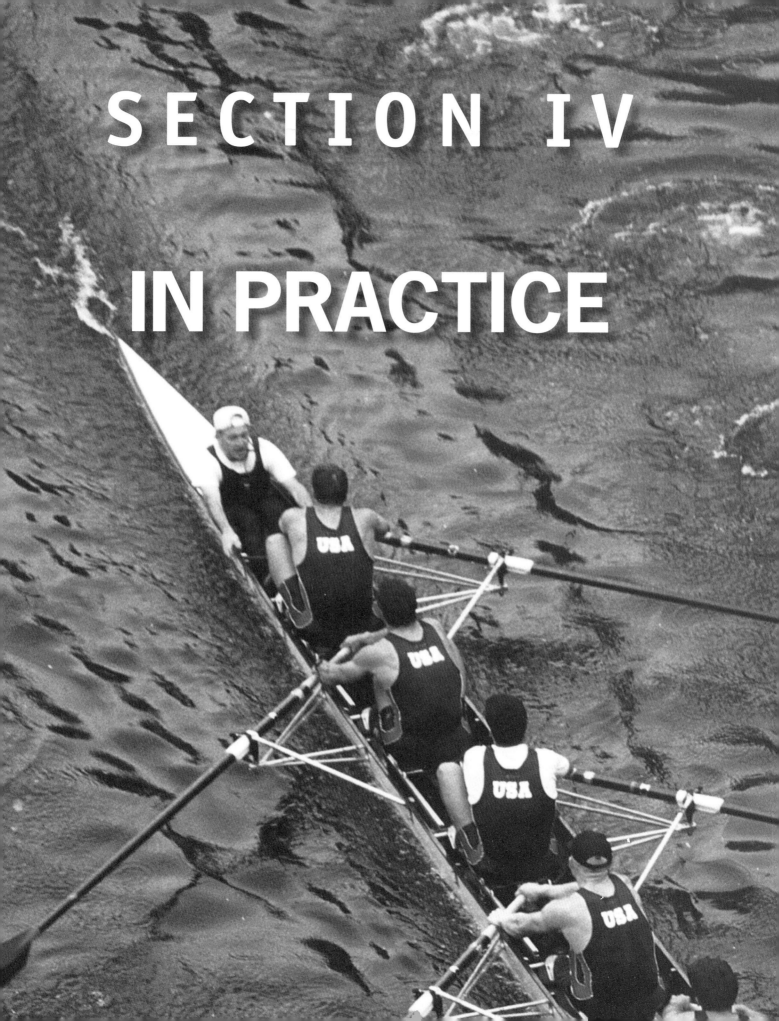

SECTION IV

IN PRACTICE

Focus principal development on student learning

By Joan Richardson

Being a principal is one of education's most challenging and important jobs. Virtually everyone agrees an effective principal is essential for a successful school. But the expectations for principals have changed dramatically during the careers of most of those in service today. And, as the demands have changed, the number of educators interested in taking those jobs has declined.

Faced with that conundrum, the need for quality professional development for principals has become more crucial than ever. But, what, exactly, does good professional development for principals look like?

"Unfortunately, principal development, which has traditionally been given an even lower priority by school systems than teacher development, too often turns participants into passive recipients of information rather than active participants in solving important educational problems," NSDC Executive Director Dennis Sparks wrote in the April 2000 *Results*.

Sparks suggested there are four crucial components of quality learning programs for principals: standards-focused, intellectually rigorous, job-embedded, and sustained.

Roland Barth, creator of the respected Harvard Principals Center and a frequent writer and presenter about principal professional development, agrees. "My strong bias is that the best professional development for principals occurs at the school. It comes in the interactions with teachers, where teachers and principals work together to develop curriculum, to design an evaluation system, to tackle a problem, and learn together," he said.

LEADING BY EXAMPLE

Jefferson County Public Schools in Louisville, Kentucky, has provided that sort of exemplary learning program for its middle school principals.

"Until several years ago, professional development for principals was really done by the shotgun approach. It wasn't necessarily connected to specific student outcomes. Now, it's very much job-embedded, it's ongoing, and it's sustained," said Sandy Ledford, assistant superintendent for districtwide instructional services in JCPS.

Louisville's principal professional development program has four components:

- A more-or-less traditional institute learning arrangement that includes principals and teachers;
- Regular staff development days for principals that focus on a single area of instruction;
- A cohort strand in which principals learn with other principals who share a common interest; and
- Individual professional development plans and a peer evaluation program.

STANDARDS-BASED IMPROVEMENT

Each summer, JCPS middle school principals and the teacher leadership teams from their schools meet for a three-day institute focused on learning about the standards for a particular academic area and examining data for their school's performance. During the institute, the principal and teachers jointly develop a school improvement plan and a year-long professional development plan for their building.

"Five or six years ago, the norm was that principals might be at these meetings long enough to introduce someone from central office or maybe an outside consultant. Then, they would leave. Now, principals are not only participants, they are leaders. They are actively learning. When they leave, they are knowledgeable about what needs to be done in their buildings and how various resources are needed to support that," said Cheryl DeMarsh, director of middle school instructional support.

Ledford believes this influences principals' feeling about their own effectiveness. "It's clear that they feel they can make a difference in the student achievement in their schools. They are much more confident about their own knowledge and their own skills," she said.

FOCUSED LEARNING

The monthly meetings for JCPS middle school principals have also been transformed. "It used to be that we spent our time talking about the discipline code, talking about policies, going over this detail and that detail. We were not building capacity," said DeMarsh.

Principals meet for a full day once a month with the day divided into two learning pieces. Time spent on "administrivia" has been dramatically reduced.

During the morning, principals share a common learning period. For two years, the mornings have focused on writing in the middle grades. The district's writing specialist has spent 18 hours with principals, teaching them about writing standards and what classrooms should look like if students are writing to high standards. The principals have brought in student writing samples and spent time studying those samples and comparing them to state writing standards.

"The whole point of this is to help them develop their skills as instructional leaders in writing," said Ledford.

After two years of this work, Ledford was anxious to examine the results in the state's writing assessment. In 13 of the district's 24 middle schools, students improved their writing scores; in the other 11, scores either remained the same or declined.

"Even though we know what the inputs have been, we don't know how much has been implemented. So, our next step is to do some action research around writing. We will be looking at the writing scores to see if, in fact, any of the principals' learning has paid off," Ledford said.

COHORT GROUPS

The afternoon portion of the principals' monthly meeting is the component that Ledford and DeMarsh believe is most unique. The 24 middle school principals are divided into five groups according to their interests. One group focuses on integrating technology into instruction, another on developing leadership skills, and three groups on learning more about "knowledge work" in order to guide teachers' work in that area.

The cohorts were formed after principals responded to a self-assessment which they designed themselves. They based the self-assessment on what they believed were the 20 most important indicators for high-performing schools and used it to identify areas in which they needed to learn the most.

A coach guides the work of each cohort and stays with them over time. The coaches are former middle school principals or educators with some knowledge about the topic. The coaches also have their own professional development for this role.

DeMarsh's cohort on knowledge work initially read and discussed articles, spent time with a district specialist exploring the critical components of knowledge work, and doing assessment tasks. They later spent several months developing a survey for teachers to determine their focus for the current school year.

"The beauty of this is that they've grown to be real collegial. They're very open to hearing from each other. They're very open to talking to each other," Ledford said.

PRINCIPAL EVALUATION

A smaller component of the principals' professional development program is their tri-annual evaluation. By board policy, three principals and a central office administrator are included on every principal evaluation team. At the start of each school year, in consultation with the evaluation team, each principal creates an individual growth plan.

Each year, one of the three principals in the group has a summative evaluation. During mid-year, the three principals meet at that principal's school for at least 90 minutes to talk in detail about that principal's growth. Principals can provide artifacts, create a portfolio, lead a walk-through of their buildings — whatever they believe will demonstrate how they've met their goals.

Although the central office administrator signs off on the evaluation, each of the other principals must sign the evaluation.

ABOUT THE AUTHOR

Joan Richardson is director of publications for the National Staff Development Council.

When hearts meet minds
District's leadership team uses the power of synergy in work with principals

By Ellen H. Kahan, Tony Byrd, and Lara Drew

Ask almost any principal why he or she feels called to this vocation. Why select a leadership role with endless demands and a relentless pace? The principal will tell you that he or she took on this daunting task to make a positive impact on the lives and education of children, to be an instructional leader. This is a noble goal that is all too soon mired in the realities of school management. The job becomes one that may only be focused erratically on leading instruction.

This occurs despite inspirational stories about a few great leaders in schools who have elevated their leadership above the common experience. Research tells us what will lead to the creation of great instructional leaders. The challenge is to heed what the research says.

SETTING OUR FOCUS

The elementary leadership team of Edmonds School District #15 in Lynnwood, Wash., has been struggling with this challenge for several years. We have dismantled outdated practices to focus on instructional leadership and maintain our course despite efforts to pull us away. We believe our professional learning must maintain a sharp focus on three components:

1. Building a collaborative community of principal leaders;
2. Deepening content knowledge, particularly in literacy; and
3. Strengthening supervisory skills to improve classroom instruction.

Professional growth opportunities to meet the distinct needs of principals must be provided through different venues, including large groups, small study groups, and individual coaching support.

These emphases for professional learning seem obvious for a team of principals. Indeed, they are the specific goals cited in research about successful practices. But the road to implementing our program of professional learning has been challenging, primarily because it requires a shift in belief and practices, which creates anxiety. Many principals are highly successful building managers, meeting the wide range of demands they face each day. There was not universal acclaim in our group for this new emphasis on instructional leadership, but principals must become instructional leaders to improve what transpires every day between teacher and student. Creating strong instructional leaders who understand best teaching strategies and can supervise, coach, and motivate effective teaching is essential to reaching that goal.

CREATING A LEARNING COMMUNITY

Building a community of leaders is vital to improving instructional leadership. School districts and the community have inadvertently placed school leaders in competition with each other for better test scores, higher enrollment, or community accolades. All of that is contradictory to the environment required for collaborative professional growth in an organization.

Our elementary leadership team was a friendly group, but not a collaborative team. To become a team, we had to meet each other on a personal level, as individuals with our own hopes, frustrations, and experiences. Only then would we be a trusting community that would grow and learn together, recognizing each other's strengths and gifts and supporting each member.

To develop effective collaborative groups, we use small-group learning structures within our larger meeting time. This is most important when the focus is on a topic that some leaders may be successful with, while other leaders are still in the learning stages. In the past, individuals skilled in a particular area were invited to stand in front of the whole group and share what they know. This lecture-style presentation does not effectively support the learning needs of everyone in the group and can even create resentment. Our approach is to have small professional learning groups tackle difficult topics either in place of or following a large-group presentation. In small groups, people feel safe asking questions and seeking help from each other. While people may have different skill levels, no one person is set up as the "expert," and they are able to grow together.

Sometimes, small groups use protocols to structure the discussion. Our experience is that leaders struggle with protocols. Regardless of the established structure, leaders tend to want to jump in to solve a problem. Learning to ask open-ended questions to help a colleague examine a problem without offering a solution is a valuable skill for coaching colleagues or teachers, but it is also a slow skill to develop. Protocols also ensure that the discussion keeps moving forward rather than having individuals repeat the same response again and again.

Like a class meeting, our large weekly meetings often start with the entire group of more than 30 sitting in a large circle. This brings a sense of unity and team to the group. Taking from the writing of Parker Palmer, we incorporate time to reflect together. Inspired by poetry, storytelling, or powerful prose, our shared time to reflect brings us together as a team of trusting and committed individuals, rather than a group of people trapped together at a meeting.

Summer retreats provide extended periods of time to build our community. Over the last several years, they have evolved from half-day to whole day to three-day retreats as trust grows and group members share a deep desire to work closely with one another.

As collaboration and trust have risen among group members, our discussion about the challenging work we do has become more open and honest. True collaboration is becoming the norm.

DEEPENING CONTENT KNOWLEDGE

Deepening the content knowledge of a principal is critical to becoming an instructional leader. Principals must understand what students need to know and be able to do, and they need to be able to identify specific strategies teachers can use to enhance student learning. Principals, together with a teacher from their building and district staff, meet for content learning sessions and focused classroom demonstration lessons throughout the year. During these sessions, principals and teacher leaders reflect on their learning and think about how to share

JSD, Spring 2008 (Vol. 29, No. 2)

what they've learned with staff. Between sessions, district literacy coaches and the director of elementary education provide support to individual principals around planning professional learning and supporting individual teachers based on the new content learning and the school's improvement plan. The director of elementary education and principals go into classrooms to learn to identify what is being taught and to think about how to have conversations with their teachers about their practice. We believe that by deepening our principals' content knowledge, we enhance their ability to have meaningful and focused conversations with teachers about the most important aspect of teaching and learning — student learning and instruction.

STRENGTHENING LEADERSHIP

At the core of our elementary leadership structure of professional learning is our weekly meeting. At these meetings, we engage as a large group in professional learning, primarily on issues of leadership style. Ours is a district with collaboration and shared decision making as its core value, making the requirements for effective leadership especially challenging. Principals sometimes fear that facing tough issues with reluctant staff members will end in their being "voted off the island." To build a collaborative school team, principals must have exceptional people skills that engage, influence, and inspire. Professional learning must effectively address how principals can talk with teachers about instruction and coach them to improve their practice. In addition, principals must feel confident in creating school-based professional learning, growing teacher leadership, and leading staff discussions on instruction.

SMALL COLLABORATIVE GROUPS

Small-group work with principals is designed to enhance these leadership skills and is often part of our weekly meetings. For example, small cohorts recently

Edmonds School District #15
Lynnwood, Wash.
Schools: 36 (21 elementary, 3 K-8, 4 middle, 5 high, 3 special programs)
Enrollment: 20,098
Staff: 3,903
Racial ethnic mix:

White:	66%
Black:	6%
Hispanic:	10%
Asian/Pacific Islander:	14%
Native American:	1%
Other:	2%

Limited English proficient: 8%
Languages spoken: 77
Free/reduced lunch: 24%
Special education: 13%

spent three weeks examining case studies, with each principal focused on his or her work with one specific teacher. Principals presented case studies and consulted colleagues to glean strategies and practice skills that would more effectively support that teacher. We also practiced formal classroom observations as an avenue for coaching teachers. We observed a video of a teacher conducting a classroom lesson. Then, in small groups, we strategized questions and coaching techniques to use in a preobservation conference to help a teacher develop the strongest possible learning experience for students. Following that, we discussed the feedback that might be most successful in a post-observation conference.

Professional learning for principals must provide the opportunity to examine issues specific to the culture and context in which principals lead. This is most effectively done through small-group and individual collaborative dialogue. The Critical Friends Group (CFG) model is another successful process for small-group collaborative work that has been used by one team of principals as a tool for personal growth. This team of five principals and one district leader meet every two weeks to discuss two specific questions:

1. What does good instruction look like?
2. How do principals discuss that good instruction with teachers?

To answer these questions, this CFG reviewed videos of teaching, completed walk-throughs at each classroom in their buildings, observed teachers, discussed the definition of "good instruction," and used the book Change Leadership, by Wagner et al. (2006), as a knowledge backdrop and a reflective tool. These principals valued this time together, as evidenced by these comments:

"Our CFG has provided me the professional and personal support I need to be courageous in my leadership, take risks, and open the conversations with teachers that I may have avoided in the past. I also know I have close colleagues who will push my thinking and provide honest feedback."

— Steven Burleigh, principal of Westgate Elementary

"Learning takes time, and we need regular, sustained time together to think deeply and learn. That will be the only thing that will change our practice."

— Christi Kessler, principal of Sherwood Elementary

"Stepping into the role as learner of content and learner as self is not a comfortable thing to do. Working with our CFG gives me the courage to be uncomfortable with conviction."

— Hawkins Cramer, principal of Cedar Way Elementary

INDIVIDUAL SUPPORT

Personal influence and modeling expectations are powerful teaching tools. In keeping with that, the director of elementary education and the supervising assistant superintendent meet with each principal several times a year for a coaching session. Together, the group completes a walk-through, paying specific attention to implementation of best literacy practices. Principals are coached to maintain their focus on instructional leadership. The group develops and monitors a plan for the professional learning in each building, including the identification and growth of teacher leaders.

These conversations also clarify special materials or professional opportunities required by schools. District administrators can provide materials or expertise already available and draw from the same information to plan for unmet needs.

MEETING THE CHALLENGE

Professional learning for elementary leaders continues to evolve in our district. There are competing demands for our time as a leadership group, but we are insistent that we stay focused on instruction and leadership. We struggle with the principal's changing role. We are discovering that the power of our collaborative team keeps us focused and creates a synergy that engages our minds and hearts in the work. Together, we are becoming powerful instructional leaders, committed as a team to each other, to the development of our knowledge, and to exceptional instruction in all of our schools.

We can't say yet that our work as an elementary leadership team is having a direct impact on student achievement. What we do know is that our school leaders are increasingly able to have authentic discussions with teachers about grade-level learning expectations, subject content, and proven effective instructional techniques. Principals are developing skills to have difficult conversations with teachers about the quality of instruction. They are learning to ask teachers probing questions about their practice and to hold them to high performance expectations. Leaders are taking the professional learning community structures from our leadership team into their schools to create a culture of trust and adult learning. We know that a trusting climate, collaborative learning communities focused on student achievement, and a constant focus on improving instruction are characteristics of high-achieving schools.

REFERENCE

Wagner, T., Kegan, R., Lahey, L., Lemons, R.W., Garnier, J., Helsing, D., et al. (2006). *Change leadership: A practical guide to transforming our schools.* San Francisco: Jossey-Bass.

ABOUT THE AUTHORS

Ellen H. Kahan is an assistant superintendent, Tony Byrd is an assistant superintendent for teaching and learning, and Lara Drew is director of elementary education for Edmonds School District, Lynnwood, Wash.

10 rungs to proficiency
District partners with universities to create Principals' Academy

By Pete Hall and Rick Harris

In the Washoe County School District (WCSD), in Reno, Nev., school leaders climb a steep ladder from the moment they contemplate a career in administration. Fortunately, they are supported at each step in the process, thanks to the Principals' Academy. This approach helps principals fulfill their critical mission of providing a link between policy and student achievement, articulating vision and strengthening instructional delivery, working directly with students and teachers, and playing a key role in a district's administrative agenda. WCSD principals follow an articulated plan of career development that supports their growing expertise for the sake of improved student achievement.

The Principals' Academy is a 10-tier approach to recruiting, building, developing, and strengthening principal leadership. Following the tenets of the professional learning community concept (DuFour & Eaker, 1998) and driven by the active instructional leadership vehicle of the walk-through process (Werlinich, 2004), the 10-tier model professionalizes the principalship, from prenovice to distinguished expertise. The Principals' Academy is a collaborative effort of the WCSD, the University of Nevada, the University of Phoenix, the University of Pittsburgh, and WestEd.

Covering 6,600 square miles, WCSD is Nevada's second-largest school district. Since its inception in 2001, the Principals' Academy has provided leadership training, mentorship, coaching, and professional learning to practicing administrators and other professionals in many roles throughout the school system. Along that journey, every aspect of each tier holds to the guiding principles of the Principals' Academy.

THE 10-TIER APPROACH TO PRINCIPAL DEVELOPMENT

Tier 1: Diving into administration

The foundation of the 10-tier model is a recruiting tool designed to introduce school administration to the participants. Principals encourage their lead teachers, instructional coaches, and other staff with clear leadership strengths to participate in a series of workshops.

These five three-hour sessions provide the framework and background knowledge for certified personnel interested in entering administration. The first three sessions are designed around the eight dimensions of

GUIDING PRINCIPLES OF THE PRINCIPALS' ACADEMY

- All academy activities and events will be professional and high quality.
- All activities will have current principals involved in planning, instruction, and mentoring.
- For activities that include direct instruction, instructors:
  - Should be guides, not directors.
  - Use the Socratic method rather than merely teaching facts.
  - Will help principals see other perspectives and push their limits.
  - Will show respect for principals' opinions.
  - Will focus on activities that are intellectually stimulating.
  - Will include principal discussions and reflection in all activities.
  - Will exhibit passion and humor.

leadership outlined by the WCSD principals' evaluation system. The remaining two sessions reintroduce participants to the driving forces behind district leadership emphases: the walk-through process and professional learning communities. Current WCSD principals lead all of the sessions.

Tier 2: Apprenticeship

The Principals' Academy joins the University of Nevada, Reno, and the University of Phoenix (Nevada campus) to offer for-credit internships for new and aspiring administrators and doctoral candidates. This program gives the intern practical experience outside of his or her current school setting, offering new perspectives and information. Collaborating with established leadership teams and principals, the interns work directly with students, staff, parents, teachers, and other administrators on a variety of initiatives at the school and district level.

Tier 3: Leadership institute

Recognizing that many lead teachers and deans are almost ready for their first administrative position, the Leadership Institute provides relevant preservice training to aspiring administrators. Educators who hold or are close to achieving administrative certification can attend Institute sessions led by Principals' Academy instructors and faculty of the University of Pittsburgh or the University of Nevada, Reno. The sessions include such topics as budgeting, teacher evaluation, public relations, data-driven dialogue, and many others. In addition, these candidates are eligible for short-term administrative assignments as needed by the district, where they will receive mentoring support.

Tier 4: Deanship

An early step into the administrative realm is the post of dean of students. Like an assistant principal, but with a teacher's salary and no authority to evaluate staff, this position provides a range of administrative experiences. A dean cohort meets monthly to discuss challenges, share ideas, and support one another. Led by a building-level administrator teamed with a Principals' Academy leader, these meetings offer opportunities for problem-solving, networking, and continued administrative preparation. Participants receive recertification credit.

Tier 5: New administrator training

All new principals and assistant principals participate in the "First Years" training series. First- and second-year administrators are divided into cohorts that meet regularly with peers, network with experienced mentor principals, and engage in challenging problem-solving exercises. Mentors meet with smaller communities of new administrators to engage in team walk-throughs, cooperative job shadowing episodes, book studies, and other collaborative efforts to build relationships and leadership capacity in newer administrators.

Tier 6: Mentorship

Both active and retired principals and assistant principals provide a number of services to the district through the Principals' Academy as mentors. Some mentors coach first- and second-year administrators; others work one-on-one with aspiring administrative candidates. A select group of mentors assists specific schools with their school improvement processes and helps identify strengths and areas of need, while other mentors serve as instructors in Principals' Academy workshops. Realizing that providing ongoing support for the mentoring program is essential, all mentors meet on a regular basis to share strategies and methods for effective mentoring.

Tier 7: Academic initiatives

The Principals' Academy has been instrumental in designing and implementing several school district academic initiatives. Ongoing learning sessions provide

PARTICIPANTS DISCUSS THEIR EXPERIENCES

"Involvement in the Principals' Academy has made me feel like a valued member of the administrative team."

— Kim Brant, dean of students, Glenn Duncan Elementary School

"I learned more from my deanship than any other setting I could imagine. This experience has solidified my conviction to become an outstanding administrator."

— Derek Cordell, dean of students, Swope Middle School

"The experiences, classes, seminars, and trainings benefit not only us as instructional leaders, but also those with whom we make daily contact … our teachers and students."

— Michael Higgins, dean of students, Incline Elementary School

"I have grown professionally through the reading of research and the action research I have been able to implement at my school."

— Gloria Geil, principal, Veterans Elementary School

"The doctorate cohort has been an invaluable experience for me. I have been able to work with peers who are currently practicing in the field on projects that have been relevant and engaging. The professors are knowledgeable, the coursework rigorous, and the hours convenient. It is the best way I can imagine a working administrator completing this program."

— Reagan Virgil, assistant principal, Traner Middle School

"The National Board process required me to look closely at my current practices. As a result of this 'forced' reflection, I targeted areas that needed improvement. This introspection led to my National Board goals, which will improve my skills as a leader benefiting teachers and children."

— Bob Deery, principal, Mathews Elementary School

JSD, Spring 2008 (Vol. 29, No. 2)

principals with the research-based information they need to lead their schools. Workshops cover the walk-through process, differentiating supervision, professional learning communities, struggling teacher assistance, and other topics. This tier is perhaps the most comprehensive stage, as the Principals' Academy has ample resources to prepare, support, and empower school leaders in these areas. The Principals' Academy was also influential in creating the district's new principal evaluation system, in partnership with the University of Wisconsin at Madison. The system has been so effective that the district is building a similar tool for assistant principals and deans.

Tier 8: Veteran administrative support

Typically, newer administrators garner most of the professional learning focus in most school districts. However, the Principals' Academy ensures that all principals receive the tools, skills, strategies, and learning that combine to build and sustain effective leadership. Veteran principals and assistant principals use Principals' Academy funding to attend national conferences, participate in regional trainings, and host skilled consultants at district-level or school-level workshops. The Principals' Academy advisory team (seven distinguished K-12 principals) designs and co-facilitates the workshops with senior directors and consultants.

Tier 9: Executive doctorate

In fall 2006, the Principals' Academy and the University of Nevada, Reno, created an executive doctorate program. The coursework is based on the eight leadership dimensions outlined by the Principals' Academy framework document:

1. Vision
2. Student achievement
3. Political, social, economic, legal, and cultural context of learning
4. Communication/interpersonal
5. Instructional leadership/supervision
6. Organization/management
7. Decision making
8. Professional development

Instructors include university professors, district-level administrators, and distinguished principals as selected by the Principals' Academy. Participants can earn a doctorate degree in instructional leadership, while the Principals' Academy furnishes the materials and provides stipends for instructors.

Additionally, the district superintendent works alongside the advisory board to select candidates for the program.

Tier 10: National Administrator Board Certification

The Principals' Academy is participating in a collaborative partnership with the National Principals Initiative, the University of Pittsburgh, the University of Nevada, the Nevada Association of School Administrators, the Union Pacific Principal Partnership, and WestEd to establish a National Administrator Board Certification Program. Rigorous in its time and content demands, this program has established a voluntary system of advanced certification for school administrators that leads to an additional pay increase (8%, similar to National Board Certified teachers) and an increased level of professionalism. The first cohort has begun its work in the program, and the Washoe County School District has been selected to serve as a pilot host. The collaborative partnership plans for this certification program to potentially serve administrators regionally and even nationally.

PRINCIPAL DEVELOPMENT FOR POSITIVE CHANGE

On a variety of measures, the results demonstrated by WCSD students indicate the success of Principals' Academy initiatives: In 3rd-grade reading, student proficiency rose from 47% in 2002 to 56% in 2006; in 5th-grade math, student proficiency rose from 50% in 2002 to 62% in 2006; in 8th-grade writing, student proficiency rose from 62% in 2002 to 70% in 2006; and the high-school graduation rate of 73.9% dwarfs the state average of 64.9%.

Developing school principals as instructional leaders is essential to implementing meaningful school improvement (LaPointe & Davis, 2006). To answer that monumental challenge, the Principals' Academy attracts and supports individuals from the time they show interest in administration all the way through the continuum as expert building principals. As Tom Brown, principal at Galena High School, stated, "I would not be in the position I am in, nor would I be able to effectively handle the challenges of my position, without the constant support and resources the Principals' Academy and the Academy's leadership has provided me over the past five years."

REFERENCES

DuFour, R. & Eaker, R. (1998). *Professional learning communities at work: Best practices for enhancing student achievement.* Bloomington, IN: National Educational Service.

LaPointe, M. & Davis, S. (2006, September/ October). Effective schools require effective principals. *Leadership 36*(1), 16-19, 34, 36-38.

Werlinich, J. (2004). *Werlinich on walk-throughs. Washoe County School District Principals' Academy programs and services manual.* Reno, NV: Washoe County School District Principals' Academy.

ABOUT THE AUTHORS

Pete Hall, a graduate of the Washoe County (Nev.) School District's Principals' Academy, is principal of Sheridan Elementary School in the Spokane (Wash.) Public Schools.

Rick Harris, deputy superintendent of the Washoe County School District in Reno, Nev., is also director of the Principals' Academy.

This article was adapted with permission from the Winter 2006 issue of The Launching Pad, published by Education Hall.

Washoe County School District
Reno, Nev.

Number of schools: 95 (65 elementary, 15 middle, 15 high)
Enrollment: 63,046
Staff: 7,220
Racial/ethnic mix:

White:	56%
African-American:	4%
Hispanic:	32%
Asian/Pacific Islander:	6%
Native American:	2%
Other:	0%

Limited English proficient: 27%
Languages spoken: 57
Free/reduced lunch: 33%
Special education: 13%
Web site: www.washoe.k12.nv.us

Guiding hand of the superintendent helps principals flourish

By Gene Spanneut and Mike Ford

Whether by design or by chance, superintendents communicate their beliefs about what is important educationally and the roles they expect their principals to fulfill. Superintendents who champion the development of their principals as instructional leaders begin by establishing common understandings with them about why principals' instructional leadership is necessary for school success. They reinforce this by actively providing support for their principals to develop and refine their effectiveness as instructional leaders.

"I'm hooked on visiting classrooms, observing artfully crafted lessons and students engaged in purposeful learning," said Janice Driscoll, principal of the intermediate school in Phelps-Clifton Springs, N.Y. "It's all coming together now, and I'm enjoying being able to share what's going on in classrooms and, more importantly, to encourage teachers to share what they're doing and seeing in their students."

Phelps-Clifton Springs, commonly called Midlakes, is a centralized public school district located in rural upstate New York. Superintendent Mike Ford has two fundamental beliefs about the academic performance of the 1,860 students enrolled in his K-12 school system. First, he believes that they are all capable of high levels of academic achievement. Second, he believes that students' opportunities to perform at those levels can be realized by developing the capacity for principals to grow and excel as instructional leaders. This growth happens when school leaders deliberately design and implement measures tailored to the needs of the school system.

To develop principals as instructional leaders, Ford and his colleagues first define the specific areas where the district needs to improve instruction. In Midlakes, districtwide performance on state elementary English and language arts assessments was quite low. The district commissioned an audit of its program, and the two elementary principals, the director of curriculum and instruction, and the superintendent reviewed the audit and prepared a plan. The audit produced two strong findings: the need for a literacy coach at the elementary level and a recommendation that the principals be present in classrooms more frequently to monitor and support instruction. One of the two principals, Karen Cameron, is an adjunct professor in the reading department at a nearby college and taught a course on literacy coaching. The other principal, Janice Driscoll, has a strong desire to improve student performance on state assessments. With these two leaders in place, the team decided on a novel approach: principal as literacy coach.

To support such instructional leadership approaches, superintendents must provide principals with resources that will allow them to put their plans into action. Increasing the capacity of principals as instructional leaders does not alleviate the management needs of their schools. Superintendents can find ways to meet those demands by removing obstacles that impede principals' progress. For example, when the Midlakes principals became literacy coaches, Ford created the position of dean of students to free those principals from some managerial duties. This permitted Cameron and Driscoll to spend time regularly in classrooms and gave them time to provide monthly training sessions for all teachers and teaching assistants. This new position also allowed the principals to function as leaders of learning when they observe teachers, provide coaching, interact with students, and actively model instructional strategies.

EXPLORING LEADERSHIP THROUGH PLCS

The district explores the importance of principals as instructional leaders through professional learning communities (PLCs). DuFour (2003) describes how superintendents use PLCs by employing a tactic described as "one that is loose and tight, a strategy that establishes a clear priority and discernable parameters and then provides each school and department with the autonomy to chart its own course for achieving the objectives" (p. 2).

When he meets with principals, Ford provides practical examples of the connections between their instructional leadership and students' academic accomplishments. For example, he crafts the agenda for his biweekly administrative leadership team meetings with an emphasis on learning and engages the principals in purposeful discussions about "growing people." The team explores ways they can help teachers improve their skills, expand their knowledge, and find ways for them to

Phelps-Clifton Springs Central School District
Clifton Springs, N.Y.

Number of schools: Four (one primary, one intermediate, one middle, one high)
Grades: K-12
Enrollment: 1,860
Staff: 360
Racial/ethnic mix:

White:	97%
Black:	1%
Hispanic:	2%
Asian/Pacific Islander:	0%
Native American:	0%
Other:	0%

Limited English proficient: 0%
Free/reduced lunch: 31%
Special education: 14%

demonstrate leadership. These conversations drive district priorities and build principals' capacity to lead at the building level.

To boost the district's expertise in effectively using PLCs, Ford arranged for all Midlakes administrators to attend a four-day institute on PLCs in summer 2004. Principal Cameron noted, "The opportunity to attend the institute on PLCs with the other principals in the district allowed all of us to hear the same information and dialogue and reflect on the new learning. It provided the time for us to discuss the possibilities and plan for their implementation."

The district also paid for 10 members of its Professional Development Committee to attend the National Staff Development Council's summer conference in each of the past three years. They chose sessions on PLCs to further enhance the school system's use of the model in the district. Teams now exist in Midlakes at the elementary and middle school levels. In the elementary

JSD, Spring 2008 (Vol. 29, No. 2)

schools, each grade level is a PLC; at the middle school, the math and the English and language arts departments are PLCs. Time is built into the schedules so that each team can meet at least once a week. Team meetings are devoted to discussions about what is being taught, what students are learning, and how well they are learning it. The analysis of assessment results is a central theme.

Team leaders, who received training in facilitation skills, lead meaningful conversations about student learning and instruction. The principals meet regularly with them to ensure the alignment of priorities and to assist in planning and problem solving.

The central message they communicate is that leadership, rather than being a one-person title, is "a shared activity in [their] schools" (Oduro, 2004, p. 24).

DEVELOPING LEADERS OF LEADERS

As leadership becomes a staff-wide responsibility in a school, the superintendent and principals are ready to explore links between principals' instructional leadership and successes in the core business of their schools. Ash and Persall's Formative Leadership Theory (2000), for instance, suggests that principals function as "Chief Learning Officers…[who] focus more on the learning opportunities provided to students and on the work students do" (Ash & Persall, 2000, p. 16).

When districts work to develop principals as chief learning officers, the district is creating leaders of leaders. This evolution of leadership roles helps the district establish leadership as a distributed responsibility with teachers. From this perspective, principals work "collaboratively with teachers in planning, scheduling, and leading students in academic work (Ash & Persall, 2000, p. 17).

Shared leadership is an important organizational value in Midlakes. The leadership team has created avenues for teacher leadership to emerge. Teachers serve as committee leaders, assist in building management, and facilitate curriculum and staff development processes. The leadership team encourages all staff members to provide feedback and counsel.

ONGOING SUPPORT AND LEARNING

Superintendents encourage and support their principals through targeted dialogue in a variety of areas, including shared leadership, teachers as leaders, and accountability for results, to investigate how to achieve changes in the way they define authority and power. Each summer, the leadership team at Midlakes devotes two days to dialogue about leadership. This collegial time not only fosters team and relationship building, but also encourages the development of a shared vision, and, most importantly, cohesion. In nine years, there has been almost no turnover on the leadership team.

Providing support also means that superintendents must keep their principals focused on their continuing development as instructional leaders. While specific conversations may help with this, superintendents also need to provide tools principals can use to examine their own growth. A prime example is the encouragement of principals' reflective thinking, what Rich and Jackson (2006) describe as a process through which leaders can "think about and improve upon practice as well as challenge internal faulty perceptions and beliefs [and to] see gaps in their knowledge base" (p. 12).

Reflections present superintendents with opportunities to model leadership through their facilitation of professional discourse from collegial as well as supervisory perspectives. Reflection is not only a solitary experience; indeed, "powerful reflection and collaboration is also possible when educators engage in professional dialogue with each other in small groups" (Rich & Jackson, 2006, p. 13).

Ford plans and conducts the leadership development initiatives for his principals and other administrators. Their most recent activities have included book studies (e.g. *Working on the Work,* by Phillip Schlechty and *What Great Principals Do Differently,* by Todd Whitaker), training sessions on effective observation skills, and developing action plans to achieve the district's vision for learning.

During one-on-one and group discussions, superintendents can prompt their principals to move from maintaining their current leadership abilities to identifying new areas for growth. As principals re-create their roles, superintendents can support them in seeking opportunities to lead instructional initiatives and improvements in their schools.

When principals specify what their instructional leadership roles need to be to successfully accomplish such ends, they invest in their own professional learning by creating self-expectations.

CONCLUSION

Superintendents focused on instructional leadership provide not only the rationale for their principals to realize that they can operate their schools efficiently, they can also develop within their principals the knowledge that by investing in their growth as instructional leaders, they can effectively move their schools to increasingly higher levels of success.

Superintendents also have a responsibility to communicate this message to school district constituents — especially boards of education, district employees, students, and parents. Publicly providing valid, concrete examples of how those roles have led to documented increases in student achievement highlights what is taking place, what is expected, and what will be accomplished.

Midlakes has seen encouraging results in just the first year of the principal-as-coach initiative. While only 60% of the district's 5th graders scored at the proficiency level on the state assessment in 2006, 82% met proficiency in 2007. Of the 25 school districts in the region, the 5th-grade results were 23rd in 2006 and 6th in 2007. At the 4th-grade level, the percentage of students meeting

proficiency increased from 61% to 76%, while the regional rank improved from 23rd to 10th.

Last year, principals Cameron and Driscoll learned one more important lesson when their fellow administrators singled them out as the two district administrators who made the biggest difference last year. They learned that principals grow and succeed when others have faith in their capabilities as instructional leaders, have expectations for their accomplishments, and believe their leadership will result in higher levels of success for their students and schools.

REFERENCES

Ash, R. & Persall, J.M. (2000). The principal as chief learning officer: Developing teacher leaders. *NASSP Bulletin, 84*(616), 15-22.

DuFour, R.P. (2003, May). Building a professional learning community: For system leaders, it means allowing autonomy within defined parameters. *The School Administrator, 60*(5), 13-18.

Oduro, G.K.T. (2004). Distributed leadership in schools. *Education Journal, 80*, 23-25.

Rich, R.A. & Jackson, S.H. (2006, Winter). Building the reflective capacity of practicing principals. *Journal of Scholarship & Practice, 2*(4), 12-18.

Schlechty, P.C. (2002). *Working on the work: An action plan for teachers, principals, and superintendents.* San Francisco, CA: Jossey-Bass.

Whitaker, T. (2003). *What great principals do differently: Fifteen things that matter most.* Larchmont, NY: Eye on Education.

ABOUT THE AUTHORS

Gene Spanneut is assistant professor of educational administration at the State University of New York College at Brockport.

Mike Ford is superintendent of schools for Phelps-Clifton Springs School District in Clifton Springs, N.Y.

A winding path
Tucson follows circuitous route toward professional learning for principals

By Harriet Arzu Scarborough

I s this a familiar image from not so long ago? Principals manage schools, ensuring that that nothing interrupts business as usual. They spend little time on instruction. A good principal is the one who works in a high-achieving school that has no significant management problems. Districts celebrate improved student results by recognizing an outstanding crop of students, rarely pointing to the quality of teaching in a school. Before accountability reached Tucson (Ariz.) Unified School District in 2003, we embodied this image.

In 2000, TUSD's leadership set ambitious five-year goals for the district but failed to develop a blueprint for achieving those goals. Frustrated by the lack of progress towards the goals in three years, the district designed a plan of action in 2003 that focused on school-level interventions that would improve student achievements. A significant piece of that new action plan was targeted professional learning for principals to support those interventions.

THE BIG PICTURE

To enlist the district's principals in this work, we studied disaggregated student achievement data. We could not continue to accept that we had just pockets

Tucson Unified School District
Tucson, Ariz.

Grades: K-12
Enrollment: 60,000
Staff: 3,900
Racial/ethnic mix:

White:	30%
Black:	7%
Hispanic:	55%
Asian/Pacific Islander:	4%
Native American:	3%
Multiracial:	<1%

Limited English proficient: 13.1%
Languages spoken: More than 142
Free/reduced lunch: 58%
Special education: 12.4%
Web site: www.tusd.k12.az.us

Subject	2003	2007
Mathematics	36.5% proficient	60.9% proficient
Reading	48% proficient	63.7% proficient
Writing	63.9% proficient	77.8% proficient

of excellence in our district. The student mobility statistics indicated that all of the principals needed to be instructional leaders. Ultimately, we developed the following big picture to guide professional learning for our principals.

The goal is to improve student achievement. To improve student achievement, we must have effective instruction in our schools. To improve instruction, instructional leaders must know what effective instruction is and be able to assist teachers to improve instructional practice. To help teachers improve instructional practice, we need to provide focused, quality professional development for our principals and our teachers.

We envisioned schools where students were engaged in meaningful, rigorous work, where teachers worked collaboratively to provide the best instruction possible, and principals saw themselves as instructional leaders monitoring instruction, coaching teachers, and ensuring powerful professional learning focused on the improvement of student learning. We outlined three objectives to focus the professional learning:

1. Identify effective instruction.
2. Conduct learning-focused conversations to assist teachers to improve instruction.
3. Provide quality professional learning for teachers.

REALIZING THE VISION

The professional learning for principals had four main components:

1. A seven-day course in observing and analyzing teaching, ending with one-on-one coaching visits.
2. A six-day workshop on conducting learning-focused conversations.
3. Six principal coach-led cadre visits to classrooms for application work.
4. Reading and discussion of selected professional books.

1. Observing and analyzing teaching

We knew that the only way to improve student achievement was to improve instruction. The first step was to help principals arrive at consensus about what effective instruction looks like. We discussed *The Teaching Gap* (Stigler & Hiebert, 1999) to develop an understanding of effective instruction, then visited classrooms to determine if the lessons we saw mirrored what we considered to be effective instruction. But we soon realized that we lacked a common vocabulary for discussing instruction as well as a solid foundation of knowledge. Research for Better Teaching (RBT) provided that foundation in the form of a seven-day course in observing and analyzing teaching.

We divided 105 principals into three cohorts and began the course — all principals were required to participate. Since professional learning, particularly for administrators, had never had such visibility in the district, debate raged about the use of time: "How can we be expected to run our school and be out so much?" "Why do I need to take this course?" "This is more like a university course more appropriate for beginning principals."

This course focused on the work that instructional leaders do to support and sustain high-quality teaching and to build capacity to identify what makes a difference to students and their learning (RBT, 2003). We studied key aspects of teaching within the larger areas of management, instruction, motivation, and curriculum. Soon, terms such as student engagement, momentum, provisioning, clarity, and alignment of objectives and activities became a part of our vocabulary. Additionally, we developed the discipline of using evidence to support our understanding of what we observed in classrooms. Finally, the instructor had a one-on-one coaching session with each principal. We expected that by providing this course for all principals, we would build a common understanding of effective instruction as well as how to make that the norm in all classrooms.

2. Learning-focused conversations

Another component of the professional learning for principals was a six-day course on learning-focused conversations This component of professional learning gave principals skills and tools to coach the improvement of instruction. In these sessions, principals learned processes for leading groups as well as components and continuum of learning-focused conversations. They also had opportunities to practice what they had learned and to experience various types of conversations: planning, problem-solving, and reflective.

3. Principal coach-led cadre visits

To support principal growth efforts, the district added three principal coaches to assist principals in developing instructional leadership skills. Each principal was a member of a cadre that participated in classroom visits with a principal coach. These visits, held three times a semester, were opportunities for principals to observe a complete lesson and then meet to discuss its effectiveness and ways in which the lesson could be improved.

We developed a rubric that the principals used to rate the various components of the lesson. First, they arrived at consensus regarding the effectiveness of the lesson. Next, they determined the part of the lesson on which to direct the learning-focused conversation with the teacher. When implemented effectively, we expected that this aspect of the visit would most contribute to improved student learning. Finally, cadre members discussed how to hold the learning-focused conversation. In essence, the cadre visits were opportunities for principals to apply their learning. We encouraged cadre members to focus on the strengths of the teacher as much as possible. What good elements could the teacher build on to move his teaching to the next level? How could he improve this lesson to increase opportunities for student learning?

4. Professional reading

The fourth component of the principals' professional learning was reading and discussion of selected books on leadership. This was an effort to institutionalize the concept that effective instructional leaders are engaged learners. Questions to guide the reading were

provided, and the principals discussed books during monthly leadership meetings and cadre visits. The books we discussed include: *Good to Great*, by Jim Collins (HarperCollins, 2001), *Sticking to it: The Art of Adherence*, by Lee Colan (CornerStone Leadership Institute, 2003), *The Moral Imperative of School Leadership*, by Michael Fullan (Corwin Press, 2003), and *Courageous Conversations About Race*, by Glenn Singleton and Curtis Linton (Corwin Press, 2006).

SCALING DOWN

At the end of the 2003-04 school year, we had a change of leadership that led to a reduction in principals' professional learning opportunities. However, the principal coaches picked up the pieces and provided professional learning sessions for the assistant principals and central office administrators to build their instructional leadership skills, organized them into cadres, and took them on classroom visits to apply their learning. What remained of the principals' professional learning were the cadre visits with the principal coaches to refine observing and analyzing teaching skills as well as their learning-focused conversation skills. The principals also continued their book discussions in the cadre visits.

WHERE ARE WE NOW?

While we've struggled to maintain our professional learning program for principals, we have seen success. Professional learning for our instructional leaders is a continuum beginning with a leadership academy for aspiring leaders and continued professional learning for new and veteran principals. In September 2007, our student achievement data shows some improvement. See chart above.

WHAT HAVE WE LEARNED?

Wagner et al. (2006) outline the following as the phases of the change process:

1. Preparing — laying the foundation
2. Envisioning
3. Enacting

Sometimes change fails because we are very good about developing solutions for problems that others do not think they have (Wagner et al., 2006). While we invested time conveying the need for change, we should have spent more time in the envisioning phase to establish a shared understanding of the problem, possible solutions, need for new forms of collaboration, and vision for quality instruction and instructional leadership.

Because we saw our situation as urgent, we didn't invest enough effort to generate ownership to sustain the professional learning that we needed. With the reduction in our professional learning programs after just one year, we were forced to make modifications sooner than we had anticipated.

We also have not been good about celebrating small wins. At the end of the 2006-07 school year, we are not where we would like to be in terms of principals' professional learning and student achievement, but clearly we are not where we were at the beginning of the 2003-04 school year. The level of discourse in Tucson Unified School District is much higher, principals will gladly claim the title of instructional leaders, and there is a districtwide commitment to learning for everyone — students, teachers, and administrators.

REFERENCES

Research for Better Teaching. (2003). *Course description for observing and analyzing teaching I.* Acton, MA: Author.

Stigler, J.W. & Hiebert, J. (1999). *The teaching gap.* New York: The Free Press.

Wagner, T., Kegan, R., Lahey, L., Lemons, R.W., Garnier, J., Helsing, D., et al. (2006). *Change leadership: A practical guide to transforming our schools.* San Francisco: Jossey-Bass.

ABOUT THE AUTHOR

Harriet Arzu Scarborough is co-director of Furendei Consulting Services in Tucson, Ariz. She retired from Tucson Unified School District in June 2007 and served as TUSD's senior academic officer for professional development and academics from 2003 to 2007.

Alaska's principals warm to coaching project

By Joan Richardson

In the tiny Alaskan village of Newtok (population: 321), Grant Kashatok faces issues familiar to most principals: ensuring that students make AYP this year, helping his staff become more collaborative, dealing with irate parents.

But as a principal in this ultra-remote area of the country, Kashatok also has different worries: acting as landlord for the housing where his teachers live, managing a limited supply of water and fuel to get through the harsh winters, ensuring balanced nutrition for students when fresh food is delivered only once a month. Kashatok also has an additional worry that even other bush principals don't face: His village is sinking into the waters off the Bering Sea and he must figure out how to support his students and teachers as the village migrates inland to a safer location.

But Kashatok also has a resource available to few principals: weekly coaching conversations with a retired Alaskan bush principal, Peter Kokes, who helps him navigate the usual and the unique concerns of being a bush principal. "He made a big difference for me. It's less lonely, and I always knew that whatever I told Peter stayed with Peter. That was number one with me. I could

share anything with him and there would never be any backlash," Kashatok said.

The Alaska Department of Education started the Alaska Principals Coaching Project three years ago to stem the high turnover of principals by helping educators in those jobs thrive. The project has trained 13 retired principals to coach 80 principals, all of whom have volunteered to be coached. "The point is to keep people here," said Lynn Sawyer, director of the Alaska coaching project, which uses Cognitive Coaching[SM] as its model for coaching.

Alaska represents a unique challenge in developing principals. Of its 503 schools, 125 have fewer than 50 students. The state averages 60 to 80 new principals annually, often principals who have not been exposed to the hardships of village life before taking the job. In spite of the challenges, however, initial evaluation data of the Alaskan project is showing a positive impact on both the effectiveness and retention of principals, Sawyer said.

Although coaching has become a popular and widespread way to support teachers, that has not been the case for principals. Whether in Alaska or elsewhere, Carolee Hayes, co-director of the Center for Cognitive

Coaching in Highlands Ranch, Colo., believes principals need coaches as much as do teachers. "We tend to put resources in the classroom. If it's not directly affecting kids, we don't see it as valuable. But if you coach a principal, you impact an entire school, you impact all of the teachers," Hayes said.

In a survey of 30 principals in 13 states and Canada, Hayes and Jane Ellison, also co-director at the Center for Cognitive Coaching (2006) learned that:

- Principal professional development is random and unfocused with little or no linkage to student learning outcomes.

- Principal professional development is a reaction to an event, e.g. a school incident and the need to review safety procedures.

- Less than a third of principals receive any mentoring; when present, mentoring usually is informal and focused only on first-year principals.

- While principals see coaching as valuable, the system did not provide it.

- A principals' meeting on a quarterly or monthly basis is the delivery system for most professional development; second are annual principal institutes.

- Only 20% of the respondents saw national conferences as opportunities for professional development.

Perhaps more than anything else, coaching provides principals with an opportunity to have trusting conversations with a skilled listener who is familiar with the challenges of their work and has the skills to assist them in identifying solutions. "Half of what principals deal with, they can't talk to staff about and most will tell you that nobody from central office visits them on a anything like a regular basis," Hayes said.

The Alaska coaching project and others managed through the Center for Cognitive Coaching, have three goals.

The first is to improve the craftsmanship of the principal, to help principals become more precise in their thinking and more precise about setting goals and how to achieve them.

The second is to guide them to becoming more flexible in their thinking. "We want them to learn to see other options, to ask how this would be viewed by special education teachers or by parents," Hayes said.

The third is to develop interdependence with teachers and with other principals. "They feel such a sense of aloneness. But there are resources they can draw on. They are not the only ones responsible for student achievement in the school," Hayes said.

COACHING IN ALASKA

The Alaskan principals begin with a face-to-face gathering in the fall in Anchorage where they meet their coaches and participate in some traditional professional development, typically focusing on boosting their skills in areas such as teacher evaluation. They gather again in the spring for a similar meeting. In between, they try to talk weekly to their coaches following the precepts of Cognitive Coaching[SM]. At least twice a year, the coach ventures out to each of their schools.

In the Alaska project, the coaches are learning to be coaches at the same time they are coaching principals. The challenge for the coaches, said Sawyer, is that "they're all great problem solvers themselves. They have great suggestions. They have to fight the temptation to just fix it, rather than helping the principal think it through himself."

"Getting the coaches to really use the tools of coaching with automaticity is what we're really working towards. When they do that, they set an example for the principal so they'll use the same tools with teachers," Sawyer said.

Coach Peter Kokes, who now lives in Missouri, found that conference calls with all of his principals was an effective way to work. "That way, they can collaborate with each other. They have common questions. It becomes kind of a peer counseling session. They don't have much chance to collaborate with other principals. But they're all asking the same kinds of questions," he said.

Kashatok said he found great value in the conference calls. Even though the principals were often hundreds of miles apart, the conference calls helped develop a sense of community with other principals. "So many brains were working on the same issues. We would come at things from so many different angles. We came up with many different solutions," he said.

After experiencing the collaboration with colleagues during the conference calls, Kashatok introduced the concept to his staff. "I incorporate the idea of having many people deal with one issue and coming up with the best solution. Now, we have a very collaborative school in the making," he said.

That sense of community and collaboration has also inspired Kashatok to reach out in a less formal way to a new principal in another bush school in Kipnuk, 90 miles from Newtok. "I call her once a month, and she calls me when she needs to," he said.

ABOUT THE AUTHOR

Joan Richardson is director of communications for the National Staff Development Council.

Boston structure supports school leaders

By Jennifer Welsh Takata

Bettie Nolan began her career in public health administration as a high school nurse in Boston Public Schools. After witnessing the challenging experiences of many adolescents, particularly pregnant teens, she concluded that access to better educational opportunities could support better life choices. As a result, she decided to become a school administrator in the hope that she could improve the quality of education for youth.

Nolan's decision led her down a path that she describes as "phenomenal." She applied and was accepted to Boston Public Schools' Principal Fellowship program, which prepares and supports the continued development of the district's aspiring and novice school leaders. Nolan's sentiment echoes that of other fellowship alumni who laud the direct route into school administration that the district's programs provide.

Boston Public Schools, winner of the 2006 Broad Prize for Urban Education, creates innovative programs to develop school leaders based on the idea that "school leadership is the single most important factor in schools' success" (Boston School Leadership Institute). Teachers play an invaluable role in determining the quality of classroom instruction, but a principal is, in the words of former Boston superintendent Thomas Payzant, the "teacher of teachers" who envisions, implements, and supports high-quality learning environments (Rubenstein, 2006).

The district's leadership development programs evolved under Payzant's direction in 2002-03 as part of a school improvement effort initiated in 1995. Through analysis of best practices in the field, Boston identified the "Essentials

Boston's structure

- School Leadership Institute
- Boston Principal Fellowship program
- Exploring School Administration
- New Principal Support System
- School-Based Administrator program
- Structured professional learning
- Ongoing mentoring
- Monthly networking meetings

of Whole School Improvement," a framework that has received national recognition for its results (Boston Public Schools, 2004). The framework's emphasis on leadership and professional learning led to the creation of the School Leadership Institute, which serves as the major pipeline for developing Boston Public Schools leaders.

THE BOSTON PRINCIPAL FELLOWSHIP PROGRAM

While the district offers a range of programs to recruit, develop, and support leaders, the Boston Principal Fellowship program is particularly notable. This one-year urban principal preparation program features opportunities for participants to receive hands-on experience four days a week with an experienced school leader. The fellowship includes full-time placement with one of Boston's strongest principals, 90 days of seminars and coursework, a Massachusetts Initial Principal License, an optional master's degree, consideration for administrative positions in Boston Public Schools, and membership in a lifelong professional network. Approximately one-third of those exiting the year-long program move directly into a principal or headmaster position.

The fellowship begins with a summer intensive session made up of five weeks of coursework to prepare the participants for their residencies. The courses, covering topics such as the history of schooling in Boston, leadership, and learning and teaching, are designed around key elements of leadership defined by the district to align to the district's whole-school improvement principles.

In the fall, fellows begin their school-based residency four days a week and meet on Fridays to continue their coursework. Every course focuses on a particular theoretical perspective, and fellows implement a related practical project at their school site with the support of their mentor. For example, one fellow conducted an audit of race equality at her school and developed a plan

BROAD PRIZE FOR URBAN EDUCATION

The Broad Prize for Urban Education is an annual $1 million award created to honor urban school districts demonstrating the greatest overall performance and improvement in student achievement while at the same time reducing achievement gaps among ethnic groups and between high- and low-income students.

Each year, five finalists are selected from 100 eligible school districts across the nation based on academic performance data, site visit observations, and interviews with district administrators, teachers, principals, parents, union leaders, school board members, and community representatives. To learn more, visit www.broadprize.org.

to address challenges that she witnessed. Twice a month, fellows participate in residency seminars, where a panel of principals addresses best practices on the topic. The first seminar of the month is designed around the fellows' interests and particular learning needs; the second seminar is based on the monthly theme, such as family and community engagement or race and culture in schools.

All program coursework and learning is designed to support the specific urban needs and challenges of Boston Public Schools. The program's senior leadership team aligns learning topics to the district's key challenges, such as closing the achievement gap and supporting family and community engagement in schools. Emily Cox, a program fellow, says the district "looks from the inside for certain instructors" so that, for example, the fellows learn about budgets from the district's budget department. Fellows believe that such opportunities enhance their learning by enabling them to "network within the greater school system," according to Cox.

Program leaders have learned that there are three critical factors that prepare future principals for success.

Factor 1

The first is the cohort of fellows, which provides a critical support network during residency and principalship. Fellows recognize the value in the peer network they gain as part of the program. Given the isolated nature of their position, principals appreciate finding "ways to stay enthusiastic, current, and in sync with the world outside their small buildings," said Valdez. According to Cox, "The program does an incredible job in selecting a diversity of fellows who support each other's learning and open each other's minds." While the average tenure of principals is declining nationwide, virtually all of the principals from the first fellowship cohort have remained in the same school for three years following their appointment, according to an informal review conducted in 2006. Therefore, support networks for principals may prove to be powerful tools in increasing principal retention.

Factor 2

Additionally, the school residency gives fellows an opportunity to observe and practice school leadership skills under the supervision of a successful principal who offers constructive feedback. Principal Traci Walker Griffith identified the internship as the most helpful program component because she was immersed in a school with a thoughtful, reflective, and transparent mentor whom she felt comfortable probing about his work. However, a successful residency experience hinges on the right match between mentors and fellows. Though fellows are given an opportunity to request preferred characteristics of a mentor during the admissions process, some fellows acknowledge that they come to the program unsure about what qualities are most important in a mentor principal (Levy & Neufeld, 2005). One feature that fellows later identify as critical is reciprocal learning. For instance, the "second-guess memo" assignment encourages fellows to critically evaluate an administrative choice of their mentor and write a constructive memo,

Boston Public Schools
Boston, Mass.

Schools: 144 (67 elementary or early learning centers, 17 K-8 schools, including special education and at-risk program)
Enrollment: 56,770
Staff: 9,368
Racial/ethnic mix:

White:	14%
Black:	41%
Hispanic:	35%
Asian/Pacific Islander:	9%
Native American:	<1%
Other:	1%

Limited English proficient: 18%
Languages spoken: Spanish, Haitian Creole, Chinese, Cape Verdean Creole, Vietnamese, and others.
Free/reduced lunch: 71%
Special education: 20%

which encourages dialogue and mutual learning between fellow and mentor. Cox explained that "as much as I'm taking from my school, as time passes, I'm able to give back a lot more."

Factor 3

Finally, the coursework portion of the program offers fellows an opportunity to prepare for their school-based work, especially since the program works carefully with "senior leadership to align the topics of study to key priorities and challenges in the district," according to Khita Pottinger, acting director of the School Leadership Institute. Given the pressure on school leaders to produce rapid results, fellows prefer projects that foster the application of their knowledge in the school setting rather than ones that require a lot of "sitting and listening" (Levy & Neufeld, 2005). Cox noted that their instructors are some of the top professors in New England who challenge them to connect the research and theory to their experiences in a school.

Bettie Nolan's fellowship at the Academy of Public Service in the Dorchester Education Complex is near an end. She appreciates the opportunity to work with an innovative headmaster who allowed her to observe, shadow, and participate in instructional leadership in a hands-on manner. Nolan plans to apply for a full-time position as a headmaster or assistant headmaster in Boston Public Schools. She intends to use her background in health care to become a school leader who can address the wide range of needs that each student has.

SUPPORT AT ANY STAGE OF GROWTH

In addition to the fellowship program, the district offers Exploring School Administration to reach prospective school leaders. Through after-school seminars, this program introduces the principalship and other school leadership roles to educators and community leaders who show leadership potential and have a deep knowledge of instruction but might not have considered becoming a principal. Each of the 10 after-school seminars focuses on a different aspect of the school leader's role. Participants review readings and case studies, meet with school and district leaders, and visit schools to observe principals or assistant principals in action.

The district also offers the New Principal Support System. First-year principals attend a five-day summer institute to prepare them for effective entry into their school. Throughout the year, new principals participate in monthly networking sessions, where principals discuss current challenges and "utilize their collective knowledge to support each other when facing complex issues as school leaders," said Anthony Valdez, a principal in Boston Public Schools. Principals value this support system, which enables them to "reach out to people who share the same language and passion for student achievement," said Walker Griffith.

Additionally, principals participate in structured professional learning designed to support them in addressing districtwide challenges. Monthly meetings may also take the form of school site visits, where facilitators with experience in school administration arrange one-to-one meetings at principals' schools. Principals also receive ongoing mentoring from an experienced principal selected to match the novice principal in geography and type of school. Second- and third-year principals do not participate in a formal mentoring program; however, they have a coach who assists them with leadership or operational challenges. They continue to participate in monthly networking meetings, which are organized by the principals' years of experience, as well as just-in-time sessions, which combine principals of all years.

Recognizing the needs of school-based non-principal administrators, the district has developed its most recent program, the School-Based Administrator program, to provide leadership development for school leaders.

The program serves many functions including educating teachers and recruiting them into leadership roles, providing a two-year system of support for new school-based administrators, providing professional learning that facilitates instructional improvement, creating professional networks to support sharing of best practices, and providing school-based administrators who aspire to the principalship with the skills and experiences required to be competitive candidates for the role.

CONCLUSION

While the results of Boston Public Schools' leadership development programs are preliminary, the district has been successful in developing "new cadres of leaders … who share the same passion for fulfilling the dream of proficiency for all," according to Walker Griffith.

The district provides an accelerated career path that addresses the continuum of developmental levels for leaders from both traditional and nontraditional backgrounds; it exposes future leaders to the reality of the field through a one-year hands-on residency, and builds a cohort of colleagues who serve as an ongoing support network throughout their careers in school administration. The lessons learned from the district's experience serve as a model for other school systems looking to grow and sustain strong school leaders.

REFERENCES

Boston Public Schools. (2004). *Boston Public Schools whole-school improvement: The six essentials.* Boston, MA: Author. Available at www.boston.k12.ma.us/teach/offices. pdf.

Boston School Leadership Institute. (n.d.). *About the Institute.* Boston, MA: Author. Available at www. bostonsli.org/program.html.

Levy, A. & Neufeld, B. (2005). Mid-year findings: Boston Principal Fellows (BPF). Cambridge, MA: Education Matters.

Rubenstein, G. (2006). Payzant on principals. *Edutopia, 2*(4). Available at www.edutopia.org/payzant-principals.

ABOUT THE AUTHOR

Jennifer Welsh Takata is program analyst at the Broad Foundation.

Getting personal
New York City's District Two puts priority on principals

By Liz Willen

I t's three weeks into the school year for the nation's largest school system, and Mary Timson needs a second opinion.

As acting principal of Midtown West Elementary School in New York City, Timson worries about everything from building conditions to fund-raising and reading scores. But on this rainy September morning, she is zeroing in on her teaching staff. Are their lessons sharp and focused? Are they ready for the challenges ahead?

That's where Leslie Zackman comes in.

Zackman, a veteran staff developer and principal of a small East Side elementary school, is Timson's mentor, a position taken seriously in District Two. This district includes some of the city's highest performing and most popular elementary and middle schools, along with some that are lagging behind. At the start of classes today, Zackman is at Timson's door like a personal trainer, prepared to prod, push, and encourage her newly assigned mentee.

Together, the two embark on a walk through this building in the heart of the theater district, peeking into classrooms, exchanging ideas, and making lists.

"It is so helpful to have another set of ears and eyes," says Zackman, who over the years has benefited from having veteran principals visit her school, dispensing specific advice about everything from supervision and instruction to budgeting.

This time, as Timson's mentor, Zackman will be ready to share what she has learned and help Timson zoom in on what is working, what is missing, and what needs improvement.

HOW IT WORKS

Mentoring in Community School District Two grew out of a longstanding emphasis on supporting principals and has been formally in place for more than five years.

Here's how it works: Each fall, the superintendent identifies a group of principal mentors; they tend to be the most experienced administrators who are offered a stipend along with an opportunity to take on additional responsibilities.

Great care is taken to match principals whose specific skills are in line with what another school needs; for example, a principal who has been successful working with at-risk students might be assigned a principal with a similar population.

This year, the district selected 10 senior principals as mentors. Eight are also responsible for their own building,

Journal of Staff Development, Winter 2001 (Vol. 22, No. 1)

while two are full-time principal mentors who can devote a great deal of time to their colleagues. Thirty principals are being mentored this year.

At the beginning of the school year, mentors are assigned and mentors and mentees attend a kick-off meeting, but many speak or work together even before the start of school. After that, they'll meet at least once a week, and may be in frequent phone contact.

In addition, the mentors meet with one another, as a group, to discuss mentoring and share activities and success stories.

Deputy Superintendent Tanya Kaufman says there isn't a high turnover of principals in the district; there are no vacancies at the moment.

"I think principals stay because of the collegial nature of the district and the support they get, and the strong professional development they are offered here. There is a proud feeling to be in District Two," she says.

HIGH PRIORITY

There is nothing new about mentoring, but it's easy to understand why many city principals say they have no time for it in a staggeringly poor and troubled school system of 1.1 million students and roughly 1,100 schools. Only half the city's public school students graduate on time; one out of three were in danger of failing last spring, and principals and teachers are constantly lured to more lucrative suburban jobs.

Nonetheless, mentoring takes a high priority in District Two, as it has since former superintendent Anthony Alvarado built an enviable staff development program in nearly a decade at the helm. Alvarado left in 1998 to become chancellor of instruction in the San Diego, Calif., system.

Alvarado believed principals should have a strong instructional vision and play a large role in training, evaluating, and hiring teachers. In turn, he personally visited every school in the district, issuing the kinds of

formal reviews that kept principals constantly on their toes, even in the many small, experimental buildings where they are called by their first names.

The Alvarado legacy continues, and today's District Two principals take part in leadership teams, meet on their own for dinner and discussion, or tap into an informal network of support.

"It's easy to forget that you have someone to call for any reason," Shelly Harwayne, the district's acting superintendent, tells several dozen principals gathered in a midtown Manhattan conference room a week into the school year. Harwayne reminds the group that she, too, was a principal who sought advice from her peers, and remembers, "It was the little things that kind of killed you."

"You know each other. And you trust each other," Harwayne adds, while Deputy Superintendents Kaufman and Bea Johnstone hand out sheets of paper, asking principals to detail their challenges and concerns, and to describe what makes a mentoring relationship work.

As they sip tea and nibble cookies, the principals are ready with low-key support, questions as simple as "How is it going?"

"I get tired at around 3:30 p.m.," acknowledges one principal, describing the post-dismissal slump, a time of day when the building empties out but much work remains. Another wants advice on slowing down, reacting less, and becoming a better listener.

At no time, though, does the meeting turn into the usual gripe session about overcrowding, low salaries, and crumbling buildings. There's little dwelling on the inevitable rough patches that are part of the landscape for urban principals, like problem kids, pesky parents, and inexperienced teachers.

District Two is clearly the kind of place where principals throw life rafts to one another, but in past years they've spread out a bit, offering to mentor principals in Brooklyn and parts of the Bronx, and spreading their philosophy of teamwork.

Journal of Staff Development, Winter 2001 (Vol. 22, No. 1)

STRESSFUL JOBS

One-on-one mentoring programs aren't easy to come by in city schools: Efforts to pair all new principals with a "buddy" principal several years ago ultimately fizzled out, recalls Jill Levy, who heads the Council of Supervisors and Administrators, the union representing city principals.

Time pressures and the day-to-day stress of surviving the job made the mentoring program nearly impossible to keep in place — almost as tough as keeping principals in the city.

"Nobody wants these jobs. The stress is too high," Levy says. "The New York City principal is responsible for everything in, around, and related to the school — and that includes every aspect of school life, from the time kids leave home until they go home and beyond. If you had a stress barometer of zero to 100, the levels would burst right through the top."

Already this year, there are more than 200 principal vacancies and 680 vacancies for assistant principal jobs, Levy says. "We used to get several hundred applicants for a job. Now we get two or three."

District Two noticed a dwindling pool of applicants, so administrators created their own training program to create new leaders, collaborating with nearby Baruch College School of Public Affairs, another way they focus on solutions rather than on the problems.

In District Two, principals don't dwell on the stress of their jobs as much as they discuss ways to cope with it. Often, that is where the mentor fits in.

"I can say I'm having a bad day, and my mentors have just been there for me," says Timson, who has relied heavily on veteran principals Carmine Farina at PS 6, Ann Marie Carrillo at PS 116 and Anna Switzer of PS 234, a TriBeCa school whose top reading scores are the envy of the school system.

FRINGE BENEFIT

Many principals say the support they get from their colleagues is part of what keeps them in the job. Eric Byrne, principal of the progressive PS 183 on the East Side, says he turned down a job in an affluent Long Island school district, where he could have had a higher salary, a secretary, and even a coveted parking spot.

But Byrne is staying put, in part to pay a debt to the many mentors he's had, including Kaufman, the deputy superintendent. Kaufman was once principal of PS 183 and shares Byrne's passion for a school where 43 languages are spoken, where children of doormen and janitors learn alongside the kids of prominent physicians and cancer researchers from nearby Sloan Kettering and the United Nations.

Kaufman, he says, "is the person I go to with everything. I will put anything on the table with her, and it doesn't scare me that she is the deputy superintendent."

But the list of principals Byrne has sought advice from is a long one. When he needed suggestions about kindergarten staffing, he called Zackman. To find out why his school was losing students to the ever-popular PS 6, Byrne marched his entire staff to the building, asking them to observe veteran principal Carmen Farina. In turn, he asked Farina to walk through his school and give him some advice.

Instead of lecturing Byrne, Farina "helped me to focus," says Byrne, adding that in his old school, staff development "meant going to a workshop. Here, it is our language and our legacy. I don't think this kind of support exists anywhere else."

ABOUT THE AUTHOR

Liz Willen is a freelance writer in New York City.

Sharing the mystery
Leadership program adds support to the administrative mix

By John Norton

On a quiet residential street in Chapel Hill, some of North Carolina's newest principals pick through the remains of box dinners as they sit in small groups, sharing war stories and reflecting on a collection of first-person essays, *The First Year as Principal.*

The conversation, held in the home of a Principals' Executive Program (PEP) staff member, begins with frustrated tales of unopened mail, unanswered phone messages, unmanageable students, and unsympathetic veteran teachers. After 10 minutes or so, the talk turns from the unavoidable minutiae of school administration to deeper — and potentially more worrisome — issues of school leadership.

A young principal shares the challenge of communicating his vision to an aging school staff in a neighborhood that has become poorer and more blighted with time. After two years of frustration, he believes he's turned the corner. "We have new teachers coming in, teachers with a different attitude

For more information about PEP, visit its web site at www.ga.unc.edu/pep, or phone (919) 996-4173, fax (919) 962-3365.

about the kids we have today. Teachers will stay in a high-risk school if they believe they can make a difference."

A bearded man in his mid-30s reveals that he's the fifth principal in seven years at his high school, where he arrived in October with no previous principal experience. "The teachers are still waiting to see if I'm the 'flavor of the month,'" he says. His first priority has been to create a safe school. "I'm accessible, but teachers complain that I'm not in classrooms enough. That's my frustration. You're supposed to be an instructional leader, but you have all this other stuff to do — all the paperwork, the discipline, the appeals of student suspensions."

A young principal from an isolated mountain county near the Virginia border has just replaced a 25-year administrator. Many of the teachers in his elementary school are approaching retirement. "They've accepted me very well," he says. "The thing I've struggled with is new ideas. It's hard to get them off the dead horses."

Sitting quietly in a corner of the comfortable living room, Darryl Powell nods as each newly minted

Journal of Staff Development, Winter 2001 (Vol. 22, No. 1)

administrator relates the mystery and frustration of school leadership. After two years as director of PEP's Leadership Program for New Principals, Powell can predict the issues that will arise in these small group sessions.

"We used to invite brand-new principals into our program, but we learned fairly quickly that they're too preoccupied with opening their first schools and surviving their first year on the job to fully engage in this work," says Powell, a former elementary principal and high school English teacher. "Now principals must be at least in their second year, and we prefer the third year. When they have some experience under their belts, they really get more out of the training because they have real context. The issues we discuss are not theoretical to them anymore."

The PEP curriculum covers typical principal challenges, he says — from dealing with difficult people and negotiating with parents, to managing teachers and using best practices in instruction. But there's another side, too, he says: "They have an opportunity to reflect together about the side of the job that people don't see ... and that is to try and really understand how they fit into the world of the principalship."

PEP's role, Powell says, is to help principals "make sense of their own experiences in the school and to balance out the role they believe they're supposed to play with the role they have to play."

MATURE PROGRAM, NEW FOCUS

Established in 1984, the Principals' Executive Program is one of the oldest of nine state-supported initiatives for the professional development of educators. PEP operates under the auspices of the Center for School Leadership Development, an umbrella organization attached to the University of North Carolina's General Administration.

More than 2,800 school administrators — including half of the principals currently working in North Carolina

– have completed at least one of PEP's residential programs. PEP began, says Director Kenneth D. Jenkins, "as a fairly traditional administrator training program, with a strong emphasis on school law and the nuts and bolts of school management." Over time, PEP's programs have expanded and diversified to keep pace with the evolving demands and expectations placed on school administrators. When Jenkins arrived in 1998, he brought the perspective of a professor of educational leadership and former school principal who understood the growing pressures on school administrators to be not only site managers, but leaders of school reform.

"When I first got here, PEP's three programs were of a 'one-size-fits-all' model," Jenkins says. "Principals were considered to be interchangeable, and there was one approach designed to 'fix' them. The programs — one for principals, one for assistant principals, and one for central office administrators — were semi-clones, all looking curiously alike, both in content and in structure."

Expanding a talented core staff with specialists in leadership and technology, Jenkins set out to reinvent PEP's professional development offerings. The trio of "one-size-fits-all" programs was replaced with nine year-long seminars: The Leadership Program for Assistant Principals, the Leadership Program for New Principals, the Higher School Performance Program, the Leadership Program for Career Principals, the Leadership Program for High School Principals, Principals as Technology Leaders, the Central Office Leadership Program, the Leadership Seminar in the Humanities, and the Principal Fellows Seminars. A 10th program, Developing Future Leaders, helps school systems address principal shortages by encouraging teachers with leadership potential to pursue administrative careers.

The curriculum focuses on "both the hard and soft edges of school leadership," Jenkins says, and seeks to augment university studies. On the 'soft side,' Jenkins adds, participants learn "the importance of relationship building ... that leadership is inherently moral, and that the perception of their integrity is the basic sustenance of effective leadership."

The program uses a variety of instructional techniques, including didactic lectures, interactive discussions, Socratic seminars on key readings, case studies, problem or project-based learning, independent studies in skills-intensive technology clinics, as well as networking and conversations with each other.

RESIDENTIAL APPROACH TO TRAINING

One aspect of PEP that has not broken with tradition is its reliance on residential training. Most participants travel to UNC's main campus in Chapel Hill a half-dozen times during the school year, for sessions that last two or three days each. (A few programs, including the year-old "Future Leaders" initiative, are offered in other regions of the state.)

Powell and Jenkins say the residential approach is the most economically feasible and will likely continue as PEP moves into a state-of-the-art training facility now under construction on the UNC campus.

How does PEP's "you come to us" training system match up with the national trend toward job-embedded, results-driven professional development? Jenkins believes PEP's revamped curricula, which relate seminar training "to the nature of the job being confronted," address the issue, at least in part. Before 1998, he says, "the curriculum was unaligned. It was a collection of what someone thought principals needed. There was no attempt to serve anyone else's agenda except our own." Today, each curriculum is aligned to either the State Board of Education's Strategic Priorities or to the 10 Standards of Professional Practice established by the state Standards Board for Public School Administration. PEP also incorporates the six leadership standards promulgated by the Council of Chief State School Officers.

PEP continues to fine-tune curricula to emphasize the connection between its seminars and the realities of school leadership and management. "At the end of many of our session weeks, we typically ask our folks to design an action plan to use what they've learned. We call it 'next steps.' When they return, we start the program week with 'new learnings.' Some report on what they learned when they tried to apply the knowledge and skills they gained in the previous session. That, too, embeds the learning in the jobs they do."

Last year, PEP experimented with a system of on-site mentors in its Higher School Performance Program (HSPP) — training designed to support principals in schools designated as "low performing" under North Carolina's high-stakes accountability system. The experiment met with mixed success, says Shirley Arrington, who assumed leadership of HSPP last summer.

The experiment relied primarily on retired principals and superintendents who were asked to make least one on-site visit, "doing walk-throughs, talking to them about their concerns, and offering suggestions and support. We also did 'temperature checks' by phone." But Arrington says some participants never saw their mentors. Arrington believes a better system can be developed that relies on active principals in nearby districts who can develop peer partnerships with PEP participants.

BREAKING DOWN ISOLATION

Although they agree that on-site support would be a plus for PEP's programs, both Jenkins and Arrington believe that PEP's emphasis on building networks among seminar participants provides a viable and longer-lasting alternative.

Darryl Powell describes this bonding as "one of the wonders of PEP. By the end of the program, you see people wearing their shirts, singing the song — there's this whole campfire kind of stuff that will go on over time.

Journal of Staff Development, Winter 2001 (Vol. 22, No. 1)

They're full of esprit de corps and hopefulness and 'we're going to get it done.'" That process begins from the first day, he adds, "when principals look around and see others who are in the same boat they're in."

Two years ago, PEP research associate Anita Ware surveyed a sample of PEP graduates to determine "satisfaction" and to gather ideas about needed program changes. "We found that one of the most valuable parts of the program is having a chance to be with other principals and being able to talk about things in a safe environment and not worrying about it getting back to your supervisor. It's not that the conversations are negative — most of them aren't — but they are in a safe place where they can reveal some of their uncertainties in a way they can't do back home."

Jenkins says PEP graduates report "consulting" with program colleagues years after graduation. Since the mid-1990s, with the emergence of the Internet and the convenience of e-mail, PEP's graduate networks have grown stronger and more durable.

The advent of instant Internet communication and web-based resources has helped PEP address another issue peculiar to North Carolina — physical isolation. While North Carolina's status as a "rural" state is rapidly becoming an anachronism, pockets of the population remain relatively isolated in the mountain counties along the Tennessee-Virginia border and throughout the inland coastal areas that lie west of the state's jagged shoreline and remote Outer Banks.

PEP is cognizant of the special problems of rural school administrators, Jenkins says. He points to the organization's "Future Leaders" program as one example of PEP's commitment to helping small and rural communities identify and develop hard-to-find principal talent through a "grow-your-own" approach. PEP's new emphasis on interactive technology also links isolated principals with critical friends.

IMPACT ON PERFORMANCE

Does participation in PEP change the way principals do their jobs? Jenkins concedes that the lack of follow-up in PEP's programs makes it difficult to be accountable. He says finite resources limit follow-up to self-reported data at present.

Research associate Anita Ware says most of PEP's evaluation data "is at the satisfaction level." Over the last two years, Ware has interviewed samples of PEP graduates to determine whether and how PEP programs have influenced their job performance. "It usually comes back to comments like: 'It validated a lot of my own beliefs about what should be happening in schools,'" she says.

The array of PEP programs and the difficulty faced by all professional development programs in connecting training with results makes the development of a reliable evaluation system a long-term project. "We definitely want to measure impact," Ware says, noting that PEP is under pressure from the state legislature to show clear evidence of results. "But we are just really in the very beginning stages of deciding how we can do that."

Jenkins is convinced, however, that PEP participants "do apply, albeit selectively, the stuff they learn, sometimes as soon as they return to their 'real' worlds. Participants are constantly telling us, through our listservs, of things they actually did with what they learned.

"For example," he says, "they are better able to see how they have put restrictions on their ability to lead by focusing on the easier tasks of managing — something we stress constantly in our programs. They talk of increased classroom visitations, or changing the content of faculty meetings from administrative items to a combination of administrative and instructional matters. They tell us that they use their deeper knowledge of the law to solve particular problems more effectively and efficiently. We have a lot of anecdotal evidence of changed practices. I'm not sure it's hard evidence, but superintendents tell us they are more effective as school leaders."

THE JOY OF SCHOOL

During the opening session of the Leadership Program for New Principals last July, Jenkins offered a warning he shares with each new PEP class. "Schooling can be hazardous to your intellectual health," he says. "That's ironic, but the school train travels very fast and in only one direction. The job is far too busy every day to leave much time for reflection. Yet we don't learn much from pure experience; we learn from reflecting on experience. That's your job during the time you spend with us."

And Jenkins offered some advice about emotional health as well.

"Every day, find somewhere in your school where you can find 15 minutes of joy, 15 minutes of excitement about teaching and learning," Jenkins urged the often-harried rookie leaders. "Don't deny yourself the joy of school."

ABOUT THE AUTHOR

John Norton is a freelance education writer based in Little Switzerland, N.C.

Journal of Staff Development, Winter 2001 (Vol. 22, No. 1)

Intern at work
Chicago program helps leaders test-drive principal's job

By Elizabeth Duffrin

On a humid August morning, Principal Frances Oden of Beethoven Elementary in Chicago places yet another urgent phone call to the central office. The time is 10:30 a.m. So far today, Oden has attempted to reopen two teaching positions that the district mistakenly closed. She has calmed a frantic teacher and disciplined a student. Now a mother is at the front desk, complaining that her daughter was sent to high school with the wrong test scores on her transfer form. Those scores appear to be missing on the district computer system, and Oden can't find her printed copy — vandals tossed her files out the window last spring. The voice on the phone won't release the girl's scores without a written request.

Nearby, apprentice principal Dyrice Garner cheerfully drafts a request for the missing scores on a yellow pad. It's a learning experience, she explains later.

Garner owes that experience to LAUNCH, or Leadership Academy and Urban Network for Chicago, a joint venture between Chicago Public Schools, the local

LAUNCH is located at 221 N. LaSalle St., Suite 1550, Chicago, IL, 60601, (312) 263-8101. Its web site address is www.cpaa-class.org/LAUNCHpg/launchhome.htm

principals association, and Northwestern University. Now in its third year, the program gives aspirants a chance to sit in the principal's seat.

"The principal's job is so complex that any knowledge or skills you can gain before you start are going to heighten your chances for success," LAUNCH director Ingrid Carney says.

About 30 fellows employed in Chicago Public Schools are selected each year for the five-week summer course and five-month paid internship. All are assistant principals, teachers, or central office personnel and have earned administrative certificates.

LAUNCH is organized around the district's seven leadership standards, including instructional leadership and school management. Those standards guide the application process, the summer session, and the internship.

Finalists in the application process are rated on how well they meet the leadership standards as they role-play the part of a principal. The simulation, run by a Chicago non-profit organization, is based on one

INTERNSHIP TIPS

What makes a good internship for aspiring principals? Cynthia Norris of the University of Tennessee, who studies principal preparation, offers these tips:

1. Choose mentors skilled at teaching adults.
2. Train the mentors.
3. Make the internship full time or it's not a quality internship.
4. Tailor it to individual needs.
5. Focus it on principal leadership standards adopted by your district or state. That keeps it from being haphazard.
6. Partner with a university to expose interns to ideas from outside the district so it's not just a cloning process.

developed by the National Association of Secondary School Principals.

Applicants are confronted by an overflowing inbox, for example, or a consultant acting out the part of a problem teacher. Trained observers take notes, and for those accepted to the program, the internship will target their weakest areas.

LAUNCH interns are released full-time from their regular duties. That allows them to be paired with a district principal who is best suited to mentor them.

Interns and mentors are carefully matched after interviewing each other. The goal is to give the intern new experiences, and the mentor new ideas. Since Garner's home school is an academically selective magnet school and Oden's serves a housing project, there

For more information about the Aspiring Principals Program and Big Picture, call (401) 456-0600 or see its web site at www.bigpicture.org.

has to be some good exchange of skills and knowledge, Carney says.

PROGRAM STRENGTHS

That freedom to match mentors and mentees make LAUNCH unusual, say several experts who study principal preparation.

The quality of the internship is tightly bound to the quality of the mentor, explains Cynthia Norris, a University of Tennessee professor of educational administration who has researched principal internship programs. When a mentee remains in the school to which he or she already is assigned, it's very difficult to predict what kind of internship experience may result. Principal interns typically are not released from their full-time jobs, she says.

LAUNCH has additional strengths that other districts would do well to emulate, according to Kent Peterson, a professor of educational administration at the University of Wisconsin-Madison who has just published a study of principal preparation programs around the country, including LAUNCH. The program's strengths include the length and structure of its semester-long internship, the design of its in-depth summer session that builds camaraderie, and the professional network among participants, Peterson says.

Chicago's state-of-the-art program has a price tag to match. Foundation grants cover the $400,000 annual budget for the summer session and the program's overhead costs. The school district pays a $35,000 salary to each intern.

The investment could be considered steep since no graduate is guaranteed a principalship. In Chicago, elected councils at each school hire the principal. To date, 10 graduates have been given contracts, and the district has placed another six as interim principals. Still, LAUNCH fellows can use their skills in whatever positions they hold, says Carney. "All of these people are already serving in leadership capacities, whether it's as an assistant principal or a teacher leader."

Journal of Staff Development, Winter 2001 (Vol. 22, No. 1)

SCHOOL REFORM GROUP FOCUSES ON THE TOP

Aspiring principals in four states have earned administrative certificates without setting foot in a university classroom. The Big Picture Company, a Providence, R.I.-based school reform group, teamed up with several universities to offer certification through a structured internship in the Aspiring Principals Program.

"I have always thought that taking courses at night to learn to be a leader was not the way to do it," says Dennis Littky, Big Picture's co-director and principal of Rhode Island's state-commissioned laboratory high school. "I've had many people in my schools become principals — they had to go to school at night to get the piece of paper — but they learned to be a principal from me."

One reason for the national principal shortage, he believes, is that the job seems unappealing to those best-suited to lead. The principal's role traditionally has been a managerial one — an image that university programs tend to perpetuate, he notes. Working under dynamic leaders, in his experience, is the best way to draw talented people into the profession and to train them "in vision, in moral courage, in how you treat people. You learn by being in that culture."

During the program's two-year pilot, Big Picture selected seven highly regarded principals as mentors, including Deborah Meier of Mission Hill School in Boston and Dennis Littky of "The Met," The Metropolitan Regional Career and Technical Center in Providence, R.I. Each of the seven had a doctorate and was nationally recognized, says Charles Mojkowski of Johnson & Wales University in Providence, a partner in the program. The principals then were appointed adjunct professors of the university so they could grade their students.

These principals identified an individual at their own school to mentor, someone whom they saw as a potential leader.

Interns met state licensing requirements for principals, just as in a university program. Instead of classroom assignments, they met those requirements on the job, through longer-term projects addressing the needs of their schools (e.g., orientation for new teachers, a parent involvement initiative) as well as day-to-day tasks such as managing a budget or leading a faculty meeting.

Brian Straughter, assistant principal at Mission Hill School in Boston, said his internship was "more rigorous and more enlightening than the traditional program. It wasn't reading about what would happen if. … The readings tied back to the real faces that we deal with every day at school."

Straughter, who already had his administrative certificate, worked with teachers and parents to develop a plan for the principal's evaluation.

Participants also meet regularly outside their schools to listen to speakers on topics they request, to discuss readings, and to share their work.

In July, the first seven aspiring principals earned their certification from Johnson & Wales or Lewis and Clark College in Portland, Oregon. This year, Big Picture is limiting the project to districts in Rhode Island and the Boston area to give mentors more direction and support. Some erred in assigning interns "things that are strictly management and not instructional leadership," such as lunch duty and bus duty, explains program coordinator Elizabeth Wilson Rood. "It was hard to do quality control when people were far away." The principals in the program to that point were in such disparate locations as Oregon, Massachusetts, New York, and Rhode Island. Currently, 17 faculty are interning full time and will earn certification from Northeastern University in Boston or a consortium of four Providence schools: Johnson & Wales, Rhode Island College, University of Rhode Island, and Providence College.

Journal of Staff Development, Winter 2001 (Vol. 22, No. 1)

Teachers are released full time from their classroom duties for the one-year program. Their school districts foot the bill, in part through grant money.

Big Picture recently won a $1.3 million grant to expand its program from Wallace-Reader's Digest Funds' $150 million Leaders Count initiative. Within three years, Big Picture hopes to create five to seven new offshoot centers in states including New Jersey and Vermont, according to Rood.

The program will limit its growth, however. "In order for us to maintain our quality, we need to stay small in terms of numbers," Rood explains. Instead, Big Picture hopes to make its biggest impact as a model for university principal licensing programs to replicate.

The Leaders Count initiative reports that three-fifths of all school districts say they are unable to attract enough quality candidates to the principalship. Internship-based university programs are the key to countering that shortfall, Littky believes

"That's how were going to reform schools," he insists, "… through getting different people and better prepared people to run schools."

In the future, LAUNCH will increase its efforts to market candidates to local school councils, she adds. Currently, councils tend to select new principals from staff at their own schools.

PREPARING

The program's long-term benefits can only be assessed after principals are in their schools for a period of time, says Peterson.

Yet, he adds, "I honestly do not know of a program that has this much preparation for aspiring principals anywhere in the country."

Day-long sessions in LAUNCH's summer academy are hands-on and intense.

In one activity, LAUNCH fellows break into three teams to draft a plan for improving instruction in a school on the district's academic probation list.

Teams review written reports and school data before meeting the principal for a two-hour question-and-answer session. They visit the schools to observe classes and interview staff, then draw up an improvement plan and present it to the principal for a critique.

The week-long activity stresses the need for principals to enhance teachers' knowledge and skills, says LAUNCH co-director Al Bertani. Professional development becomes a real linchpin in the school improvement plans they present.

LAUNCH activities also aim to model good professional development.

"You were up, you were talking, you were mobilizing things," says graduate Susan Kurland, now principal of Nettelhorst Elementary. "It was fun to be there, and that's what you want for teachers."

Inspired, she had her own staff work in teams to revise the teachers' handbook, presenting their revisions in song or pantomime.

Administrative programs often have a lot of interesting speakers, but not a sequenced and organized curriculum, notes Peterson. Here, sessions are carefully sequenced and zeroed in on a core set of skills and knowledge, he says.

MANEUVERING

Dyrice Garner says managing a school budget is one of her weaknesses, so this morning's closed teaching positions provide yet another learning opportunity. "What we have to do now is get a memo to Karen Bertucci — she's in budget — and explain to her that these numbers should not have been closed," Oden explains.

In all, LAUNCH has more than 70 specific activities for meeting the seven standards that guide the program. Although no intern covers them all, Garner will work on a wide range of projects, from helping teachers develop

Journal of Staff Development, Winter 2001 (Vol. 22, No. 1)

assessments that align with curriculum to screening outside agencies that provide services such as gang intervention and tutoring.

Curriculum development and community outreach are long-term projects often neglected in semester-long internships, says Bruce Barnett, a University of Northern Colorado professor who studies principal preparation. As principals report spending ever more time building support networks, he says, experiences that allow interns to connect with the community-at-large are critical.

Garner divides her time between planned projects and job shadowing. From her front row seat in Oden's office, she hears and sees everything, she says.

Much of the learning is incidental, such as today's lesson on maneuvering through bureaucracy.

As Oden dials up one office after another, she provides a running commentary: "With test scores, always call student assessment. … Always write down who they transfer you to. … Now I'm going to call Donna back in an hour if I don't hear from her."

These tips are important, explains Carney.

"If a principal is not resourceful enough to know how to navigate central office and find answers … then the teachers might lose confidence in you."

OPEN RELATIONSHIP

LAUNCH fellows who have worked as assistant principals say the internship gave them a more in-depth look at the principalship. For one, interns take on a wider range of duties than do assistant principals. The interns also must spend two weeks at a second school — a high school if their expertise is elementary, or vice versa.

And because their mentor is their teacher rather than their boss, they gain new insights. One mentor shared mistakes she'd made during her career, from buying too many programs to mishandling conflicts with parents, says Assistant Principal Latunja Williams-

Fowler. "I think some things principals hold tight and close to the heart. The mentor-mentee relationship is a lot more open."

LAUNCH graduates who became principals say the program has made a difference in how they do their jobs. Larry Garstki of Sauganash Elementary would have overlooked his PTA. "Forging a relationship with them has been so important to my success here, and I might not have realized that resource in the past," he says. Brenda Thomas of Fairfield Elementary would have fired a number of teachers. Instead, she used the team-building exercises LAUNCH taught her to unite the faculty. At the end of one weekend retreat, they were ecstatic, she says.

And first-year principals get continuing support from LAUNCH. Regular meetings with Carney and Bertani keep them abreast of district deadlines and give them a chance to network.

LAUNCH grads say they keep in close touch, calling each other constantly for advice and sometimes just to vent, reports Interim Principal Melverlene Parker of Hirsch High.

"Oftentimes principals are tossed [in] like new teachers. And you're on your own," she says. "We've got an excellent support group."

Peterson believes LAUNCH could serve as a model for districts grappling with a shortage of qualified principal candidates.

So far, LAUNCH directors have "focused their energies on serving their local clients, not on getting national visibility" the way that better-known principal preparation programs have, he adds. "This is a major program [for] developing urban leaders that has not gotten the attention it deserves."

ABOUT THE AUTHOR

Elizabeth Duffrin is a Chicago-based freelance writer.

Journal of Staff Development, Winter 2001 (Vol. 22, No. 1)

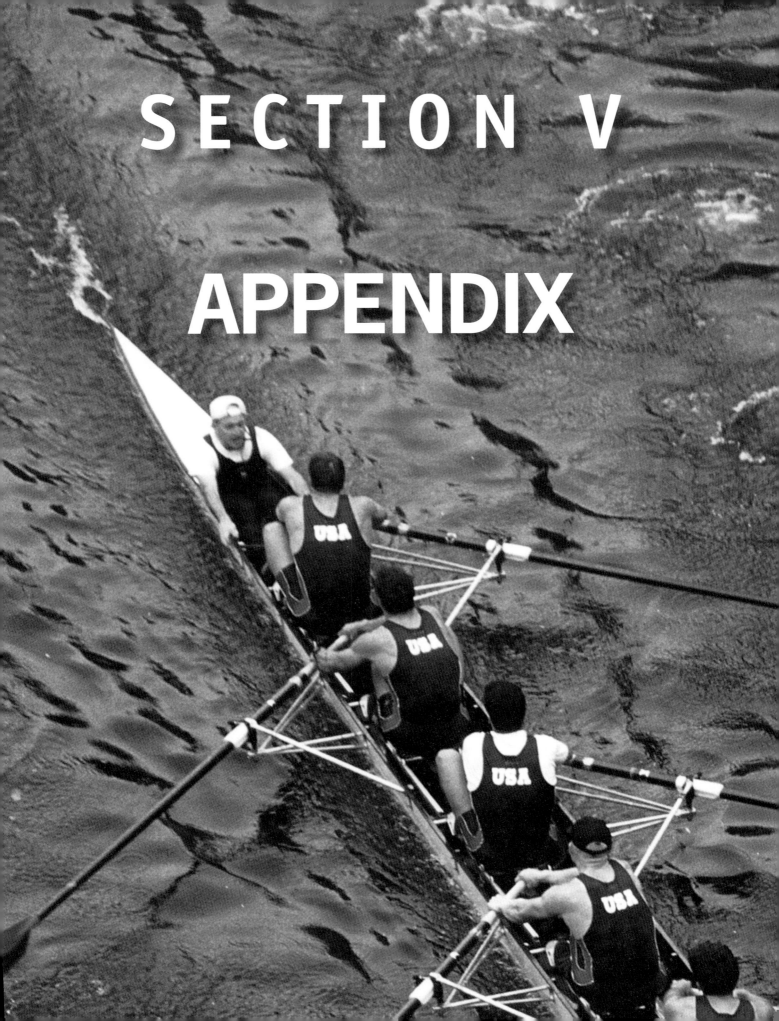

SECTION V

APPENDIX

Resources

For additional information on professional learning for leaders, see:

Beyond transformational leadership
Day, C. (2000). *Educational Leadership, 57*(7), 56-59.
A 1998 leadership study commissioned by the United Kingdom's National Association of Headteachers (the equivalent of principals in the U.S.) revealed several leadership qualities: values-led, people-centered, achievement-oriented, inward- and outward-facing, and able to manage a number of ongoing tensions and dilemmas. A discussion of each is included.

Building a new structure for school leadership
Elmore, R. (2000). Washington, DC: The Albert Shanker Institute.
www.shankerinstitute.org/Downloads/building.pdf
Five principles for a model of distributed leadership focused on large-scale education improvement are: improving instructional practice and performance; continuous learning; leaders who model the values and behavior that represent the collective good; leadership that flows from expertise, not title; and reciprocal accountability.

Developing principals as instructional leaders
Fink, E. & Resnick, L. (2001). *Phi Delta Kappan, 82*(8), 598-606.
Principals in New York City's District 2 improved student achievement by creating cultures of learning in their schools as the district has devolved decision-making authority and resources to schools. The authors tell how a community of principals was built on strong interpersonal relationships and a sustained focus on teaching and learning.

Leadership for school culture
www.eric.ed.gov/ERICWebPortal/Home.portal?_nfpb=true&ERICExtSearch_SearchValue_0=stephen+stolp&ERICExtSearch_SearchType_0=kw&_pageLabel=ERICSearchResult&newSearch=true&rnd=1204047981736&searchtype=keyword

Stolp, S. (1994). East Lansing, MI: National Center for Research on Teacher Learning. (ED370198)
A discussion of the principal's role in changing school culture by acting with care and concern for others, working to develop shared visions of what the school should be, and working on team-building.

Relationship leadership
http://www.aasa.org/publications/saarticledetail.cfm?ItemNumber=3224
Dyer, K. (November, 2001). *The School Administrator.*
How well you lead an organization may come down to how you connect with others, says the director of education at the Center for Creative Leadership. Relational leadership involves being attuned to and in touch with the intricate web of inter- and intra-relationships that influence an organization.

The role of the principal as instructional leader in a standards-driven system
Cross, C. & Rice, R. (December 2000). *NASSP Bulletin, 84*(620).
This article explores four elements of effective standards-based instructional leadership: vision and commitment; high expectations and trust; effective communication; and courage to collaborate.

School culture change in the making: Leadership factors that matter
Eilers, A.M. & Camacho, A. (2007). *Urban Education, 42*(6), 616-637.
This case study provides evidence that leadership coupled with multiple and coherent district supports can result in dramatic change at a school in a short period. Survey data on school culture demonstrate an improvement in professional communities of practice, collaborative leadership, and evidence-based practice.

The school leader's tool for assessing and improving school culture
Wagner, C. (2006, December). *Principal Leadership, 7*(4), 41-44.
One of the few research-based tools that can help principals and school improvement teams measure the health of a school's culture is the School Culture

Triage Survey. The survey allows schools to evaluate three main aspects of school culture: (1) professional collaboration; (2) collegial relationships; and (3) efficacy or self-determination. These three culture behaviors provide insight into the overall culture of the learning community.

BOOKS

The constructivist leader
Lambert, L., Walker, D., Zimmerman, D., & Cooper, J. (1995). New York: Teachers College Press.

A framework for leadership that includes a comprehensive approach to issues of equity, diversity, and multiculturalism, with principles and examples to guide accountability.

The cycles of leadership: How great leaders teach their companies to win
Tichy, N. (2002). New York: Harper Business.

Tichy describes how leaders who break the cycle of authoritative command and become teachers and learners have more successful organizations.

Designing powerful professional development for teachers and principals
Sparks, D. (2002). Oxford, OH: NSDC.

Sparks' ideas on connecting the quality of teaching and leadership to school improvement, with ideas for how schools and systems can provide powerful professional development for both teachers and leaders.

Educational leadership and school culture
Sashkin, M. & Walberg, H. (Eds.). (1993). Berkley, CA: McCutchan Publishing.

This book provides an examination of the research on the nature of educational leadership and school culture, and how they are related.

Effective school leadership: Developing principals through cognitive coaching
Ellison, J. & Hayes, C. (2006). Norwood, MA: Christopher-Gordon.

A discussion of the challenges facing today's principals is followed by a clear outline for a method of coaching leaders, with specific examples.

Encouraging the heart: A leader's guide to rewarding and recognizing others
Kouzes, J. & Pozner, B. (2003). San Francisco: Jossey-Bass.

The most motivating factor in performance, the authors say, is not money but respect and recognition. They tell how to inspire extraordinary performance through recognizing and celebrating achievement.

Finding our way: Leadership for an uncertain time
Wheatley, M. (2005). San Francisco: Berrett-Koehler.

A compendium of essays about Wheatley's real-world experiences helping clients introduce more authentic, life-affirming practices into their organizations, with practical advice on applying the ideas.

How leaders learn: Cultivating capacities for school improvement
Donaldson, G.A. (2008). New York: Teachers College Press.

The founder of the Maine Principals Academy reveals what he has learned about how leaders learn best — by taking on the role and then reflecting on the actions.

Interstate School Leaders Licensure Consortium: Educational leadership policy standards
Council of Chief State School Officers. (2008). Washington, DC: Author.
www.ccsso.org/content/pdfs/elps_isllc2008.pdf

A national research panel identified the research base to update these standards for leaders.

The leadership challenge (4th ed.)
Kouzes, J. & Pozner, B. (2007). San Francisco: Jossey-Bass.

The authors identify five fundamental practices of exemplary leaders: challenge the status quo, inspire a shared vision, enable others to act, model the way forward, tap individuals' own motivations. Includes a tool for assessing leadership behavior.

Leading for results: Transforming teaching, learning, and relationships in schools (2nd ed.)

Sparks, D. (2007). Thousand Oaks, CA: Corwin Press and NSDC.

Interactive essays help school leaders learn to promote extraordinary changes, be accountable, and achieve meaningful results for schools, districts, and their personal lives.

Leading learning communities: Standards for what principals should know and be able to do

National Association of Elementary School Principals. (2001). Alexandria, VA: NAESP.

Principals speak about the importance of focusing on learning for both adults and children, and the NAESP identifies six standards the organization believes characterize instructional leadership in schools.

The moral imperative of school leadership

Fullan, M. (2003). Thousand Oaks, CA: Corwin Press.

Strategies to reshape the culture and context of leadership in schools.

Preparing a new breed of school principals: It's time for action

Bottoms, G. (2001). Atlanta, GA: Southern Regional Education Board.

Addresses the two questions: What do successful education leaders need to know and be able to do? How do you prepare and develop effective school leaders?

The principal as instructional leader: A handbook for supervisors (2nd ed.)

Zepeda, S. (2007). Larchmont, NY: Eye on Education.

This book provides an examination of learning and leading in the areas of developing a vision and culture that supports the supervision of the instructional program, professional development, and other processes to help teachers further develop their teaching.

Principle-centered leadership

Covey, S. (1990). New York: Simon & Schuster.

Principle-centered leaders need trust and patience as individuals become involved in paradigm shifts. Principle-centered leadership is based on the belief that a set of specific principles (trustworthiness, trust, empowerment, and alignment) should guide relationships and form the foundation of effective leadership.

School leadership that works: From research to results

Marzano, R., Waters, T., & McNulty, B. (2005). Alexandria, VA: Association for Supervision and Curriculum Development.

An analysis of carefully selected studies since 1970 and interviews with building principals led the authors to a list of 21 leadership responsibilities that affect student achievement.

Shaping school culture: The school leader's role

Deal, T. & Peterson, K. (1998). San Francisco: Jossey-Bass.

An in-depth look at the ways that real schools shape their culture, including many examples.

What great principals do differently: Fifteen things that matter most

Whitaker, T. (2003). Larchmont, NY: Eye on Education.

An outline of the specific qualities and practices of great principals, why these practices are effective, and how to implement them.

More information about educational leadership can be obtained from:
www.e-lead.org
E-Lead is a partnership of the Laboratory for Student Success at Temple University and the Institute for

Educational Leadership and provides free, online information about how to provide better professional development for principals. The site includes a leadership blog, resource topics around issues of school leadership development, current research, and examples of standards-based programs.

AUTHOR CONTACT INFORMATION

Jo Blasé, professor of educational leadership at the University of Georgia, Athens, Ga.; e-mail: jblase@uga.edu.

Joseph Blasé, professor of educational leadership in the School of Education at the University of Georgia, Athens, Ga.; e-mail: blase@uga.edu.

Harold Brewer, senior vice president for programs at the Centers for Quality Teaching & Learning in Raleigh, N.C.; e-mail: hbrewer@qtlcenters.org.

Tony Byrd, assistant superintendent for teaching and learning for Edmonds School District, Lynnwood, Wash.; e-mail: byrdt@edmonds.wednet.edu.

Raymond Calabrese, professor of educational administration at The Ohio State University; e-mail: calabrese.31@osu.edu.

Margaret A. Claspell, retired.

Michelle Contich, principal at Lipscomb Elementary School in Brentwood, Tenn.; e-mail: michellec@wcs.edu.

Shelby Cosner, assistant professor in the Department of Educational Policy Studies at the University of Illinois at Chicago; e-mail: sacosner@uic.edu.

Lara Drew, program director of elementary education with the Edmonds School District in Lynnwood, Wash.; e-mail: drewl@edmonds.wednet.edu.

Elizabeth Duffrin, freelance writer based in Chicago.

Rick DuFour, former superintendent of Adlai Stevenson High School District 125 and author and consultant on professional learning communities; e-mail: rdufour@d125.org.

Gay Fawcett, retired curriculum director for Mayfield City School District, Mayfield Heights, Ohio.

Mike Ford, superintendent of Phelps-Clifton Springs School District, Clifton Springs, N.Y.; e-mail: mford@midlakes.org.

Pete Hall, principal at Sheridan Elementary School in Spokane, Wash.; e-mail: petehall@educationhall.com.

Rick Harris, deputy superintendent at Washoe County School District in Reno, Nevada; e-mail: rjharris@washoe.k12.nv.us.

Judith P. Huddleston, a principal consultant in the Office of Federal Program Administration at the Colorado Department of Education; e-mail: huddleston.j@comcast.net.

Ellen H. Kahan, assistant superintendent of the Edmonds School District in Lynnwood, Wash.; e-mail: kahane@edmonds.wednet.edu.

Joellen Killion, deputy executive director of the National Staff Development Council; e-mail: joellen.killion@nsdc.org.

Linda Lambert, professor emeritus at California State University, East Bay; e-mail: linlambert@aol.com.

Ginny V. Lee, associate professor, Department of Educational Leadership, California State University East Bay; e-mail: ginny.lee@csueastbay.edu.

Suzette D. Lovely, author and deputy superintendent for personnel services of the Capistrano Unified School District; e-mail: slovely@capousd.org.

Cynthia A. McMinn, retired, Mississippi Department of Education, Office of Leadership Development & Enhancement.

Joseph Murphy, professor of education at Vanderbilt University, Nashville, Tenn.; e-mail: joseph.f.murphy@vanderbilt.edu.

Joye Hall Norris, director of the School of Education & Child Development at Drury University; e-mail: jnorris@drury.edu.

John Norton, education writer/consultant based in Little Switzerland, N.C. and co-founder of the Teacher Leaders Network; e-mail: jcroftn1@mindspring.com.

Parker J. Palmer, author, educator, activist, and founder and senior partner of the Center for Courage & Renewal; e-mail: info@CourageRenewal.org.

Kent Peterson, professor, University of Wisconsin-Madison Department of Educational Leadership & Policy Analysis; e-mail: kpeterson@education.wisc.edu.

Joan Richardson, editor-in-chief of *Kappan*; e-mail: jrichardson@pdkintl.org.

Pat Roy, educational consultant; e-mail: cooppat@cox.net.

Harriet Arzu Scarborough, co-director of Furendei Consulting Services in Tucson, Ariz.; e-mail: scar7227@q.com.

Gene Spanneut, assistant professor of educational administration at the State University of New York College at Brockport, N.Y.; e-mail: spanneut@verizon.net.

Dennis Sparks, independent consultant and emeritus executive director, National Staff Development Council; e-mail: dennis.sparks@comcast.net.

Jennifer Welsh Takata, program analyst at the Broad Foundation; e-mail: jtakata@broadfoundation.org.

Eddy J. Van Meter, professor emeritus in the college of education at the University of Kentucky.

Liz Willen, associate director for the Hechinger Institute on Education and the Media at the Teachers College, Columbia University; e-mail: Willen@exchange.tc.columbia.edu.

NSDC'S PURPOSE

Every educator engages in effective professional learning
every day so every student achieves.

NSDC STAFF

Stephanie Hirsh, Executive director

Joellen Killion, Deputy executive director

Leslie Miller, Director of business services

Carol François, Director of learning

Hayes Mizell, Distinguished senior fellow

Dennis Sparks, Emeritus executive director